Brutal Artistry

Books by Thomas Hauser

Non-Fiction
Missing
The Trial of Patrolman Thomas Shea
For Our Children (with Frank Macchiarola)
The Family Legal Companion
The Black Lights: Inside the World of Professional Boxing
Final Warning: The Legacy of Chernobyl (with Dr Robert Gale)
Muhammad Ali: His Life and Times
Muhammad Ali: Memories
Arnold Palmer: A Personal Journey
Confronting America's Moral Crisis (with Frank Macchiarola)
Muhammad Ali: In Perspective
Healing: A Journal of Tolerance and Understanding
Muhammad Ali & Company
Miscellaneous
With This Ring (with Frank Macchiarola)
A Beautiful Sickness
A Year at the Fights

Fiction
Ashworth & Palmer
Agatha's Friends
The Beethoven Conspiracy
Hanneman's War
The Fantasy
Dear Hannah
The Hawthorne Group
Mark Twain Remembers
Finding The Princess

For Children
Martin Bear & Friends

Brutal Artistry

Great Fighters and Great Fights

Thomas Hauser

ROBSON BOOKS

First published in Great Britain in 2002 by Robson Books, 64 Brewery Road, London, N7 9NT

A member of **Chrysalis** Books plc

British Library Cataloguing in Publication Data
A catalogue record for this title is available from the British Library.

ISBN 1 86105 584 6

Typeset in 11/14pt Times by FiSH Books, London WC1
Printed by Creative Print & Design (Wales), Ebbw Vale

From the dedication to
Muhammad Ali & Company

I've often said that some of the best people I've ever met are in boxing, and some of the worst people I've ever met are in boxing. This book is dedicated to the best.

Contents

Round 3: Other Fighters

Round 4: Issues and Curiosities

Author's Note

The articles I've written about professional boxing have been published in the United States in three books: *Muhammad Ali & Company, A Beautiful Sickness*, and *A Year at the Fights. Brutal Artistry* contains the best of these articles plus several new ones.

Special thanks are due to Secondsout.com, Houseofboxing.com, HBO Boxing, Showtime Boxing, and *Boxing Digest* under whose aegis many of the articles in this book first appeared.

Round 1

The Brits

I've had the pleasure of meeting Henry Cooper several times; most recently in January 2001, when we had tea in London and talked for this article.

Sir Henry Cooper

It's a moment frozen in time, fixed in the collective consciousness of a nation. A memory that has been conjured up, told, and retold so many times that for many in England it has become the equivalent of religious lore.

In one corner, a brash young American named Cassius Marcellus Clay Jr. The 21-year-old Clay had won a gold medal at the 1960 Olympics in Rome and was undefeated in eighteen professional fights with fourteen knockouts. He was loud, cocky, and beginning to irritate people as much as he charmed them.

And in the other corner, Henry Cooper: the patron saint of modern British heavyweights. The 29-year-old Cooper had been born in Bellingham, Kent, and been fighting professionally since 1954. He'd won the British and Commonwealth heavyweight titles in 1959 and would hold them for a record ten years.

The date was 18 June 1963. Clay entered the ring wearing a crown embedded with imitation precious stones and a red robe emblazoned with the words 'Cassius the Greatest'. Prior to the bout, he'd predicted that he would knock Cooper out in round five, and 55,000 fans had jammed into Wembley Stadium to see if 'Our Henry' could make the American eat his words.

For three rounds, two minutes, and 55 seconds, everything went as Clay had planned. From round one on, he was in control. By round three, Cooper was bleeding badly and it appeared as though the bout would end whenever Cassius wanted it to. But instead of taking care of business, Clay seemed intent on prolonging the Englishman's agony and making good on his prediction of a fifth-round knockout.

Then THE PUNCH landed. 'Henry's Hammer', the British called it.

3

'It came from a long way back,' one ringside observer later wrote, 'with Cooper lungeing forward as hard as he could. It caught Clay on the side of the jaw, and Cassius went over backwards through the ropes. He rolled back into the ring and got dazedly to his feet, gazing off into the distance, starry-eyed. He wobbled forward, gloves low, and started to fall, but his handlers caught him. Wembley Stadium was in an uproar.'

But the round was over. And for British fans, a tale of woe followed. Earlier in the fight, Clay's trainer, Angelo Dundee, had noticed a split on one of Clay's gloves on the seam near the thumb. Now, with his fighter in desperate straits, Dundee, in his own words, 'helped the split a little, pulled it to the side, and made the referee aware that there was a torn glove. Dundee later reminisced. 'I don't know how much time that got us, Maybe a minute, but it was enough. If we hadn't gotten the extra time, I don't know what would have happened.'

But Clay did have the extra time. And in round five, a barrage of punches ripped open the skin around Cooper's eyes, causing a torrential flow of blood. The fight was over, as Clay had predicted, on a fifth-round knockout.

Henry Cooper is now 66 years old. He retired from boxing in 1970 with a record of forty wins, fourteen losses and one draw. He's still a hero in England; the most beloved fighter in the history of British boxing. Last year, he served as national spokesman for a campaign encouraging people age 65 and older to get flu shots. Cooper's message – 'Get your jab in now!' – was in print ads and on television for weeks on end. Healthcare personnel later reported that many citizens coming into clinics said simply, 'I want a Henry Cooper.'

Cooper is also Chairman of the Executive Committee of The Variety Club in London. In that capacity, last year he supervised thirty golf tournaments that raised more than one million pounds for charity. He does extensive fundraising to support a school for mentally handi-capped children. And in perhaps the ultimate tribute, he has been knighted by Queen Elizabeth.

Cooper still cuts a striking figure, with rugged features and an aura of honesty and decency about him. He and his wife, Albina, have been married for forty years. One of their sons operates a charter boat. The other is a chef in an Italian restaurant. They have two grandchildren – Henry James, age six; and Lilly Maria, who's two years old. With his boxing days far behind him, Cooper plays golf with an eleven handicap. 'I shoot my 85s,' he says. 'Take eleven off, and I'm all right.'

As for boxing, Cooper has a lot to say about the sweet science today. 'It's killing itself,' he says with dismay. 'If it keeps going the way it is, there will be no professional boxing in England in ten years. It's not boxing now. It's fighting. You're supposed to learn your basic defensive moves as a kid. But trainers today don't know their trade, and fighters aren't being properly schooled as amateurs or professionals. They're not learning defensive skills any more. All their trainers tell them to do is go forward.'

'There are too many one-sided fights,' Cooper continues. 'You have all this hype for thirty minutes. Searchlights, posing in front of the searchlights, lasers, dancing, bands. Then the fight lasts a minute and a half. In the old days, there were one-round fights, but people didn't know which ones they'd be in advance.'

Cooper supported the decision of the British Home Office to allow Mike Tyson to fight Julius Francis in England. 'Tyson's done three years in prison,' he said at the time. 'How long does he have to keep paying for it? We know he's a bit of a nutcase, but they're talking about Julius Francis losing money if Tyson isn't allowed in.'

And despite the debacles surrounding Iron Mike's fights in the United Kingdom against Francis and Lou Savarese, Cooper's opinion on the matter is unchanged. 'What's the worst crime?,' he posits. 'It's not rape; it's murder. Don King has killed two men that we know of. Don King served time in prison [for manslaughter]. Yet we allow Don King to come here and promote fights. Why should Tyson be any different? Besides,' Cooper notes. 'If Tyson wants to fight Lennox Lewis in London, you know they'll let him in.'

And who does Cooper think would win a bout between Lewis and Tyson? 'Tyson was a great fighter for the first few years of his career,' he answers. 'He's still dangerous. The last thing a puncher loses is his punch. But Tyson has lost it mentally and physically since then. There's no movement; he's getting hit. I think Lennox will stop him. You have to measure fighters by the standards of their era,' Cooper continues. 'Jack Johnson, Jack Dempsey, Joe Louis, Rocky Marciano, Muhammad Ali and Larry Holmes all had great talent and a great fighting brain. In my view, they were the greatest heavyweights ever. Lennox Lewis is in the next group. He's a good fighter and he dodges no one.'

Meanwhile, Cooper's own place in British boxing history is secure despite his 'Achilles heel' – the tendency to cut.

'If you gave Henry a rough towel, you needed a basin to catch the blood,' says Hugh McIlvanney, England's foremost sports journalist. 'When he fought the serious Americans, you wouldn't have bet him. But he was a good boxer. For a man of his weight, he was a wonderful puncher. He fought to the limit of his powers and never let anyone down. He was a marvellous presence for the game.'

And McIlvanney's American counterpart, Jerry Izenberg, adds, 'If Henry Cooper had a different facial bone structure, he would have been heavyweight champion of the world. He could punch; he could box; he came to fight; he always gave people trouble. But at the end of almost every fight, he was red with his own blood because those jagged edges betrayed him.'

Cooper himself prefers not to dwell on the cuts. He has a different memory to look back on – round four on the night of 18 June 1963. 'The greatest heavyweight ever,' he says. 'And I had him on his bum. It's still vivid in my mind. I remember everything.'

'I was confident going into the fight,' Cooper continues. 'Clay, which was his name then, had looked good against big guys, but small quick fighters like Doug Jones had given him trouble. And he was a novice inside fighter. He hadn't learned how to defend himself in close. I only weighed thirteen-and-a-half stone [190 pounds], but I was messing him up inside. Then I knocked him down. And when I looked in his eyes, I knew he was gone. The eyes register everything. There's no way he would have come around in one minute. But Angelo saw that the stitching on the glove had ripped a bit. That's what you pay top trainers for.'

Hugh McIlvanney says simply, 'If Ali had gone out with only one minute's rest, it might have been over.' That conforms to the view of BBC boxing commentator Harry Carpenter, who viewed Clay between rounds and later reported, 'His eyeballs were still rolling in their sockets.'

'But there's nothing I can do about it now,' says Cooper. 'And you know the rest. I was a bleeder. I'd come to expect cuts. They were part of every fight for me. It's a shame, really. If I'd had flatter rounder features, who knows. But the worst cut I ever had was against Cassius Clay. I could feel the warm blood dripping on my chest. Of course, I think about the torn glove and the extra time it bought. There's no bitterness; I'm content with the way my life has worked out. Still, I have to say, you expect to be disadvantaged like that when you're abroad. I had a fight in Germany when I knocked my opponent down in the second round and they rang the bell a minute early. Then, when I knocked him out in the next round, I was disqualified. If Clay had been fighting a German in Germany, they would have let the fourth round go another ten seconds in the pandemonium after the knockdown and he would have been knocked out. I never asked for that. All I wanted was a level playing field. And to have it happen the way it happened in England was a bit hard.'

There was a second fight between the two men in 1966, but it was little more than a postscript to the first. Cassius Clay had become Muhammad Ali. He was heavyweight champion of the world by then and well respected as a boxer with an aura of menace about him.

'Ali was a quick learner,' Cooper remembers. 'By the second time we fought, he'd learned how to defend himself inside. Whenever I got near him, he'd clamp down on me like I was in a vice, hold on until the referee made us break, and step back out of harm's way.'

Cooper fought valiantly, as he had three years earlier. But this time, there was no left hook. Otherwise, things were pretty much the same. Ali stopped him on cuts in round six.

And as for what might have been had Cooper won the first fight –

'Probably I would have fought Sonny Liston next,' Cooper acknowledges. 'I always thought the press built Liston up more than he deserved until Ali exposed him. If you were a mover and a good boxer and could punch a little, you could beat Liston, so I would have been confident going in. As for Ali, even if I'd won, someday he still would have become heavyweight champion. Joe Louis lost before he won the title. Jack Dempsey lost before he won the title. Ali was such a brilliant boxer, he was destined to become heavyweight champion of the world.'

Cooper, of course, would have his own destiny. 'You think you've got all the honours you're going to get,' he says with pride. 'And then this letter arrived in the mail. I saw the return address, 10 Downing Street, which is the office of the Prime Minister. I opened it up, and the letter said, "You are under consideration for knighthood. Will you accept?" I showed the missus. She couldn't believe it. We were sworn to secrecy for seven weeks. Then we went for the big event. You're allowed to bring three guests, so I took my wife, my youngest son, and my grandson, which was what my older son wanted. It was at Buckingham Palace, and no one does ceremony like the British. They tell you the etiquette before you go. You kneel before the Queen, and she touches you with a sword on your shoulder. There's a bit of small talk. The Queen said to me, "You had a long career, didn't you, Mr Cooper?" I told her, "I did, ma'am; seventeen years." Then she shook hands with me. And according to the etiquette, when the Queen shakes hands with you, you know it's over. You don't keep talking to her.'

So there it is. Lennox Lewis might be 'The King'. Naseem Hamed might be 'The Prince'. But Henry Cooper is a knight. That much is clear when an admirer approaches and asks Cooper if she can have his autograph. He signs with a flourish:

Best Wishes,
Sir Henry Cooper

The first time I talked at length with Lennox Lewis was when I travelled to his training camp in the Pocono Mountains on 4 July 2000. This article was the result.

Lennox Lewis: An Appreciation

On 9 June 1899, James J Jeffries claimed boxing's heavyweight crown by knocking out Bob Fitzsimmons in the eleventh round. Jeffries was American, and Fitzsimmons was British. More than one hundred years passed from that date until an Englishman again held the undisputed heavyweight championship of the world.

Now the heavyweight champion is English-born. And the Brits ignore him. They holler about Naseem Hamed. They fixate on Mike Tyson. They wax nostalgic about Henry Cooper. Hey, gang; wake up and smell the roses. Lennox Lewis is boxing royalty.

The standard knock on Lewis is that he's dull. Some perceive him as aloof, moody, and arrogant. Others see him as shy. Either way, Lennox's trainer, Emanuel Steward, acknowledges, 'Lennox is kind of reclusive. When he's not with his friends, he likes to sit in his room, watch TV, and be by himself.'

But let's take a look at what Lennox Lewis brings to the table.

First, Lewis is a quality fighter. Over the years, he has beaten the likes of Evander Holyfield, Michael Grant, Andrew Golota, Razor Ruddock, Tommy Morrison, Ray Mercer and Frank Bruno. In 1993, when Lewis was the mandatory challenger, Riddick Bowe relinquished his WBC heavyweight crown rather than face him. In 1996, Mike Tyson did the same. The sole loss on Lewis's record is a second-round knockout at the hands of Oliver McCall in 1994. And although Lewis was in trouble at the time, the stoppage was premature.

As for his personal side, Lennox Lewis one-on-one has a genuine warmth about him. His voice is soft and, at times, lyrical. He has a good sense of humour and considers himself 'a citizen of the world'.

'After all,' he notes, 'I'm British by birth; my parents are Jamaican; I was brought up in Canada; and I spend a lot of time in the United States. That makes me a true world champion.'

Lewis also offers the following:

- 'I want to be a special person; someone with a positive gleam about me, so I can do special things and make people happy. Sometimes I fantasise about having special powers – flying like Superman or having ESP – so I can zoom in and save people in distress.'
- 'I'm a goal setter. When I was growing up, my mum and I didn't have much money and I wanted a waterbed that cost $450. So I went out and put together a dance. My mum worked the kitchen; I sold tickets; and I made $500.'
- 'Watching the news on television makes me sad. It's all about people being raped and killed and suffering and war.'
- 'My heroes are people who have done positive things. My mother. Nelson Mandela. Bob Marley. Bob Marley gave an entire island an identity and made its people proud.'
- [When asked whether he would rather be heavyweight champion of the world, the international chess champion, or a rock star] 'That's a good question. Let me hear the choices again. Wow, that's a tough one. I guess, heavyweight champion first; world chess champion second; and a rock star third. But all of them are good.'
- 'I like nature, and I love animals. I hate hunting. I don't understand why anyone would want to kill an animal for sport. Isn't it enough to enjoy the beauty of them? It was great to go to Africa and not see a single animal in a cage.'
- 'I met the Queen. She's very petite. She kind of looked up at me and said, "My, you're a big fellow".'
- [Regarding his famous dreadlocks] 'Now and then, I go for a steam and get my hair tightened. There's one place I go to in New York, another in London, and one in California. But there are very few people I let touch my hair. There might be some Delilahs lurking around, so I have to be careful.'

Much of the public's lack of interest in Lewis stems from the fact that he's a private person. 'I am what I am,' he says in response. 'I don't want to be an open book. I'm happy to be the one who's watching and observing. I enjoy partying, but not in limelight places. I don't need cheap publicity like Mike Tyson. The public doesn't know me yet, but that's all right. Eventually, people will get to know me. And I hope, when that happens, I'll be known for my good qualities. But I want it to happen naturally.'

In this age of confessional television and Monica Lewinsky telling Barbara Walters about Bill Clinton's sexual proclivities, that's a refreshing attitude. And it underscores the tiresome nature of the public inquiry into Lewis's own sex life, which he has every right to consider private. I mean, let's get real. Mike Tyson stares at Razor Ruddock at a press conference and says, 'I'm going to kiss your fat lips and make you my girlfriend' – and people ask whether or not Lennox is gay?

Still, that does bring us back to Tyson, whose presence shadows Lewis's life. It's Tyson, of course, who has threatened to rip Lewis's heart out, eat it for dinner, and then feast on Lewis's children (he has none) for dessert. Tyson today is a train wreck waiting to happen. But he remains the best one-punch knockout artist in boxing, and Lewis–Tyson would be a perilous fight.

'In chess,' Lewis observes, 'even the simplest moves are danger-ous.' The same can be said about any move that one makes in the ring with Tyson. In the past, Lennox has had problems with stamina. He has looked his best against tall opponents. And his overhand right takes longer to deliver than Tyson's hook. A lot of people don't want to see Lewis–Tyson happen. Ironically, Tyson might be among them.

Meanwhile . . . Pay attention, England! Who would you rather have your children look up to and model themselves after – Lennox Lewis or Mike Tyson? Who would better represent the world of boxing – Lennox Lewis or Mike Tyson? You don't have to worry about picking up the newspaper and reading about Lennox Lewis and drugs, or Lennox Lewis and some woman who was assaulted in a bar or raped in a hotel room. With Lennox Lewis, there are no ugly histrionics; just decency, dignity, and grace.

When Lennox Lewis fought David Tua in November 2000, Lewis and Emanuel Steward gave me access to the champion's camp.

Lennox Lewis and Emanuel Steward

At the end of a week in which American democracy became as chaotic as professional boxing, two foreign nationals fought on American soil for the heavyweight championship of the world. When they did, in the eyes of many, the third man in the ring wasn't referee Joe Cortez. It was Emanuel Steward.

Steward was born on 7 July 1944. A national Golden Gloves winner, he has worked as an electrician, an insurance salesman, and a cosmetics distributor. Along the way, he began training fighters and turned the Kronk Gym in Detroit from a neighbourhood recreational centre into one of the most famous gyms in the world. Over the years, he has worked with 25 world champions. He has been named Manager of the Year twice and Trainer of the Year three times by the Boxing Writers Association of America. Those are 'legendary' credentials.

Steward was in Oliver McCall's corner on the night of 24 September 1994, when McCall defeated Lennox Lewis to capture the WBC heavyweight crown. He began working with Lewis before the deposed champion's next fight (a fifth-round knockout of Lionel Butler) and has been with him ever since. Lewis–Tua was their fourteenth fistic collaboration.

'There's a special bond between a fighter and his trainer,' Steward says in describing his job. 'Often, they're the closest two people in camp. Look at the young men who become fighters. Many of them never had a father at home when they were growing up. Or if the father was there, he wasn't a positive influence. So when the relationship between a fighter and his trainer is right, oftentimes the trainer becomes a father figure and the fighter's best friend. The two men develop similar thought patterns and become spiritually synchronised with one another. Now with Lennox, things are a little different. Lennox isn't looking for a father figure. He's his own man. In a lot of ways, he's made it through life on his own. Lennox was separated from his mother when he was young. And when they were finally reunited, he saw that his mother was looked down upon and treated badly by a lot of people. That hurt Lennox and made him very wary of people. It's one of the reasons he's so conscious of loyalty. Tommy Hearns was different. Tommy was loyal, but if someone turned his back on him after a defeat, Tommy would shrug and say, "That's human nature; people want to run with a winner." Lennox isn't like that. Lennox demands loyalty from the people around him. There's also a tough street side to him, but most people never see it. And he's very sensitive, very intense, and more competitive than most people imagine.'

'In terms of working together,' Steward continues, 'Lennox and I caught on to each other's thought patterns very quickly. We work exceptionally well together. The first week at camp, we plan a mental strategy for the fight. For example, when Lennox fought Holyfield, I knew it was important to never let Evander get his rhythm. So we developed a strategy where Lennox's jab was the key. He should never stand still and just block Evander's punches because, even if he blocked them, that would allow Evander to get his rhythm. It had to be jab, jab, jab. And we do that together. Lennox watches tapes of his opponent before a fight, and I value his input. You know, you can't dominate your fighter in training. You have to listen to him and work on what he wants to do too. But it's not just about throwing the jab or an uppercut. Sometimes it's about finding the spiritual key that turns a fighter on. When Buster Douglas fought Mike Tyson, he fought well over his head because he was motivated by his mother's death. I had an amateur fighter once – a young man named Rodney Trusel – who was motivated because he wanted to outshine his older brother. Every fighter is different. You have to get into the mind-set of your fighter, and that's particularly true with Lennox, who has a mind of his own. For example, against Ray Mercer, Lennox started backing against the ropes, blocking punches and firing back. He'd done it in training, and he was doing it in the fight. That wasn't what I wanted, but there are times when you have to work off what your fighter is doing. Don't spend the fight arguing with him because, if you do, you'll win the argument and lose the decision. So what I did to motivate Lennox was, after the eighth round, I said to him, "Remember, I told you once that someday you'd be in a fight where your natural talent and skills aren't enough; that you'd just have to go out and outfight the other guy to win. Well, that time is now." And Lennox responded. He went out and plain outfought Ray Mercer the rest of the way to win.'

Lewis, for his part, remembers the Mercer fight well and says, 'I believe in myself because I've been through tough fights. Razor Ruddock was tough in the beginning, but Mercer was easily the hardest fight I've been in.'

As for Lennox Lewis versus David Tua, prior to the bout, one could have made a pretty good argument in favour of the Samoan. The durability factor; the relative ability of both men to take punishment in general and the big punch in particular; the fact that Tua had never been badly hurt, never been on the canvas, and never been cut as a pro. Moreover, Tua is only 27 years old and had seemed not to wear down during his fights, whereas Lewis is 35 and there were questions regarding his stamina.

Still, Steward was confident before the bout, declaring, 'People say that David Tua has never been hurt. That sounds good, but the truth is, Tua seldom gets hit clean because he keeps his chin tucked down very nicely and picks off punches with his shoulders. And Tua has never been hit by anyone as big and strong as Lennox, so I don't know how good a punch David Tua really takes. But we'll find out. The fight Lennox and I looked at a lot in training camp was Tua against Hasim Rahman. That fight showed how to beat Tua and also what can happen if you get careless against him. But most of all, it showed Tua's vulnerability against a taller opponent. And believe me, not only is Lennox a big man; he uses his height. The key to this fight will be to keep Tua preoccupied with Lennox's jab and then smash him with right hands. Tua's only hope is to get inside, but that will be very difficult for him. Lennox has been working on hand speed for this fight. And he's been working a lot to build up his arm strength. He wants to be able to control Tua inside with his arms. Tua will force the fight and force Lennox into some explosive situations. But David Tua is stepping out of his league. If he thinks he's prepared to fight Lennox, he's mistaken.'

Steward was right. Lewis looked good in round one, throwing a stinging jab and occasional right hands. Then he put the right in mothballs and went almost exclusively with his jab, controlling the fight like a cat toying with a mouse. The crowd had come in anticipation of a slugfest, and more than a few onlookers began booing with the realisation that they were watching a tactical fight. But, hey; it's called 'boxing'.

'I was conserving energy,' Lewis explained later. 'Everyone was talking about how dangerous Tua is late, so I wanted to make sure I had something left at the end. Also, even if I land a hundred punches, all he needs is two good ones. That's what Tua was looking for all night, one or two good punches; so I wanted to be careful. I'm a more confident fighter now that I've unified the title, and that makes me a better fighter. But I said "confident," not "foolish". A fighter should never think he's invincible. The first fight against Oliver McCall taught me that.'

Also, it's worth noting that the lack of excitement was more Tua's fault than Lewis's. Lewis was winning, and Tua was losing. Thus, it was incumbent upon the challenger to change the pace of the fight, and he never did. Instead, Tua kept coming forward without really forcing the action and waited for Lewis to make a mistake. In fact, from round nine on, Tua looked as though he had stopped trying to win altogether and was simply going through the motions. By the end of the evening, the champion had landed 300 punches to 110 for the challenger, and the decision was no longer in doubt. Emanuel Steward was correct in observing, 'Lennox shut him down completely. He made David Tua look like a sparring partner.'

As for what comes next, Lewis says he'd prefer to fight less often in 2001 than in the past. 'Four fights in twelve months put me in front of the public,' he acknowledges. 'But I'd like to slow down a bit now and not have more than two fights next year.'

The most frequently mentioned opponent for Lewis is, of course, Mike Tyson. The champion appears to want the fight. 'Beating Tyson would add to my legacy,' he says. But in the next breath, he voices doubt that the bout will happen, noting, 'Riddick Bowe called me names and then joined the Marines. Maybe Tyson will join the Marines.'

Meanwhile, boxing fans can count on one hand the number of world-class fighters who have gotten better in their mid-thirties. But that's what seems to be happening with Lennox Lewis. Lewis himself agrees with that evaluation and gives much of the credit to Steward. 'I've worked hard to improve my technical skills,' he says, 'and a lot of what's happened is due to Manny. The first thing he corrected in me was never having my head go past my front knee, and I've been getting better and better ever since. But even now, there's things I see other boxers do in the ring that I want to be able to do, so I'm still improving.'

Steward responds with equal praise, declaring, 'Lennox is a perfectionist. He has fast hands and explosive power, which is a devastating combination. He can box and he can punch. He's still learning and, once he catches on to something, he's got it. He's physically big, and we're not talking big and clumsy. He's fast and well-coordinated. The old perception of Lennox as a big old clumsy boy with dreadlocks is gone now. And Lennox is more relaxed in the ring these days than ever before. He was always confident, but his belief in himself has grown and he's more comfortable with his skills. And another thing; Lennox wants to be great. He talks with me about that a lot now. It's not just about winning fights. He wants to be recognised in history as a great heavyweight champion. That's one of the reasons he wants to fight Mike Tyson. If you think about it, the only two major heavyweights of Lennox's era that he hasn't fought are Bowe and Tyson. And neither guy wanted to fight him. In fact, both guys gave up their WBC championship belt rather than get into the ring with Lennox. Lennox wants Tyson badly so he can show the world how much better he is than Tyson.'

Meanwhile, let's give Lennox Lewis credit. In a little less than a year, he has fought Evander Holyfield, Michael Grant, Frans Botha and David Tua. He has become boxing's dominant heavyweight. No nickname; no frills. Just Lennox Lewis: Heavyweight Champion of the World.

I collaborated with Marilyn Cole Lownes for a 'styles' piece on the scene in Las Vegas for Lennox Lewis versus David Tua.

The Epitome of Style

Last month, the heavyweight championship of the world was contested by an Englishman of Jamaican parentage who grew up in Canada and a Samoan who grew up in New Zealand. That's a far cry from years past when boxing's most coveted prize seemed as American as apple pie. But as Bob Dylan once wrote, 'The times, they are a-changin'.'

Boxing styles are changing too.

In the old days, heavyweight championship fights were contested at venues like Yankee Stadium and Madison Square Garden. Now, as often as not, they take place at Las Vegas sites like Mandalay Bay – an eleven-acre 'tropical rain forest and South Pacific water environment' featuring a huge swimming pool with an air machine capable of producing six-foot waves that roll on to an artificial beach.

In the old days, the audience for fights was virtually all men, and virtually all of them wore suits, ties and proper hats. Now the crowd is mixed, and fashions run the gamut from men in fur coats to women wearing next to nothing at all.

In the old days, the apparel fighters wore into the ring was fairly simple. Black trunks for one fighter and white for the other, accessorised by black gloves. The robes were terrycloth, although a champion might opt for satin. Then colour television came along, and the gloves turned red for better viewing. Muhammad Ali stretched the envelope further with tassels and a beaded robe given to him by Elvis Presley. After that, Hector Camacho wore a leopard-skin loincloth into the ring, and things got out of hand.

It all culminated on 11 November 2000, with Lennox Lewis versus David Tua; a contrast in styles if ever there was one.

The six-foot-five-inch Lewis looks like a graceful Michelangelo sculpture. He's carefully groomed with no tattoos and a clean wholesome look. He's also almost always impeccably dressed; the most stylish champion since Ali. Patrick Drayton estimates that he has designed fifty suits for the champion, which are then cut and stitched by the famed Savile Row tailor, Fallen & Harvey.

By contrast, the five-foot-ten-inch Tua looks like a sumo-wrestler with a punch. He is, shall we say, a more casual dresser than Lewis. Or phrased differently, David Tua makes Lou Duva look like the Duke of Windsor.

And then there was the matter of the fighters' hair.

Once upon a time, Lewis's hanging dreadlocks would have been a source of controversy. By his own reckoning, they haven't been cut in eight years. By contrast, Tua's hair rises upward toward the heavens like the coiffure of a well-known boxing promoter. 'I'm not trying to look like Don King,' Tua explained recently. 'I just thought I'd try something new. People expect that of me. I'm Tuaman.'

Thus, it came to pass that, during a week in which the American Presidency hung in the balance, the dominant story in Las Vegas was David Tua's hair. The Lewis camp expressed concern that (1) Tua might load his hair with chemicals that would get into Lennox's eyes and impair his vision; and (2) a hard gel applied on fight night would turn the challenger's hair into dozens of spikes, any one of which could become the equivalent of a thumb in the eye.

Larry Merchant put his hand in Tua's hair the day before the fight and pronounced it 'natural', but Lewis remained unconvinced. 'You never know what compounds a man might put in his hair at the last minute,' the champion reasoned. Then Marc Ratner (Executive Director of the Nevada State Athletic Commission) promised a close examination of Tua's hair in the dressing room immediately before the bout, and that calmed things down a bit.

Meanwhile, what did referee Joe Cortez think about the controversy swirling around Tua's hair?

'I wish he'd give me some,' the balding referee said.

When the hour of reckoning finally arrived, the crowd was in its sartorial glory. Among the more noticeable feminine fashions on display were sequined zebra-striped trousers, bronze leather suits, and mink coats draped over silk in a manner reminiscent of Rat Pack era glamour. Considerable attention was also paid to a particularly striking beauty showing ample cleavage in a magenta satin dress, matching jacket, and rhinestone sandals with an ankle strap and four-inch heels. None of the women had hair more bouffant than Tua.

Lewis entered the ring as a knight in white satin with red lettering on his trunks. Tua wore black trunks with white trim. As the fight wore on, the challenger's hair was never a factor. But Lewis's jab did make it a bad hair day for Tua.

One of the nice things about being a writer is getting to know the people you write about. Meeting Naseem Hamed in January 2001 was no exception.

In Search of Naseem Hamed

The public image of Naseem Hamed is of someone who's loud, arrogant, flamboyant and obnoxious. That's the part of his persona known as 'The Prince'. But Hamed is a complex person, and most people who meet him are surprised at how nice he is. Or phrased differently, many people who root hard against 'The Prince' find themselves rooting for Naseem.

Hamed began fighting professionally at age eighteen. At present, his record stands at 35 wins and no losses with 30 knockouts. At the relatively young age of 26, he's financially secure and the preeminent featherweight in the world.

Also, despite Hamed's manic public image, he has handled his success well. He's a positive person. He knows who he is. And rather than fall victim to the roller-coaster ride of fame, he is in many ways thoughtful and well grounded.

Hamed's character has been shaped by myriad influences, foremost among them his family, his religion and his natural talent. He was born and raised in Sheffield, which offers an environment very different from London. Sheffield is an industrial town with high unemployment. And while Hamed might be on stage away from home, in Sheffield he keeps largely to his family and himself. The core of that family is his parents, who were born in Yemen; four brothers, four sisters, a wife, and two sons, who will celebrate their first and third birthdays later this year.

As for who he is, Hamed offers the following:

- 'I have a lot of respect for my parents, and I'm so grateful to them for my upbringing. My biggest hero is my father; the way the man is; what he believes; the way he raised nine children in a foreign country with none of us ever getting in trouble. My father taught me values and manners and how to speak with people. And my mother taught me how to treat women; to be right and honest with women and not treat them as secondary people. One of my biggest satisfactions is being able to look after my family with the success I've had in boxing. And I want to bring my children up the same way my parents brought me up.'

- 'The most important thing in my life is to worship Allah. I believe that everything is created by Allah, and everything is created by Allah for a reason. I want people to know that I'm a Muslim, and I want to be a vehicle for Islam. I thank Allah for everything I have and everything that I'm going to get. The gifts Allah has given me go far beyond boxing.'

- 'I believe that Islam is God's final religion. I believe that Allah loves to be worshipped in a certain way and accepts only one religion, and that religion is Islam. That's a harsh statement to make, but I will also say that no one can tell another person that he or she is going to hell because no one except Allah is all-knowing and no one except Allah is entitled to judge. Only Allah knows what will happen to virtuous non-believers.'

- 'I'll never forget my pilgrimmage to Mecca. It was fantastic to see so many people. People of all colours and people from all countries; millions of people as far as my eyes could see and as wide as my eyes could see. And not one person looked at anybody in a wrong way. Everyone was there for one purpose: to worship Allah. It gave me strength and purified my soul.'

- 'I created "The Prince". If all I did was sit at a press conference and say things like, "I've trained hard; I'll do my best," no one would care. But when I'm loud and cocky, it makes people switch on their televisions and that means I'm doing my job. It's the same thing with my ring entrances. When I started fighting on television, SkySport came up with a few ideas and I added to them and people liked it. It's one of the reasons people come to see me fight. It sells tickets. There's a show; there's music; and then there's a proper fight. And there are times when I like being The Prince. It lets me say things that are fun to say but, without a fight to promote, I'd tell myself not to go that far.'

- 'I don't have anything against my opponents. I don't want to hurt them, and I don't want them to hurt me. All I want to do is win. But if I ever lose – or worse, get knocked out – I'll hold out my hand and say to the man who did it, "Congratulations; you were the better fighter tonight." '

- 'People ask, why don't I move up in weight and fight Mayweather and Corrales and Frietas. I started as a flyweight. Now I'm a natural featherweight. With my height and frame and the way I punch, I'm perfect at 126 pounds. Why should I move up? I'm a perfectionist. I like to do things in the best way, and I fight best at this weight. There's no reason I should disadvantage myself and go into the ring at less than my best to please other people. Hey; sometimes I think of myself as a heavyweight. I'd have been a great heavyweight. But at the end of the day, I've come to realise that I'm a five-foot-three-and-a-half-inch guy, and I have what I have, and I have to be grateful for it.'

- 'I was on pilgrimmage when I heard about Paul Ingle. I hoped and prayed for him in Mecca, and I still do. He's in every one of my prayers. As soon as I got back to Sheffield, I went to the hospital. Paul's eyes were closed. They told him, "Naz is here." ' Finally, he opened his eyes and I told him, "Paul, I want you to know; if there comes a time when I fight Mbulelo Botile, I'll dedicate the fight to you and I'll beat him for you; not to hurt him, but to win for you." Paul couldn't speak, but he put his thumb up. And that was a very moving moment for me; to know that Paul understood.'

- 'What makes me sad? Ignorance makes me sad. Sinful people make me sad. People who are asleep and don't realise why we're here make me sad. My father smokes and it's hard to get him to stop. That makes me sad. People smoke, they take drugs, they drink alcohol. And it's like going to someone and saying, "Here's a cup of poison. It won't kill you, but it will start you on your way." They wouldn't drink the poison; but if it's camouflaged, they will.'

All of that brings us then to 7 April: Naseem Hamed versus Marco Antonio Barrera.

Confidence is important for any athlete, and it's particularly important for a fighter. Hamed is supremely confident. In Islam, he has found something larger than himself to flow into. It's true that there are times when he looks like a less-than-complete boxer; particularly when he's under pressure. But Barrera is a one-dimensional fighter, and Hamed should be able to beat him with speed.

Also, with the possible exception of Mike Tyson, Hamed is pound for pound the hardest active puncher in boxing and among the hardest punchers ever in the featherweight division. When a fighter hits as hard as he does, it often renders other considerations irrelevant.

In the days leading up to 7 April, Naseem Hamed will be in 'Prince mode'. But once the bell rings, it won't be an act.

One of the challenges in writing is to find a different angle to a story that hundreds of other writers are covering. Watching Naseem Hamed rehearse his ring entrance prior to fighting Marco Antonio Barrera was part of that process.

Illusion, Reality and Naseem Hamed

Las Vegas is the capital of illusion. Whatever fantasy you have, the men and women who run the casinos will help you pursue it. On 7 April in Las Vegas, illusion and reality collided for Naseem Hamed, and his carefully constructed world came tumbling down.

Hamed made his United States ring debut in 1997 with a fourth-round knockout of Kevin Kelley at Madison Square Garden. At the time, HBO was committed to developing The Prince into a media sensation. There were giant ads featuring a sneering Hamed on bus shelters throughout Manhattan, a 50-foot-wide billboard in Times Square, national advertisements, luncheons, bus trips, even a 40-foot banner in Los Angeles; all designed to raise Hamed's profile in the United States from ground zero to the sky at a cost of one million dollars. On fight night, 150 seats were removed from the Garden's normal seating plan so The Prince could dance down a 200-foot runway amid flashing strobe lights and confetti before somersaulting over the top rope into the ring.

But after the Kelley bout, HBO became an enabler for Hamed. In the succeeding years, he fought two shot fighters (Wilfredo Vazquez and Vuyani Bungu), three guys who couldn't punch (Wayne McCullough, Paul Ingle and Cesar Soto), and one guy who couldn't take a punch (Augie Sanchez). Finally, Hamed came to understand that he needed a true inquisitor to prove his claims of ring greatness. Enter WBO super-bantamweight champion Marco Antonio Barrera.

Barrera had 52 wins coupled with 3 losses and 38 knockouts. In his four defining fights, he had scored a victory over Kennedy McKinney in the first *Boxing After Dark* show ever; lost a disputed decision to

Erik Morales; and suffered two defeats at the hands of Junior Jones. In his most recent bout, he looked impressive in stopping Jesus Salud. Barrera would be Hamed's toughest opponent ever.

Hamed–Barrera was The Prince's pay-per-view debut in the United States and his first fight in Las Vegas. The promotion was a tribute to his showmanship and the skill of both pugilists. The formula it followed was simple. Put the two best fighters in any weight division in the ring together, and you're likely to have a good fight. The bout was marketed as the heavyweight championship of featherweights.

The task of readying Hamed for battle fell in significant measure on the shoulders of Emanuel Steward. Ever since Naseem left Brendan Ingle, he has in effect had two trainers. Before each fight, Steward comes in for several days at the start of training to plan strategy. Then Oscar Suarez takes over the day-to-day chores, and Emanuel resurfaces from time to time before assuming command a week or so before the fight. On fight night, they're co-trainers although Steward has the lead role in the corner.

Steward had been with Hamed for four fights before Barrera, and he spoke glowingly of his charge. 'Naz has an uncanny ability to sense things in the ring,' the trainer said. 'He's very smart and adaptable during a fight. He has the ability to trap his opponents in a slugfest. And when he does, he has unbelievable punching power. His punching power is phenomenal early and late. And Naz attacks from unorthodox angles, which means his punches are even more devastating because often the opponent doesn't see them coming. And he's tough inside. He's a rare gifted kid who always finds a way to win.'

Steward loves big fights. But for this one, he'd been spread pretty thin. He had wanted Hamed to train in Las Vegas, so he could continue his own work with Lennox Lewis and also spend time on a movie with Wesley Snipes. But Hamed had opted for a gated community in Rancho Mirage, where a conference centre was converted to a makeshift gym. For six weeks, the fighter had lived in this compound, leaving only on Fridays for a two-hour round-trip to a mosque in the town of Hemet. Steward flew in by charter plane twice a week until 1 April, when Hamed broke camp and flew to Las Vegas.

'When I started working with Naz, I was amazed at the way things had been done before,' Steward said shortly before the fight. 'Prior to our association, Naz had never done roadwork. He'd never been to a real training camp. He was still preparing for fights surrounded by kids at an amateur centre in Sheffield. He'd never even had his hands properly wrapped before sparring. In fact, when Naz sparred, he and his sparring partners never punched to the head because they were afraid of hurting their hands. I know that's hard to believe, but it's true. It's only in the past two years that Naz has become a true professional fighter.'

But if Hamed was getting better, so was Barrera. And Steward knew it. 'Everyone is saying that this will be an easy fight for Naz,' the trainer cautioned. 'But I just don't see it. Barrera has become a complete fighter. He began his professional career in Mexico when he was fifteen. That means he completed his amateur training as a pro and became a champion before he was seasoned. He's like a lot of these Mexican kids, who lose some fights early because they haven't fully learned their trade. But Barrera's defence has gotten a lot better since he lost to Junior Jones. That fight is long in the past. Back then, Barrera was a kid fighting for money. Now he's a complete fighter. Now he rolls away from punches that used to catch him solid. And the Morales fight showed me that he's the kind of fighter who rises to the occasion. I thought Morales was going to beat the hell out of him. But in the end, believe me, Barrera won that fight. And he looked very good against Jesus Salud. Regardless of Salud's age, it was an impressive performance. So Barrera is good. And what I'm most worried about is, Naz throws lungeing punches and, when he misses, he's off balance when he finishes up. That's why he gets knocked down so much. It's not that he's hurt as much as he's off balance. I've never really seen Naz hurt, on or off his feet. But Barrera can take advantage of Naz being off balance. And if Naz doesn't shorten his punches and keep his left hand close to his chin, Barrera could nail him.'

Lest anyone think that Steward was just blowing smoke and hyping the fight, it had to be remembered that he'd predicted a relatively easy win for Lennox Lewis over David Tua and had gone so far as to say before that fight, 'David Tua is stepping out of his league. If he thinks he's prepared to fight Lennox, he's mistaken.'

Adding to Steward's concern before the Barrera bout was the fear that Hamed was underestimating his opponent. Naseem was working with two Mexican sparring partners. 'He's getting used to smashing Mexicans,' one entourage member noted. But Hamed was coming off a 230-day layoff; the longest of his career. 'Naz should have had tougher sparring; more sparring and better sparring partners,' Emanuel acknowledged several days before the fight.

As the bout approached, both fighters were confident. 'I've seen his weakness. I'll win; I'm sure,' Barrera offered.

'We're both in the same boat,' Hamed countered. 'For both of us, it's the fight of our lives. There will be a collision; I promise you that. Someone is going to get knocked out, and it won't be me.'

On the afternoon of the fight, Hamed sat in his suite on the 29th floor of the MGM Grand Hotel and watched the videotape of a documentary entitled *a/k/a Cassius Clay*. Occasionally, he sipped water that had been brought to him from an underground spring that runs through Mecca. The water is believed to be blessed. Hamed had ingested a bit of it every day since his training began.

At 2.30 p.m., Hamed left his hotel suite. Ten minutes later, accompanied by several family members and friends, he arrived at the Grand Arena and journeyed to its upper reaches to the point where his ring entrance would begin. There, standing on a platform, he examined six signs that would be spotlighted for his entrance. Three of the signs bore the name of the prophet Muhammad. The other three bore the inscription 'Allah'.

'How do I get up to this platform before the fight?' Hamed queried.

'An elevator lift will bring you up,' the man responsible for the technical direction of The Prince's ring entrance answered. 'You'll be back lit; there will be smoke. Once the fog dissipates, you walk down two steps to this white-tape "X" right here. Fountains will rise behind you and confetti will rain down.'

'I don't want to get any confetti on my body.'

'No problem. It will be way behind you.'

'How do I get from here down to the ring?'

'You have two options. Option number one is a fly-rig. Once you're strapped in, it will lift you off the platform. As it goes up, flame projectors will shoot out, and then you'll fly down.'

Hamed crossed the platform to examine the fly-rig. Somewhat sceptically, he pulled at the two supporting cables.

'Are these little things all that hold it up?'

'They're steel cables,' he was told. 'Each one is capable of supporting 980 pounds.'

'Before I ride down in that thing, I want to see someone else do it first.'

'We can show you the pyrotechnics and fountains too.'

'I want to see the dangerous part first.'

Someone from the technical crew sat down on the fly-rig, and a harness was strapped around his waist.

'Good luck,' Hamed offered.

The fly-rig lifted up off the platform, and Hamed watched intently as it descended one hundred feet to the floor below. Then he turned to the director.

'What's Plan B if I refuse to do this?'

'You walk down.'

'That's a lot safer, isn't it.'

The remark was a statement; not a question. Hours before the biggest fight of his life, Naseem Hamed was deliberating whether or not to take the risk of flying on a thin steel contraption to a boxing ring. One had to wonder why he'd be willing to put that extra pressure, perhaps even fear, on himself moments before the fight. The answer was twofold. First, he was aware of his obligations as a showman. The Prince is expected to be bigger than life. And second, in the past, Naseem Hamed had fed off the frenzy of the crowd.

Once again, Hamed stared down at the ring below. 'Maybe they should just put a rope up here,' he suggested, 'and I can swing down like Tarzan.' Then, wordlessly, he walked down the arena stairs, climbed into the ring, and looked back up at the platform. 'All right,' he called out, standing in ring centre. 'Show me what it will look like.'

The director narrated the effects as the demonstration unfolded.

'First, there will be smoke and lights; then the effects. Effect number one will be an airburst with the platform empty. As you come into view on the elevator lift, ten flame-throwers will shoot up. That's effect number two. Number three will be a six-second fountain.'

At this point, the demonstration stalled. There was no fountain.

'We've got a dead battery,' someone shouted.

The dead battery was not lost on Hamed, who was being asked to trust these people and their technology on a one-hundred-foot drop to the ring.

A new battery was inserted, and the six-second fountain blazed. That, in turn, was followed by effect number four; twenty sparklers flaming downward, creating the illusion of a waterfall.

'Have you added up how long the whole thing will take?' Hamed asked.

'The fly-rig will take a maximum of forty seconds from lift-off to the floor.'

'Not just the flight; the whole thing. I'll want to get to the ring.'

'That depends on how long you spent on the platform before you take off.'

'Can the whole thing be done in under three minutes?'

'Absolutely.'

Hamed was businesslike and polite at the same time. 'I want to ride down on that thing myself,' he told the director. 'I need to know exactly how high and how fast it will go.'

Hamed walked back up the stairs to the platform, where his father was waiting. His father expressed concern over the safety of the fly-rig. Naseem has total respect for his father. If his father said, 'Don't do it,' most likely, he wouldn't. But Mr Hamed left the decision to his son.

At 3.35 p.m., Hamed was harnessed into the fly-rig. 'Let's do it,' he said with bravado. The flight from the platform to arena floor lasted thirty seconds. At 3.40 p.m., Hamed left the arena. He had been there for over an hour.

Outside, a light rain was falling. 'It means something when it rains on the day of a fight,' Hamed told his father. 'A desert rain. Allah is bestowing His blessing upon us.'

* * *

Virtually everyone in the media agreed that Hamed–Barrera shaped up as a good fight. And virtually everyone in the media was picking The Prince. The match-up was seen as the equivalent of a test for a gifted student who had studied hard and was expected to pass. Hamed was a solid three-to-one favourite.

As the moment of reckoning approached, the MGM Grand Arena was awash with British and Mexican flags. Both groups of followers were fervent. The Brits were loud and the Mexicans were louder. The atmosphere had the chaotic passionate feel of a World Cup football contest.

Meanwhile, a problem was unfolding. As of 6.45 p.m., Hamed still hadn't arrived at his dressing room; the fight was scheduled to start at eight o'clock; and the fighters' gloves had yet to be chosen.

The glove controversy had been brewing since the previous day's weigh-in. The fighters' contracts called for both boxers to wear Reyes gloves. The Nevada State Athletic Commission had agreed to requests that Hamed be allowed to wear green gloves and Barrera yellow. Then, at the weigh-in, Barrera had chosen a pair of yellow gloves for himself. But Hamed had first choice of gloves under the contract and, changing his colour preference, he decided suddenly that the pair chosen by Barrera was the one he wanted. Thereafter, everything degenerated into uncertainty and the unorthodox colours were discarded.

At 6.48 p.m., finally, Hamed arrived in his dressing room. Two minutes later, Marc Ratner (Executive Director of the Nevada State Athletic Commission) entered with six pairs of red Reyes gloves. Naseem began trying on the gloves. In the background, rap music incorporating the word 'motherfucker' blared. Hamed looked up angrily. 'Turn that off,' he ordered. The room fell silent. 'Who put that on?' he demanded. There was no answer.

One by one, Hamed tried on the gloves, with Ratner placing the discards in a large black plastic bag. None of the gloves satisfied the fighter.

'I'm sorry to be taking so long,' Hamed told Ratner.

'That's all right,' Ratner responded. 'These are your guns. Take your time, and make sure you have the right ones.'

At seven o'clock, three more pairs of gloves were brought into the dressing room. Finally, after Hamed had examined every glove and pumped a series of punches into Oscar Suarez's outstretched hands, a pair marked 'Naz #1' was chosen. Then Ratner journeyed to Barrera's dressing room, where Emanuel Steward was watching Barrera's hands being taped. Ratner set the remaining eight pairs of gloves on a table. A Barrera second walked over and, without looking twice, pointed to a pair at random.

Referee Joe Cortez entered Barrera's dressing room and gave the fighter final instructions. Then he went to Hamed's dressing room, but was refused entry because the fighter was deep in prayer. Finally, at 7.25 p.m., Cortez was allowed in. Hamed's hands were still not taped, nor had he taken off his street clothes. With Cortez waiting, Naseem went into a back room and changed into his ring garb. He was moving deliberately at his own pace; completely in control of the situation, meeting his own strategic and emotional needs; or so it seemed.

At 7.30, Hamed reappeared in leopard-skin boxing trunks, ring shoes and a plain grey T-shirt. Cortez gave him final instructions. Emanuel Steward and a second from Barrera's camp returned from the Mexican's dressing room, and Hamed's hands were taped. Over the next hour, he would glove up, warm up, remove his right glove to retape his thumb, and warm up again. Meanwhile, Barrera waited stoically.

'Everything is already written,' Hamed said to no one in particular. 'Allah knows now who will win.'

As for the fight itself, it can be said simply that Barrera fought a brilliant tactical fight, counterpunching for much of the evening and getting off first when he wanted to. Meanwhile, Hamed spent most of the night looking for one big punch and never found it. The Prince might be a great puncher, but Barrera exposed him as a less-than-great boxer. Neither Hamed's ring skills nor his confidence had ever been so sorely tested and, on this particular occasion, he came up short.

Also, as the fight wore on, Hamed's corner seemed to slide into chaos with his two trainers giving him diametrically opposed instructions. Indeed, after round nine, Suarez told him, 'I know you're going to take him out now, but not with one single shot. Concentrate more on his body. Work the body.' Meanwhile, sensing the urgency of the moment, Steward implored, 'You've got three rounds to go. Every punch has to have knockout on it. All you got to do is land one shot. You may miss three or four, but if you land the fifth, you can still knock him out.'

The judges' decision was unanimous for Barrera: 115–112, 115–112 and 116–111. Anyone who gave Hamed four rounds was being kind to him. Steward himself said afterward that his fighter won three rounds maximum.

In the dressing room, Hamed's father did his best to console him. 'This is a sport,' he told his son. 'There's a winner and a loser. You won them all before tonight, and now you've lost one. There's no shame in this.'

As for Hamed himself, he took his first loss like a champion. His performance in the ring might have validated his critics, but his serenity and grace afterward disarmed them. 'I make no excuses,' he told the media. 'Barrera boxed well. He won the fight clearly. Credit is due to him. He was better than me tonight. I can accept this defeat because it comes from Allah. It's part of Allah's plan for me, and I accept what was written.' And then, somewhat pensively, Hamed added, 'If I can find out the reason for this, I will.'

In truth, it was a hard loss to swallow. Hamed had expected to win big against Barrera; cement his place in boxing history with a victory over Erik Morales later this year; and retire from the sweet science in the near future as a ring immortal. The chapter of his life after boxing had seemed to be beckoning. Now the dream of retiring undefeated is gone for ever.

Eventually, there will be a rematch. It's in the fighters' respective contracts, and Hamed says he wants one. Maybe he'll win it. People made the mistake of overestimating Naseem Hamed as a fighter before this bout. They shouldn't make the mistake of underestimating him as a fighter after it.

When Lennox Lewis's rematch against Hasim Rahman took place, I wrote about it in part through the eyes of Marc Ratner (Executive Director of the Nevada State Athletic Commission), who let me follow him around in the days leading up to the fight.

Guilty Pleasures:
The Rematch, Marc Ratner, and Las Vegas

For many people involved with boxing, there's a guilty pleasure in following the sport. And those feelings can be even more pronounced when a fight is tied to the pleasures of Las Vegas. Still, Marc Ratner, Executive Director of the Nevada State Athletic Commission and the point person for boxing in Las Vegas, has built a national reputation for integrity and competence.

'My philosophy,' says Ratner, 'is to have a level playing field when fights come to Nevada and to be as fair and efficient as possible.'

From time to time, it's suggested that Nevada's casinos exercise more influence with the commission than they should. Ratner himself states the obvious when he says, 'The reason we have as much bigtime boxing as we do in Nevada is because it brings customers into the casinos.' But in the next breath, he notes, 'I don't deal with the presence of the casinos as much as the commissioners might.'

The heavyweight championship rematch between Lennox Lewis and Hasim Rahman was a special moment for Ratner. One year earlier, Las Vegas had hosted Lewis versus David Tua against the backdrop of a disputed presidential election. Now the backdrop was more ominous. September 11 and the anthrax scare that followed had traumatised America. The eyes of the world would be focused on Las Vegas and its flagship event. The city that urges visitors to forget all worldly cares would be a tempting target for terrorists; particularly when one considered the nationalities of Lewis (the Brit) and Rahman (the American) with Rahman's Islamic heritage thrown into the mix.

'This is a big fight for Vegas because the town has been quiet lately,' Ratner said several days before the fight.

The promotion swung into high gear with a final press conference three days before the bout. There's a different feel to a Don King event. King adds excitement; he's part of the show. And Rahman–Lewis wasn't just for the heavyweight championship. More importantly for King, the outcome of the bout would determine who controlled the heavyweight champion of the world.

King was Rahman's exclusive promoter, but he had no paper on Lewis beyond the rematch. Also, Lewis was tied to HBO whereas Rahman, at King's urging, had eschewed a long-term TV contract to remain a free agent.

'A TV contract is only an insurance policy for losing,' King told the assembled media. 'I don't want to know what Rock gets if he loses. I want to know what Rock gets when he wins. This is what you call "rolling the dice; winner take all." Rock ain't no one-night stand.'

Meanwhile, behind the scenes, Ratner was at work. On Wednesday morning, he met with Mandalay Bay security personnel and representatives of the Metropolitan Police Department to discuss safeguarding the fight site. Next, he sat down with representatives of both fighters and Don King Productions for an organisational meeting. That was followed by a rules meeting with officials from the world sanctioning bodies that had put their championship imprimatur on the bout.

'We have an organised format for big fights,' explained Ratner. 'But not everything can be anticipated. I suppose the most bizarre situation we ever had was the "Fan-Man" incident [when a nut parachuted into the ring midway through Bowe–Holyfield II]. Nothing in the boxing manual told us how to handle that one. The Tyson–Holyfield bite incident was difficult to deal with. And of course there was the ugly aftermath to that fight on the casino floor [Nevada officials refer to it as an "alleged shooting incident"].'

Rahman and Lewis weighed in on Thursday. Hasim tipped the scales at 236 pounds; Lennox, ten pounds heavier. That same day, Dr Margaret Goodman, the neurologist who serves as medical director of the Nevada State Athletic Commission, administered the final pre-fight physicals. The fighters' bloodwork and other tests had been conducted earlier. This was a general check of lungs, temperature, blood pressure, pulse, eyes, ears, possible hernia symptoms and the like. Goodman knew both fighters, having worked with them before. She examined Lewis first, engaging him in conversation as she probed.

'How are you feeling?'

'Good,' Lennox answered.

'Any recent colds or the flu?'

'No.'

'What will you have for breakfast on Saturday?'

'Eggs and sweet plantains, fried.'

'When will your last meal be?'

'Around four o'clock.'

'What will you have?'

'Pasta.'

The examination was over in less than ten minutes. The most significant finding was that Lewis's nose appeared to have been broken since the last time he'd fought in Las Vegas. The cartilage on the right side had collapsed, and he couldn't draw air through his right nostril as well as before. Also, Lennox's blood pressure was higher than before previous fights; 150 over 88. And his pulse was eighty, which was faster than his past pre-fight norm. He seemed nervous.

Rahman was next, and Dr Goodman repeated the process. Hasim appeared to be more relaxed than Lennox; as though he were enjoying the ride. His blood pressure was 120 over 80 and his pulse was in the mid-sixties, both of which were normal for a relaxed well-conditioned professional athlete.

'What will you eat for your last meal before the fight?' Dr Goodman queried.

'I don't know. Probably pizza.'

The physicals seemed to confirm the pre-fight buzz; namely, that Rahman had 'gotten inside Lewis's head'.

The Hasim Rahman who settled into Las Vegas appeared confident and focused, but there were doubts about Lewis. Many of those doubts sprang from the first meeting between the two men, when Rahman knocked Lewis out in the fifth round. 'Lennox was winning every round and just got hit,' trainer Emanuel Steward said. 'It's part of boxing.'

'The punch was a great punch,' Lewis added. 'But I never put my left hand in position to block it. My defence wasn't like it should have been. I wouldn't say I was cocky or arrogant. I think those are the wrong words. But I may have taken him a bit lightly and didn't realise he was able to throw a punch like that. I'm going to make sure my defence is up in a better position this time. There's no way I want to get caught by that punch again.'

Still, a man can't go swimming without getting wet. And a fighter can't get in a boxing ring without getting hit. Wisdom decreed that some of Rahman's punches would get through to Lewis again. And more to the point, Lennox seemed to be in denial regarding some basic facts relevant to their first fight.

'I wasn't able to get off the canvas because the referee counted too fast,' Lennox said of that night. 'The ref was trying to count me out as fast as possible. When I was getting up, he stopped the fight.'

Steward adhered to the party line, also claiming the stoppage had been quick. 'When Lennox went down,' Steward said, 'the referee started counting like he was in a race. I know that for a fact because I was there. I've seen guys in heavyweight championship fights hurt much worse than Lennox was and come back to win. Larry Holmes did it against Earnie Shavers and Renaldo Snipes. Evander Holyfield was hurt worse than that in the second Ruiz fight, and they let it go on. The round was almost over. If the referee had given Lennox a normal count, he would have been able to go on. This was the heavyweight champion of the world defending his title. You give the man a chance.'

To many observers, Lewis's cavalier attitude toward Rahman in South Africa, his failure to train at altitude before the fight, and a suspect chin had more to do with the outcome of Lewis–Rahman I than the referee's count or a lucky punch. Indeed, Lennox had seemed to be tiring badly in round five and had been hit with a damaging right hand moments before the knockout blow. Thus, if one were looking for wisdom in Steward's remarks, it might have been in the message that Lennox had to fight a careful fight the second time around. That is, even if attitude and altitude weren't problems, there was still the matter of a suspect chin. Lewis's chin, it was posited, had kept him from the ranks of boxing greats.

He might not have a glass jaw; but there's always Lenox china.

Meanwhile, Rahman had his own take on things. He saw Lewis as a limited pugilist ('Jab...counterpunch...jab...counterpunch'), lacking in versatility and without heart. As for claims of a quick count in South Africa, the champion noted, 'You saw the fight. The referee counted to ten. He could have counted to twenty, and Lennox wouldn't have been able to go on. They refuse to deal with the truth.' Rahman concluded, 'They just can't accept that I have his number.'

Rahman claimed to have Lewis's number outside the ring too. There was growing personal enmity between the two men, accentuated by the champion's frequent allusions to rumours that Lewis is gay. An ugly TV-studio brawl in August brought the matter to the fore and, throughout fight week, Rahman continued his taunts.

'Is Lennox gay?' a reporter asked on Wednesday.

'How many children does Lennox have?' Rahman countered. And then he added, 'Emanuel is trying to make his baby nice and comfortable.'

Lewis sat stoically through it all. 'I have to store my emotions up and save them for the fight,' he said. 'I'll do my damage in the ring.'

Still, there were doubts. Even Emanuel Steward conceded, 'Lennox has an extremely complicated make-up mentally. You can talk to Lennox and still not know what's going on in his mind. Lennox thinks too much. Sometimes, I look at Lennox and it looks like he's playing chess in the ring. But it's not a chess game; it's a fist fight.'

Meanwhile, Rahman seemed pleased with where the fighters were psychologically. 'I've heard them say that I'm a journeyman; I'm a bum; I'm nothing,' he noted. 'But now Lennox is fighting the biggest fight of his life, and it's against me. I know I humiliated him. I knocked him out. I took his title. The facts speak for themselves. I'm in his head, big; you know what I'm saying? I can punch hard, and Lennox knows that now. But the thing is, even though he's aware of it this time, there's nothing he can do to stop it. I humiliated this man. I knocked him out, and the same thing is coming this time only faster.'

The day before the fight, Rahman seemed totally relaxed. He was walking the hotel, mingling with fight fans. He even went to the Orleans Hotel and Casino to watch one of his stablemates, Davarryl

Williamson, knock out Andre Kopolov on ESPN2's *Friday Night Fights*. Then he ate dinner at Raffles Cafe.

On the surface, all of the psychological signs appeared to favour the champion. His body language radiated confidence, whereas Lewis's seemed to radiate doubt. When the rematch was first announced, the odds had been four to one in Lennox's favour. By fight night, those numbers had been cut in half.

Meanwhile, behind the scenes, Marc Ratner was doing his job. The Nevada State Athletic Commission runs a tight ship, and 17 November was no exception. The first bout was scheduled to begin at 3.00 p.m. Lewis–Rahman was slated for nine o'clock. Ratner arrived at the arena at 1.30. He measured the ring canvas to make sure it conformed to specifications; then climbed into the ring and walked every square foot checking for dead spots. Next, he examined the ring ropes. 'We're down to a science on the big fights,' he said. No detail was too small for scrutiny.

At 2.15, the commission officials who would be working the card gathered at ringside, and Ratner reviewed each person's responsibilities. The level playing field he sought could be tilted by accident or design. Either way, as far as Ratner was concerned, a tilt would be unacceptable. His final words to the group were, 'This is a big night for us; a huge heavyweight championship card. Have fun and concentrate on your jobs.'

The undercard fights began. As they progressed, Ratner walked the floor, making certain that everything was in order; saying hello to casino executives and sanctioning body officials, ushers and security guards; greeting everyone with the warmth of a friend. Someone asked if he was nervous. 'Not really,' he answered. 'I get nervous if I'm compiling the scoring of the judges between rounds and the scores don't look right to me. When that happens, I say to myself, "I hope we have a knockout tonight." But other than that, I'm usually OK.'

As is his custom, Ratner visited the dressing room of every under-card fighter before each bout ('Welcome to Las Vegas...I'm glad you're here...Good luck...'). And he repeated the process afterward ('Good fight...Congratulations...Are you all right?...').

The Mandalay Bay Events Center began to fill up. The fight had caught on within the boxing community. The arena was sold out.

At 7.50 p.m., Ratner and referee Joe Cortez entered Lewis's dressing room. The room was silent.

Cortez gave Lewis the standard rules review and pre-fight instructions. 'Are there any questions?' he asked the fighter.

'Is there a standing eight count?' Lewis queried.

Cortez said there wasn't. Then he and Ratner journeyed to Rahman's dressing room. Loud voices and pulsating music filled the air. Cortez repeated his pre-fight instructions, closing again with, 'Are there any questions?'

There were none.

Ratner left. At 8.15, he returned to the fighters' dressing rooms one last time with the gloves that would be worn during the fight. Lewis had an intense, almost haunted, look on his face. Rahman seemed like a man preparing to go to a party, as though he intended to pick up in this fight where he'd left off in South Africa.

Forty-five minutes later, with the crowd roaring, Lewis left the sanctuary of his dressing room and made his way to the ring.

Three minutes later, Rahman followed. But now, there was a change in the champion's visage. The cockiness was gone. There was no longer any joy in his face. The absence of joy was to be expected. But more telling, the aura of confidence present all week had been replaced by a look of worry and concern.

Lewis had been storing up the meanness, anger, cruelty, even hate, that would be necessary for him to do what he had to do. Lewis was coming into the ring with an attitude.

By contrast, Rahman had been too relaxed in the days leading up to the fight. In the process of talking the talk, he seemed to have never prepared mentally to walk the walk. He'd been so busy trying to get inside Lennox's head that he had never fully readied his own.

Yes, Rahman had gotten under Lewis's skin. Now, he was about to pay the price. The party was over.

In boxing, 'big' is often a state of mind. In the ring, Lewis looked far more than ten pounds bigger than Rahman.

The bell rang. In round one, Lewis sliced open the skin above the champion's left eye with a jab. Then, still jabbing, he kept him at bay, boxing and punching from the first round on. Rahman's best hope seemed to lie in surviving until the middle rounds, when the rhythms of their first fight might repeat. But it wasn't to be. Midway through round four, Lewis threw a left hook that grazed the champion's chin and moved his head back into the line of fire. A monster right hand that landed flush on the jaw followed. Rahman plummeted to the canvas, rose through an act of Herculean will, and pitched back to the canvas again. It was over at 1.29 of round four.

Amid the tumult, Margaret Goodman crossed the ring to tend to Rahman. Bleary-eyed, lying on his back, the deposed champion's first words were, 'What happened?'

'You got knocked out,' Dr Goodman told him.

'I didn't see the punch.'

A minute passed. Rahman gathered his senses. Then, looking up, he saw a replay of the knockout blow on the giant screen above him.

'Wow!' he said to no one in particular. 'He's the real champion.'

Never before had two such dramatic knockouts with such dramatically opposite results been juxtaposed in championship bouts between two men.

After leaving the ring, Rahman went to his dressing room, retreated to the adjacent bathroom alone with his wife, dressed quickly, and left. In another room down the corridor, Lennox Lewis sat on a wooden bench with a quiet smile on his face. 'I knew what I wanted to do,' he said. 'And I went out and did it. I was keeping everything I felt inside me, saying, "OK; you'll pay come fight time."'

Meanwhile, back on the floor of the arena, Marc Ratner was addressing the Nevada State Athletic Commission personnel who had worked the fight. Everything of importance that had just transpired was critiqued. Then paycheques were distributed to the per diem employees with thanks for a job well done.

Audley Harrison is an enigma of sorts to a sporting public that wants more from him than he has been willing to give so far.

Audley Harrison

Audley Harrison has an attitude.

'I've always been opinionated,' says the man who triumphed in the super-heavyweight division at Sydney to become the first British boxer in 32 years to win an Olympic gold medal. 'I'll only do things on my own terms; never on anyone else's, unless their ideas match mine. Whatever social system or institution I've been in, I've rebelled against the authorities. I hate people telling me what to do. I could never be a middleweight and have people telling me I had to lose a certain number of pounds. Most people are afraid to speak out and put their neck on the line, but I'm true to myself. I'm a shepherd; not a sheep. I'm a non-conformist, a rebel. I love proving people in positions of authority wrong.'

It's not lost on Harrison that, when he was younger, people would cross the street to avoid him. Now they cross over to ask for his autograph. 'Being a public figure is a role,' he says. 'It's a game. Most people get tired of playing it after a while, but it's part of my job.'

Harrison was born in London to parents of Jamaican heritage. When he was four, his mother left home to live with another man.

'I honestly couldn't tell you what she was like,' Harrison says in his memoirs. 'All I know is that she was a nurse, continues to live in north-west London, and has had three more children. It's a quarter-century since she left home, and I've seen her only three times since then. She has stuck with the guy she married second time around, so she can't be that bad. But there's no bond between us. She's just another woman.'

Harrison's father, a plasterer, raised his four sons on his own. He considered giving them up for adoption, but decided not to when he learned that child welfare authorities would be likely to place them in separate homes.

'My dad is a decent hard-working man who has lived his life obeying the law,' says Harrison. 'He taught us all the difference between right and wrong.'

Nonetheless, Harrison was a textbook example of a child from a broken home who went wrong. He was expelled from two schools, developed only meagre academic skills, and was constantly in trouble with the law.

'When I was getting into trouble as a teenager,' Harrison acknowledges, 'I knew I was doing wrong. At first, it was about having fun and having an adventure. But as I grew older, mischief turned to misdemeanour and misdemeanour turned to crime. I never felt like a bad guy. I was a thrill-seeking bored teenager brought up in a tough street environment where trouble hung in the air. But the older I became, the more I lived on the edge and the more risks I took. Scraps turned from fist fights to serious assaults involving bottles, knives and knuckledusters. Most of the trouble involved showdowns with other gangs, although I did go through a bad bullying stage as I got older.'

Ultimately, Harrison was incarcerated for eighteen months after a wave of offences including vandalism, street robbery and assault. 'I knew guys who, in all honesty, were no worse than me,' he says, looking back on that time. 'But they had stabbed someone in a fight and the guy had died, and they ended up doing life for murder. I could easily have been one of those guys. I'd been in plenty of nasty fights, and it was just luck that no one came at me when I had my knife.'

Released from prison at age nineteen, Harrison resolved to turn his life around. He went back to school – 'I started at the bottom; got some basic qualifications' – and eventually earned a college degree. While in school, he held a series of jobs ranging from work as a forklift-truck driver to a stint as a lifeguard. Meanwhile, his younger brother Rodney was a member of a local boxing club, and one night Harrison went to watch him fight. Soon after, intrigued by what he'd seen, he decided to give it a try.

'I was as raw as a boxer can be,' Harrison remembers. 'But I had an instinctive feel for it. I could throw a natural jab and a natural cross. My movement around the ring and my timing were good. I had quick hands. I could think on my feet. Everything felt right, as if I'd been boxing for years.'

Harrison's first amateur bout was a second-round knockout of a local policeman in May 1992. Over time, he progressed up the ladder, winning a gold medal at the 1998 Commonwealth Games in Kuala Lumpur. But his ultimate amateur goal was Olympic gold.

Only two British boxers qualified for the 2000 Olympics. Harrison was one of them. There were sixteen super-heavyweights in Sydney, and he prevailed with victories over Alexei Lezin of Russia, Olekseii Mazikkin of the Ukraine, Paolo Vidoz of Italy and Mukhtarkhan Dildabekov of Kazakhstan. At age 29, he had fulfilled his dream.

Then it was on to Dream Two. Riding the crest of his Olympic success, Harrison turned pro with a financial flourish. Granada Media paid a large advance for his autobiography, written with Niall Edworthy. Octagon (a global sports marketing company) took him on as a client. But the centrepiece of Harrison's financial portfolio was an exclusive two-year ten-fight deal with the BBC for live United Kingdom television and radio rights to his fights. That deal, signed in January 2001, pays Harrison more than one million pounds. But oddly, the BBC failed to incorporate quality control provisions with regard to Harrison's opponents in the contract.

Therein lies the rub. On 19 May 2001, Harrison made his professional debut by knocking out an inept punching bag named Mike Middleton in the first round. On 22 September, after a period of inactivity due to a cracked rib, an overweight out-of-shape Harrison boxed six dreary rounds en route to a decision over Derek McCafferty. A second-round knockout of Piotr Jurczyk followed on 22 October. After that, a damaged pectoral muscle sidelined Harrison for the rest of the year.

There are questions regarding Harrison's motivation as a professional fighter. There's also concern that he might be too fragile for the professional demands of the sweet science, given the fact that, as an amateur, he suffered through three hernia operations, a ruptured knuckle hood, a torn tendon, stress fractures in both feet and torn ligaments in his shoulder. Doubts have also been raised regarding his training regimen. Between bouts, Harrison works with his former amateur trainer. Then, as a fight approaches, Thell Torrence and Kenny Croom fly in from the United States to sharpen him up.

In sum, Harrison hopes to follow in the footsteps of Floyd Patterson, Muhammad Ali, Joe Frazier, George Foreman, the Spinks brothers and Lennox Lewis as Olympic gold-medalists who won the heavyweight crown. But there are those who believe that comparisons with Tyrell Biggs are more appropriate.

'The British media is an interesting bunch,' Harrison says of his critics. 'I think they want me to do well, but they want me to do it on their terms. At this stage, it's about learning. People want me to get to the top, but it's important that I do it properly, which means slowly. I'll take plenty of punches and be in plenty of hard fights as my career goes on.'

'My biggest assets as a fighter are my mental strength and ability to perform under pressure,' Harrison continues. 'In the ring, you've got to be prepared to go places where normal people can't go. It's kill or be killed. I'm a respectable puncher; not a big puncher. And for a big guy, I have good hand speed and good footwork. The guys I'm fighting now are the same level opponent that Joe Frazier, George Foreman and Lennox Lewis fought early in their pro careers. Give me time. I'll get there.'

And then Harrison is on a roll.

'The press can sway public opinion, but it's not necessarily an accurate reflection of public opinion. I'm OK with the public's reaction to me as a professional so far. It's a big thing, being a British heavyweight. British fans are patriotic. They support their own. They're the most loyal fans in the world. But before Lennox, British heavyweight boxing was about fighters who were courageous, gutsy, strong, and losers. I don't want to be just another British heavyweight contender. I want to be heavyweight champion of the world. If it doesn't happen, so be it. But I think I have the talent to reach my goal. I don't fantasise. I visualise and dream, and then I make my vision a goal and do my best to turn it into reality. I'm boxing now because I want to; not because I have to. I search for adventure; and right now, that adventure is boxing. But if there comes a time when I don't want to box, either because I'm losing or because my skills have plateaued beneath the level where I want them to be, then I'm on to other goals.'

What's left then is the issue of Harrison's contract with the BBC.

There's a school of thought that neither the network nor the public is getting its money's worth as Audley fights irregularly against the softest of touches.

Harrison responds. 'In amateur boxing, there's a boy scout mentality. "Think this! Think that! Do what we tell you to do!" And nothing prepares the fighter for the pros. But I'm beyond that. I'm cool, calm and rational about the way I go about my business. Everyone, no matter what their job, wants to make as much money as they can. If they can negotiate more, they will. Fighters are paid very differently from one another, and it's not just about their boxing skills. All I did was go out and negotiate the best deal I could for myself. I did something financially that most fighters don't get to do until they're champions.

'I negotiated a good deal for myself, and that's what I got,' Harrison says in closing. 'But you can't put a price on what I did for England. What I did at the Olympics touched a nation. I was carrying other people's dreams. And I stayed amateur for ten years pursuing my goal, because I needed a gold medal to do the business things I knew I'd want to do. But that medal wasn't guaranteed. I took the risks and put in the work, and it's only fair that now I reap the rewards. What's the point of boxing for ten years and being the bravest gunslinger on the block if, at the end of it all, you have nothing to show for it?'

In sum, Audley Harrison might have broken the law when he was young, but he's not breaking any law now. All he did was go out and make the best deal possible for himself.

Over the years, thousands of boxers have been financially exploited by the system. If a boxer can go out and exploit the system for his own gain without doing anything unlawful, more power to him.

Hugh McIlvanney is a patron saint for boxing writers.

Hugh McIlvanney

One can make a strong argument that the best sports writer in the world lives in London.

There are two major awards for sports journalism bestowed annually in Great Britain. The first is the British Press Award for 'Sports Journalist of the Year'. Hugh McIlvanney has been accorded that honour eight times. The second is 'Sports Journalist of the Year' as chosen by the British Sports Council. McIlvanney won that award in each of the first three years of its existence. Then he was asked to become a judge in the selection process, which removed him from further consideration. More significantly, he is the only sports writer ever to win the British Press Award for 'Journalist of the Year'. And he's the first foreign-born writer designated by the Boxing Writers Association of America as recipient of the Nat Fleischer Memorial Award for excellence in boxing journalism. In sum, McIlvanney is a giant.

Hugh McIlvanney was born in Scotland on 2 February 1934. 'There's no point darting around that one,' he acknowledges. Four decades ago, he was working as a general news and features writer for the *Scotsman*, when the editor requested that he turn to sport. McIlvanney was reluctant, fearing that he would end up as 'nothing but a football writer'. To allay those fears, the editor gave him a copy of A J Liebling's classic work on boxing, *The Sweet Science*. 'Liebling confirmed for me that writing about sport could be worthwhile,' says McIlvanney. 'Of course, the high standard of his writing also frightened the life out of me.'

In 1962, having decided that writing about sport was in fact 'a proper job,' McIlvanney sent a letter of application and some clippings to the *Observer* in London. He was offered a position, and the rest is history. For three decades, McIlvanney and the *Observer* were synonymous with one another. Then in 1993, the *Observer* was taken over by the *Guardian*. 'At that point,' McIlvanney recounts, 'the *Observer* ceased to be the paper I had worked for for so many years. The *Guardian* was behaving like an occupying army and I had no desire to be taken prisoner, so I moved to the *Sunday Times*.'

As chief sports journalist for *The Times*, McIlvanney now covers football, boxing, horse racing and golf. He writes occasionally for magazines. And he was the literary craftsman who pieced together the autobiography of Alex Ferguson (manager of Manchester United, the world's most fabled football franchise). To date, the Ferguson book has sold 600,000 copies in hardcover, making it the best-selling sports book in the history of British publishing.

McIlvanney is also something of a pugilist himself. He is rumoured to have knocked out Norman Mailer with a single punch when Mailer challenged him to a fight. And Henry Cooper, who reigned as British and Commonwealth heavyweight champion for ten years, recalls, 'Once, when Hughie had a bit too much to drink, he wanted to fight me. It didn't come to anything. I said, "Calm down, son," and, I'm pleased to say, he did just that.'

McIlvanney, for his part, doesn't remember the Cooper incident. But he doesn't deny it either and says simply, 'It would have been a short fight and a long recuperation. If it happened, I'm thankful that Henry has a kind nature.'

As for boxing itself, McIlvanney freely admits, 'My ambivalence runs very deep. I'm aware of all the statistical evidence that boxing is less dangerous than mountaineering, and boxing is less dangerous than automobile racing. But that's not the issue. The issue is motive and a core of frightening violence. No matter how you dress it up, boxing is two men trying to batter each other senseless. And we, the public, get the charge without suffering the damage. Also, the whole circus approach to boxing that we see so much of these days appals and depresses me. The ugly babble that comes out of Mike Tyson. Laila Ali and Jacqui Frazier shamelessly plundering their fathers' good names. Professional wrestling can say, "We're just playing; no one is getting hurt." But in boxing, people *are* getting hurt. And the more I see of that show business rubbish, the more I feel I could turn my back on the sport.'

'Now, having said that,' McIlvanney continues, 'I'll add that one should examine the motives of all abolitionists. I'm tired of doctors who attack the sport and say of each knockout, "So-and-so won that fight on brain damage." People who drink get brain damage too. And some wonderful human activity has come out of boxing; moments of glory and fighters travelling to places inside themselves that few of us will ever reach. Still, the arguments against boxing are valid. And improved medical care, better pay for fighters; none of that will change the essence of it. Either you take boxing whole or not at all. If boxing were banned tomorrow, I couldn't raise a passionate outcry against the decision. Still, the truth is, as long as boxing exists, I suspect that I'll find it utterly irresistible.'

As a writer, McIlvanney professes to be 'happiest when celebrating greatness.' Thus, it's no surprise that perhaps his favourite personage to write about has been Muhammad Ali. 'Ali in his prime was the greatest figure in the history of sport,' says McIlvanney. 'He had the capacity to dream himself anew each morning and then inhabit that dream. He didn't just thrill you. He was a magical spirit of joy.'

Lennox Lewis is another favourite. 'Lennox,' McIlvanney opines, 'would have been competitive with any heavyweight in history because of his size and ability. He's a big man; he can punch; he knows how to look after himself. He's only lost one fight [author's note: McIlvanney was speaking in January 2001]. And if they'd had the same referee that night that they had when Larry Holmes fought Earnie Shavers or Renaldo Snipes, Lennox might well be undefeated as a professional. I think Ali would have beaten Lennox,' McIlvanney continues. 'Muhammad would have dazzled him and found a way to win. And George Foreman in his prime, before Ali broke his heart, had the size and punch to beat Lennox. But other than those two, I'd bet Lennox Lewis in a fight against any heavyweight ever. That's not a pound-for-pound assessment. I'd rate Joe Louis and a number of other heavyweights ahead of him pound-for-pound. But if you could match them up by way of a time machine, Lennox would be fifty pounds heavier than Joe Louis in his prime. Rocky Marciano fought at 186 pounds. There's no way that Rocky Marciano could give Lennox Lewis 65 pounds and beat him. Lennox lacks fire. Lennox lacks passion in the ring. He's a percentage player. But I'm prepared to accept Lennox for what he is, which is considerable, and I have no question about his heart.' McIlvanney says in closing, 'I just hope Lennox retires while he's still champion. He'd feel so good about it for the rest of his life.'

As for his philosophy of writing, McIlvanney says simply, 'It's important to maintain a sensible perspective on the relationship between sport and the world at large. For that reason, I've always been thankful for the years I spent writing about general news. And there should be a sound knowledge of the sport being covered. A good sports writer must be equipped to judge performances without waiting for experts to explain what he's been watching. That's not to say that one has to know all the answers, but a good writer knows the questions.'

And then McIlvanney adds modestly, 'My approach to writing is not an expectation of triumph, but a determination to avoid screwing up. When I write, I imagine people I respect scrutinising my work. I have an almost neurotic concern to avoid making a mess of it.'

One of those who McIlvanney might imagine evaluating his work is A J Liebling. 'If you couldn't go to a fight, the best commentary you could have on it was Liebling,' he says reflectively. 'Of course, Liebling had a great advantage in that he was writing about boxing. It's a writer's sport. You have courage, romance, skulduggery, excitement and moments of unspeakable horror. Liebling couldn't have written the way he wrote if he'd been writing about croquet.'

A wistful look crosses McIlvanney's face. 'You know, I greatly regret never having met Liebling. I wish I'd had the presence of mind near the end...' His voice trails off and then picks up again. 'It's one of those regrets we all have.'

No doubt, there will be writers who feel the same way about Hugh McIlvanney in the future. But those of us in the writing fraternity expect to have him active and with us for a long time.

Lewis–Tyson was a great 'writers' fight'. This was the first of three articles that I wrote about it once it became clear that the fight was going to happen.

Lewis–Tyson: The Gathering Storm

In mid-January 2002, Mike Tyson visited Jose Torres in New York. Tyson and Torres share a unique bond. In the 1960s, Torres was trained and managed by Cus D'Amato, who guided him to the world light-heavyweight championship. Twenty years later, D'Amato began the process of shaping Tyson's ring destiny.

The Tyson–Torres relationship, like many of Mike's personal interactions, has been inconsistent. But Torres is one of the few men who Tyson feels he can open up to and receive an understanding ear in return. As the two men talked, Tyson seemed on edge.

'Are you in trouble?' Torres asked.

'Yes.'

'What's the problem?'

'I have rage,' Tyson told him. 'And I can't control it.'

'If you know that, you can make it better,' Torres said. 'But you'll need help.'

One week later, Tyson's rage led to a cataclysmic explosion at the kick-off press conference for his proposed bout against Lennox Lewis. That meant, for a while, Lewis–Tyson was Lewis–Tysoff. In the weeks that followed, the charts of fight organisers began to resemble a map of the electoral college. Nevada, California, New York, Texas, Georgia and Colorado all turned their back on the contest. Washington DC, Michigan and Tennessee pursued it. Finally, the bout landed in Memphis, where Lewis and Tyson are expected to do battle on 8 June. But in deference to Tyson's peculiarities and Lewis's demands re same, the promotion has taken on a surreal quality with bizarre overtones and unprecedented contract clauses.

Let's start with some numbers.

Mike Tyson's name has become synonymous with money, and the bout's finances reflect that reality. There are 19,185 tickets priced from $250 to $2,400. The pay-per-view price has been set at $54.95, which makes it the most expensive PPV event ever. The goal of event organisers is to surpass the all-time record of 1,990,000 buys set by Holyfield–Tyson II in 1997. However, those ubiquitous 'black boxes' are more in evidence now than five years ago, and two million buys seems like an unrealistic target.

A tangled web of contracts dictates how the fight will be financed and conducted. There are contracts between HBO and Showtime; HBO and Lewis; Showtime and Tyson; HBO, Showtime, and the promotional triad of Main Events, Lion Promotions and Fight Night; the three primary promoters and Prize Fight Boxing (the local promoter); and the promotional triad and The Pyramid.

There is financial parity between HBO and Showtime on the fight. The two cable giants will split all production, travel, and marketing costs equally and share equally in the various revenue streams that flow from the bout. Main Events and the other promoters will be paid largely out of the promotion budget. But internally, there are differences. Lewis and Tyson are each guaranteed $17,500,000 by their respective networks. After HBO makes a profit of $5,000,000, Lewis will receive virtually all of the remaining profit from HBO's end. Tyson is believed to have a slightly less advantageous profit split with Showtime. Even if pay-per-view sales disappoint, this will be Lewis's biggest payday ever.

The live pay-per-view telecast of the bout will be handled by a neutral announcing team. Both HBO and Showtime will also have their regular announcers on site. If Lewis wins, HBO will televise its version of the fight on tape delay and pay Showtime $3,000,000. If Tyson wins, Showtime will air the tape delay with its announcing team and pay HBO $3,000,000.

If that sounds simple, it's not. As one HBO insider acknowledged, 'Virtually every negotiating point has been a hassle.'

Take, for example, the issue of who will be the ring announcer. Jimmy Lennon has long been identified with Showtime. Michael Buffer is thought of in conjunction with HBO. The HBO–Showtime contract says that Lennon and Buffer will have financial parity in the production budget as well as airtime parity. But Buffer usually gets more money than Lennon and is being asked by the joint promotion to take a pay cut.

Then there's the matter of which ring announcer will say what. The current script reads like the lead-in to a stilted Academy Award presentation:

LENNON: Ladies and gentlemen around the world; welcome to Memphis, Tennessee.

BUFFER: This bout is sanctioned by the World Boxing Council and International Boxing Federation.

LENNON: The officials at ringside are . . .

BUFFER: The referee is Bozo the Clown, and the three judges . . .

Lennon will then introduce Tyson. Buffer will introduce Lewis. It has been agreed that, somewhere in the mix, Buffer will intone, 'Let's get ready to rumble.' And the bell will ring.

Should Lewis win by knockout or disqualification, Buffer will announce the result. Should Tyson win by knockout or disqualification, Lennon will announce the result. If the fight goes the distance, rather than rob the moment of its suspense, the two men will alternate the reading of the scorecards or flip a coin to determine who says what. Except – and this is a big 'except' – Buffer wasn't consulted when the HBO–Showtime contract was entered into and hasn't agreed to its terms yet.

For those who are superstitious, Lewis's record in recent title fights when Buffer is not the ring announcer is 1-2-1. That includes one-punch knockout losses to Oliver McCall and Hasim Rahman and the draw in Lewis–Holyfield I. By contrast, Lennox has never lost with Buffer at ringside; but neither has Tyson, dating back to the early days for both men on ESPN.

As for Jimmy Lennon; all of Tyson's losses (Buster Douglas and both Holyfield fights) as well as his two no-contests (Orlin Norris and Andrew Golota) have come with Showtime's favourite announcer at ringside. Overall, Tyson is 10-3-2 with Lennon on hand, and Lewis is 3-0-1 (Holyfield I and II plus Rahman II and Tony Tucker).

These are the sort of minutiae that the greatest minds in the sports and communications industries are now pondering. But there remains a more troubling issue – Mike Tyson's conduct.

In some respects, Lewis–Tyson is being packaged as a real-life version of professional wrestling. But the sad truth is, the heavyweight championship is up for grabs, and virtually everyone involved with the promotion is saying, 'We can't do this because it might make Mike angry,' or 'We can't do that because everyone will find out how out of control Mike really is.'

Tyson, in essence, is saying to the world, 'I'm going to do what I want to do. Like it or leave it, and leave me the fuck alone.' He has surrounded himself with enablers and, whatever he does, there are always people who tell him, 'Yeah, Mike; you're right.'

The licensing deliberations that led to Lewis–Tyson might have addressed what Tyson does. They did not address why he does it. The man has problems and everyone associated with him, including Tyson himself, knows it.

On 30 April, Tyson met with a carefully chosen group of reporters in Maui, where he is training for the fight. Tim Smith of the *New York Daily News* was among them. 'It was bizarre,' Smith said later. 'Mike had a towel that he kept chewing on. He was very obscene, and his thoughts weren't really connected. He threw out the N-word like he was seeding a flower garden and talked about everything from Buddha to how Jesus smoked marijuana.'

The press session began with Tyson responding to a female reporter who asked about the upcoming fight: 'It's no doubt I'm going to win this fight, and I feel confident about winning this fight.' Then he added, 'I normally don't do interviews with women unless I fornicate with them. So you shouldn't talk any more unless you want to, you know.'

Thereafter, reporters were treated to a bizarre stream of consciousness:

- 'I could play the game and say I'm somebody I'm not, but I'm not that kind of person. I'm uninhibited. If I'm being interviewed by a lady, I have to say, "Hey, you're looking good." I just have to be Mike.'
- 'The people want to be lied to. That's the deal. The people don't want to believe their idol is a freak; that he likes to get fellatio. They don't want to believe that he might want somebody to stick

their finger up his butt. But the truth is, he might like that.'

- 'I think it's un-American not to go out with a woman, not to be with a beautiful woman, not to get my cock sucked. You know what I mean? I may like to fornicate more than other people. It's just who I am. I sacrifice so much of my life; can I at least get laid? I mean, I've been robbed of most of my money; can I at least get a blow job without people wanting to harass me and wanting to throw me in jail?'
- 'We all cheat on our fucking wives one way or another. Please forgive me for talking the way I am. I'm into forbidden fruits like everyone else. I want my dick sucked too. I want to love a woman too. Sometimes I want to love more than one woman. Don't crucify me because of who I am and I tell the world who I am. That's just who I am. You guys wrote so much bad about me; I don't know when the last time was that I fucked a decent woman. You said I was a fucked-up nigger. I don't know nothing but strippers and whores and bitches and all that shit because you guys put that shit on me.'

On several occasions, Tyson's adviser Shelly Finkel was heard to whisper, 'Let's get everyone out of here before he explodes.' But the session continued.

There were moments of self-pity:

- 'I wake up every morning and hate myself. I don't have any dignity left. I lost my dignity in prison.'
- 'I could be a decent guy. I could be a literate guy. I could have been a lot of things in life. But Cus got me first and I became a fighter. There are a lot of things I could have been. I could have been smart and intelligent. My family are educated people. I'm a numbskull.'
- 'My brother is a different kind of animal. He wanted to be something. My sister was so bright. My brother is so bright. I wasn't born with their intelligence. That's my problem. I was always envious of my brother. I hated my brother. Me and my brother are so different. I look at him. He's a beautiful, brilliant, strange guy.

We're not close. If he wasn't my brother, I wouldn't even like him. He wouldn't even be my type of person. Everybody loved my brother and my sister. I went to my sister's funeral. She never wanted a nickel from me. They always had more dignity and pride than me. I was heavyweight champion of the world, but they never wanted anything. I always respected them. My sister was obese. She was 500 pounds. Her heart stopped. She was 25. I was always jealous of them because they had nothing but everybody loved them. I was always nothing. Compared to them, I'm nothing. Everybody in the neighbourhood loved them. But me; I was shit. They always told me I was going to die. You ain't shit. Who the hell am I? I don't know what happened to me. I don't even know if I came from the same father.'

Then the self-pity gave way to anger:

- 'I'm the most irresponsible person in the world. The reason I'm like that is because, at 21, you all gave me $50 million or $100 million and I didn't know what to do. I'm from the ghetto. I don't know how to act. One day I'm in a dope house robbing somebody. The next thing I know, "You're the heavyweight champion of the world." I'm 20 years old. I'm the heavyweight champion of the world. Most of my girlfriends are 15, 16 years old. I'm 20 years old with a lot of money. Who am I? What am I? I don't even know who I am. I'm just a dumb child. I'm being abused. I'm being robbed by lawyers. I think I have more money than I do. I'm just a dumb pugnacious fool. I'm just a fool who thinks I'm someone. And you tell me I should be responsible? I'm angry at the world.'
- 'I offend people. I ask this lady a lewd question because I'm in a lot of pain. I have some pain I'm gonna have for the rest of my life. So every now and then, I kick your fucking ass and stomp you and put some kind of pain and inflict some of the pain on you because you deserve to feel the pain that I feel. I wish that you guys had children so I could kick them in the fucking head or stomp on their testicles so you could feel my pain because that's the pain I have waking up every day.'

- 'At times, I come across as crude or crass. That irritates you when I come across like a Neanderthal or a babbling idiot, but I like to be that person. I like to show you all that person, because that's who you came to see. I'm not in a mood right now to do a tirade. But if you said something disrespectful about my kids or my mother, I'd come out and kill you.'
- 'If I take this camera and put it in your face for twenty years, I don't know what you might be. You might be a homosexual if I put that camera on you since you were 13 years old. I've been on that camera since I was 13 years old.'
- 'You guys don't like the way I carry myself and you make names about me. Then I become insecure about that. My fuse is so short right now that, if anyone disrespects me, I might kill them.'

The following day, Tyson sat for a session with Rita Cosby of the Fox News Channel. And his thoughts were a chilling portrait of a man in pain:

- 'I don't know if I'm mentally sick, but I have episodes sometimes. I'm a depressant kind of dude. I have episodes and I'm human, but no-one cares about my health as a human; you know what I mean? I probably need to talk to somebody. But how could I talk to somebody that just looks at me when I'm really getting ready to feel this guy and put my heart out and says, "Well, time's up. Hold it, Mike; I'm sorry. Drop the 250 dollars off at the desk with my secretary and make an appointment to come back next week." I'm ready to pull out my heart with this white motherfucker. He just got me comfortable, and I'm thinking he's real and I'm getting ready to – "I'm sorry; hold that thought. Go to Mary, pay the 250 dollars, and make an appointment for next week. We're going to make some leeways, Mike. I can see that coming." Right then, I leave that place that was supposed to help me, and I leave more fucked up than I am when I first went in there. Is this a fucking game? So I stopped going; you know what I mean? I stopped going, so now they put me on this Zoloft stuff, right, and I'm so – I'm really; I'm pathetic sometimes and real shallow. I'm so dick conscious where, you know, I'm taking Zoloft and I don't get an erection. I'm just gone then, man; I'm just gone. I mean, it's ruined and rot and I'm an extreme sexual type person. I got to start taking this stuff, and it probably is making me feel a little better. But you know, it makes me feel bad because I like, you know, like I'm saying, I'm penis centred and it's just; I don't know. Now that's a big fight within itself right there, and that's not even talking about what I really have to deal with. That's not the real problem, but that turns into it. But now I got another problem to deal with; and the real problem, it just hasn't been dealt with at all. It hasn't been addressed so to speak, and I say what the fuck do I do? You don't understand the severity of what I'm dealing with.

So let me just have a couple of my episodes. Let me take care of my children. Let me screw as many women as I want. Let me smoke what I want. Let me do what I want. Let me live my life because I'm not going to let these people just tear me apart and the guys try to label me; label me a schizoid, label me a manic depressive, label me a crazy motherfucker. I'm probably more schizoid than I am anything. But if you label me so many things, you drive a motherfucker insane. I'm surprised I'm not suicidal. I haven't killed myself, but I wouldn't do that. I prefer to kill someone else than to kill myself.'

What does Mike Tyson want?

'Are you kidding?' Roy Jones Jr responds when asked that question. 'He wants to go back to jail. That's the only place Mike is comfortable. It's the only place where he feels he fits in.'

There's no doubt that Tyson is inclined towards antisocial behaviour. There's a frightening mix of sex and violence in his thoughts, and often the two converge. The world is familiar with some of the comments he has made about ripping Lennox Lewis's heart out and eating Lewis's children. In Maui, Tyson continued in that vein: 'I'll smear his pompous brains all over the ring when I hit him...I want to implant my fist in his mind. I want to reach in and touch his brain.'

But there was something more, and it was scary. Recounting an incident that occurred in Los Angeles, Tyson recalled, 'Every time I try to do something to satisfy somebody else, I wind up getting fucked. Forgive my language because, if I don't curse or say nigger, fuck or shit, you won't understand what I'm saying. I'm with my wife, and we're at this place in Los Angeles. Monica says, "There goes Lennox Lewis. Go say hi to him." I say hi, and he looks at me like, "Motherfucker! What you looking at me for?" I wanted to punch my wife in the face. She made me look like a punk. This guy just stared me down like a mad dog. I felt like my wife took my balls right from under me for this guy. She gave this punk-ass motherfucker my nuts. It made me a punk right in front of her because I wanted to be a nice guy for my wife. I wanted to show her I could change and I'm not like people say I am. I don't need a woman that says, "Go say hi to him." I need a woman that says, "That punk motherfucker wants to hurt you, baby," and starts going right at him. I need a woman to jump in there and punch him, and then I'll jump in.'

Lennox Lewis has responded to Tyson's comments with disdain. After calling Tyson 'ignorant, arrogant and an imbecile', the champion observed, 'Some of the things he's been saying make him sound like a cartoon character. When he was incarcerated, he said he was reading books. It must have been comic books.'

Still, as the object of Tyson's hatred, Lewis is understandably concerned. He is well aware that Tyson bit off a piece of Evander Holyfield's ear in the ring. And Tyson bit Lewis on the thigh during their press conference brawl in New York. Regarding the latter incident, Tyson has said, 'He [Lewis] should have died that night; those guys putting their hands on me. But I wasn't with the right crew. That's the whole thing. I was with guys who just wanted to be seen on television. If I was with the right crew, all of them guys would have been finished right there.'

Is Tyson bringing the 'right crew' to Memphis? Both the Lewis camp and event organisers have expressed concern regarding the 'element' that Iron Mike attracts to fights. There's also the risk that a high-profile event of this nature could become a terrorist target. Thus, security has been an overriding theme throughout the negotiations. Federal, state and local authorities have all become involved. Metal detectors will be employed at fight-related events. And the contracts contemplate a number of bizarre scenarios.

For example, if either fighter is disqualified on an 'extraordinary' foul – that is, a foul outside the normal realm of competition such as biting an opponent or assaulting the referee – three million dollars will be deducted from that fighter's purse and paid to his opponent. Moreover, under those circumstances, the victorious fighter's television network (HBO for Lewis and Showtime for Tyson) can decline to televise the bout on a tape-delay basis and refuse to pay its opposite number the previously agreed-upon licence fee.

Larry Hazzard (commissioner of the New Jersey Board of Athletic Control) will be the court of last resort regarding the determination of what constitutes an extraordinary foul. Other than that, Hazzard will not have an official role in administering the fight.

There will be no joint pre-fight activities for the fighters. They will hold separate press conferences and weigh in separately. The role of both entourages will be minimised at press events. On fight night, only a select few will be allowed to escort the fighters to the ring, and fewer still will be allowed into the ring before and after the fight. As the champion, Lewis will enter the ring last and be introduced after Tyson. The present plan is for each fighter to be escorted to the ring by a police guard. As the cops enter the ring, they will form a line bisecting the enclosure from neutral corner to neutral corner. There will be no ritual touching of gloves. After the fighters are introduced, the police will leave and the bell for round one will sound.

In sum, we are about to witness a fight for the heavyweight championship of the world in which one of the participants is considered so unstable and so given to criminal assaults that normal procedures aren't being followed and public appearances have to be curtailed.

'Usually,' notes one member of the Lewis camp, 'security is on hand to protect the fighter from the crowd. Here, security will be in place to protect everyone else from the fighter.'

Tyson's advocates, in turn, complain that Lewis has had his way on almost every negotiating point, including reimbursement for a $35,000 bracelet that was lost in the press conference scuffle and a six-figure sub rosa pay-out for the bite to his thigh. 'If Lennox could have his own ring, he'd demand it,' grumbles one Tyson supporter.

Sadly, all of this is obscuring the fact that Lewis–Tyson could turn out to be a great fight. 'We want this to be a major sporting event; not a circus,' HBO Sports president Ross Greenburg says. But the more Lewis–Tyson is hyped as a media happening, the less attention is focused on its fistic merits.

At the moment, Lewis is listed as a 2-to-1 favourite. Those odds are expected to drop by fight time. But most likely, this will be the first time in his career that Iron Mike has entered the ring as an underdog. That's because Tyson isn't the fighter he once was. To prepare for the young Mike Tyson, opponents were well-advised to spar with a tank that was firing live ammunition. In the ring, Tyson hasn't been 'Tyson' for a decade.

Still, Tyson appears to be getting himself into better shape for this fight than he's been in for years. Would he be in a stronger position if he'd started that process six months ago instead of last month? Absolutely. But he's still the most dangerous opponent that Lewis has ever faced.

Some observers liken Tyson to David Tua in terms of size and power. By that standard, Lennox should be able to control the bout by keeping Mike at the end of his jab all night. But Lewis's trainer, Emanuel Steward, puts that notion to rest when he says, 'Mike is a much more dangerous opponent than Tua. He punches harder. He punches well with both hands. He's faster. He fights with more intensity and puts a lot more pressure on his opponents. He's been in more big fights. There's no comparison, really.'

Meanwhile, Lewis is an interesting blend of power and fragility. He's a professional fighter, who acts like a professional and takes all of his skills into the ring with him when he fights. But Lennox has never fought anyone with the blend of Tyson's hand-speed and power. And while no one questions Lewis's heart, his chin is suspect. He isn't known for getting off the canvas to win. In fact, he isn't known for getting off the canvas. Great fighters in their prime don't lose to opponents like Oliver McCall and Hasim Rahman. And Lewis will be carrying an extra burden into the ring with him. Somewhere in his mind, he'll be worrying about Tyson's extra-legal behaviour. It won't just be a question of 'protect yourself at all times'. It will be 'protect yourself against all tactics'. Also, bear in mind that, in the rematch against

Oliver McCall, Lennox seemed a bit intimidated by McCall's craziness. And that was a night when he had dead meat in front of him.

Neither Lewis nor Tyson makes adjustments particularly well during a fight. To beat Tyson, an opponent has to take control of the bout, stand his ground, and keep Tyson busy. When that happens, as rounds progress, Mike's spirit tends to wane. But everyone knows that, at some point during the fight, Tyson will hit Lewis. The relevant questions are, 'Where, how hard, and how often?' One punch on the jaw from Mike Tyson can short-circuit a lot of fine-tuning.

Every moment of Lewis–Tyson will be marked by high drama. People who pay their money to see a circus might get their wish; or they could end up watching a great fight.

As Lewis–Tyson approached, there was an almost insatiable demand for media coverage.

Lewis–Tyson Draws Closer

Two months ago, Mike Tyson came back to New York to visit with Zab Judah. Over the years, the two men have developed a close relationship. And while some observers question whether Iron Mike has been the catalyst for changes in Judah's conduct, Zab notes that Tyson has changed too. 'When Mike got out of jail,' says Judah, 'it was like, he was different from when he went in. He came out a different person.'

Generally, when the two men are together, Tyson leads and Zab follows. This past March, Tyson led Judah to a cemetery in Queens to pay homage to Abe Attell (the legendary featherweight who reigned as world champion for nine years in the early 1900s). Attell lost only nine times in a 171-bout career. He is also widely believed to have been the bag man who carried cash from gambler Arnold Rothstein to the Chicago White Sox baseball players who participated in the fix of the 1919 World Series.

'It was weird,' Judah recalled later. 'Mike sat at the grave and talked to a dead man for six hours. He just sat there and talked. Sometimes he got up and walked around; but mostly, he just sat and talked. Six hours!'

The upcoming heavyweight championship bout between Lennox Lewis and Mike Tyson has engendered a lot of ugliness, a lot of anxiety, and a lot of passion. Most of that emotion is about Tyson. The whole world is familiar with the story of how Mike went from custody to Cus back to custody again. It has grown accustomed to his bizarre behaviour. And it has learned that, when Mike Tyson speaks, words of wisdom don't necessarily reverberate throughout the room. Indeed, given Tyson's past declarations (e.g. 'I can sell out Madison Square Garden masturbating'), it has been suggested that the traditional 'tale of the tape' for Lewis–Tyson includes the size of each fighter's male organ. One half expects Tyson to enter the ring on 8 June with 'suckmycock.com' painted on his back.

Everyone has an opinion about Tyson. Various scribes have suggested that he's 'the ultimate celebrity psycho in the midst of a public breakdown . . . a behavioural retard . . . [and] unfit for any public appearance at all, whether in the ring or out of it.' Oscar De La Hoya calls Tyson 'the worst role model in the world', and adds, 'I think he's seriously sick.' Tim Graham of ESPN opines, 'Good old Mike; never disappoints. He's often a boor, but never a bore. That's because he's insane.'

Dr Robert Butterworth (a Los Angeles-based clinical psychologist) recently put his two cents into the mix with the critique, 'We all have impulses. The brain is the mediating factor. It puts the brakes on. For Tyson, it's like an old Western. Someone shot the driver off the stage coach and no one is holding the reins.'

Olympic super-heavyweight gold medallist Audley Harrison (who had his own problems with the law and spent eighteen months in prison when he was young) observes, 'Mike's problem is, you get to a certain age in life and you should know what you want. Then you stay away from the things that make you unhappy and go to the things that make you happy. But Mike doesn't know that yet.'

Tyson's defenders claim that he's endlessly provoked by a 'poke the beast, get him to growl' mentality that pervades the media and general public. They also suggest that much of his conduct is clever marketing designed to hype his fights. But that view is credible only if one believes that Tyson spent three years in prison for raping Desiree Washington, went back to prison for assaulting two motorists after a traffic accident, and bit off a piece of Evander Holyfield's ear as part of a long-term marketing plan.

HBO has a slogan, 'It's not TV; it's HBO.' Showtime could adopt the slogan, 'It's not an act; it's Tyson.'

Tyson is in remission at the moment, but could erupt at any time. Meanwhile, his conduct is reinforced by Team Tyson; a group of enablers ranging from advisor Shelly Finkel to co-trainer Stacey McKinley.

Finkel isn't stupid, although there are times when his loyalty to Tyson compels him to act as though he is. Shelly is one of the most knowledgeable people in boxing, and it's sad to see the contortions he goes through in seeking to justify, defend, and explain away his fighter's misconduct.

McKinley takes things a step further. 'I respect Mike's views on life and everything he does,' he told reporters recently. Then McKinley added, 'The boxing ring is what we call a killing floor. I won't be satisfied unless Lewis gets some broken ribs or a broken jaw. That's what I'm looking for; I want to see something broken. We practise on how to cave in all his ribs, break his jaw, crack his skull. I've told Mike, "You've got to break something."'

Properly admonished, Tyson told Sky Television, 'I wish Lewis was dead. I wish I could kill him now.'

Lewis, in return, has labelled Tyson 'a puppy with some problems'. Meeting with the media earlier this month at his training camp in the Poconos, the champion opined, 'I think, a lot of times, Tyson is talking for his own benefit. He's trying to make himself out to be some kind of bad man, that he can say and do whatever he wants. But he's going to learn that there are repercussions.'

Then Lewis turned his attention to the brawl that occurred at the now-infamous 22 January kick-off press conference in New York. 'I was punching him, and he was biting me. I'm a fighter; he's a biter. Everybody knows Mike Tyson is a dirty fighter. I'm going to insist that he have a big lunch and dinner. I'm going to have my hair pinned up, so he can't pull my hair.'

But after that, Lewis turned serious. 'Bite on the leg; bite on the leg. That changed everything. Up until that, Mike Tyson was just another guy I was going to fight. Now I feel like anyone beating him would be a victory for decency in boxing. Tyson talks about being a victim, but anyone could say that. I could say that. I never grew up in a nice place, a nice world, but look how I turned out. Tyson can choose how he turns out. He's got to stop using his background as an excuse. It's such a silly excuse because, when you look at it, it doesn't mean anything; especially to me. I'm tired of Tyson's talk, of the attention he gets for simply being someone who can't take any control of his life. I'll be glad to see him coming into the ring because that's where it gets hard, where whatever you say doesn't mean a thing and you have to be honest and just fight.'

The architect of Lewis's fight plan will be trainer Emanuel Steward, who has been with the champion for sixteen fights. Steward projects an aura of confidence when talking about Lewis–Tyson.

'When you fight Tyson,' says Steward, 'you have to be assertive. You cannot fight a cautious fight. Tyson is used to fighting people who run from him. This time, he'll be fighting someone who wants to knock him out, who is going to be aggressive in a certain way. It could be a very exciting fight early because, even though Lennox has a great advantage technically and physically, he's liable to get excited and end up going toe-to-toe to try to knock Tyson out. It could end up being a slugfest. Tyson might land a few blows, but it won't be enough to hold Lennox off.

'Lennox isn't afraid of Mike, and Mike knows it,' Steward continues. 'I've watched Tyson. He's always had this thing about Lennox where Lennox intimidates him a lot. Mike has admitted that. In fact, he's continually making comments about Lennox intimidating him and picking on him. That's a role that Mike isn't used to. That, plus the fact that Mike doesn't want to fight Lennox, has him in a terrible state of mind. Tyson doesn't want to be at this fight. You can see that in the man's face when he speaks. And Lennox has no fear of Tyson. Lennox almost laughs at Mike Tyson. He's going to knock Tyson out. I don't think the fight will go four rounds. It will be a total mismatch after the first 45 seconds or so.'

But at times, the river of Steward's confidence seems more wide than deep. 'Tyson will be the best pure puncher Lennox has fought,' he acknowledges. 'I have a lot of respect and, to some degree, a little fear of Tyson's punching power. When Mike was young, he was the most devastating heavyweight I've ever seen in my life. And he still brings a certain rage, intensity and punching power that no other heavyweight brings into the ring. Tyson is very dangerous when he gets inside. And he's particularly dangerous with short punches. He does a great job with those little short arms once he gets in close. And Tyson is a smart fighter. He doesn't just go in there and throw wild punches. He knows where his punches are going and gets in good position. He does something that's really beautiful. He doesn't just take one step to throw a punch. Sometimes, he'll take two steps to get into position to throw a punch. He waits until he gets right under you and then, when you hold your hands out, he knows how to go up in between them. I think Tyson is going to come out and attack Lennox with more intensity and viciousness than anyone Lennox has ever fought,' Steward says in closing. 'And trying to get sparring partners to prepare for Tyson is very difficult because no one bobs and moves his head or has the speed and intensity that Tyson has when he's right.'

'I respect one thing about Tyson,' Lewis acknowledges. 'I know he has power in his punch. And Tyson is a desperate man, which can make him dangerous but it also makes him very vulnerable. I'm going to turn it on. I'm going to say to the Americans who have not shown me much respect over the years, "Hey, I'm really the very best." I'm going to ask, "Why haven't you people given me my acclaim?" And then I'm just going to take it. Tyson was a good champion once, no doubt. He matured very early, while I matured late. But when they talk about him now, they're really talking about the past. I'm operating in the present. I've answered a lot of questions about myself, fighting people like Morrison, Golota, Mercer and Holyfield. There were all kinds of questions about me; my chin, my stamina, my heart, whether I could take it when the going gets tough. Throughout my career I've answered all those questions. Mike Tyson is the last question. This is about the history of boxing in my time.'

That, of course, leads to another question: 'Is Lewis–Tyson good or bad for boxing?'

It has been fifteen and a half years since Mike Tyson first won the WBC heavyweight crown. And rather than be elevated by the sport, there are times when he seems determined to drag boxing into the gutter with him. Thus, Lewis says, 'For a long time, there has been a need to put an end to the Mike Tyson story. It has become increasingly bad for boxing. People look at the sport; they see Tyson; and they wonder how could this man, who doesn't respect women, doesn't really respect anything, become some kind of icon? The sooner the Mike Tyson story is over, the better. And the end is coming on June 8th in Memphis, Tennessee, at the end of my fist.'

But the truth is, Tyson could win. And if he does, Lewis–Tyson will send a message that contradicts a lot of what society hopes to teach about standards and accountability. It will be one of those rare sports events that has a trickle-down effect. Thus, a lot of people don't want Lewis–Tyson to happen. Bob Arum expresses their view when he says, 'Mike Tyson is the biggest disgrace in the history of boxing. It's everything that's wrong about the sport and society. He should be locked up in an insane asylum instead of having people pay to see him. Everyone is catering to an insane man.'

Arum, of course, doesn't have a stake in the promotion. But HBO does. And at times, even HBO Sports president Ross Greenburg seems ambivalent about the event. 'There was tremendous pressure put on us by the Lewis camp to make the fight,' Greenburg acknowledges. 'We would have had one very unhappy heavyweight champion if we hadn't allowed Lennox to fight Mike Tyson.'

So to repeat the question: 'Is Lewis–Tyson good or bad for boxing?'

'We'll know the answer to that on June 8th,' Greenburg answers. 'It could energise the sport. But if it's not a sporting event, if it becomes a circus, if something miserable happens...' His voice trails off; then picks up again. 'But I'm hopeful. That's why we made the deal.'

Life will be simpler for a lot of people if Lewis wins.

Meanwhile, what should boxing fans look for in the days ahead?

With Mike Tyson, one should expect the unexpected. Anything can happen. And once the bell rings, there's no script.

But one final point is worthy of mention. There has been a lot of talk lately about how Lewis–Tyson is Tyson's 'last chance'. That's nonsense. The public fascination with Tyson is such that people will always pay to see him fight. Even if Tyson is decimated by Lewis, he'll be able to fight three punching bags in a row, pronounce himself 'rededicated' to boxing, and get an infinite number of title shots. The winner of Ruiz–Johnson would fight him in a heartbeat. There's big money in a Tyson–Holyfield rematch. And if Tyson falls to the level of an aging Leon Spinks, people will pay just to see him get beaten up. Mike Tyson will fight for big money as long as he stays out of jail and wants to.

Mike Tyson took a lot of punches in Lewis–Tyson. And some people thought that he deserved every one of them.

Reflections on Lewis–Tyson

Boxing, more than any other sport, is dependent upon a single great athlete at any given time entering the public consciousness.

On 8 June, Lennox Lewis and Mike Tyson did battle at The Pyramid in Memphis. Each man hoped to establish his greatness. But their encounter was also viewed as a confrontation between good and evil.

There's a debate as to whether Tyson has suffered more at the hands of society than society has suffered at the hands of Tyson. However, it's clear that the bar has been set so low as a standard for his behaviour that he draws praise for simply being surly and not breaking any law. Alan Hubbard of the *Independent* has called him 'a deranged parody' and noted, 'The last time anything of substance came out of Tyson's mouth, it was Evander Holyfield's ear.' Jerry Izenberg of the *Newark Star-Ledger* referred to Lewis–Tyson as 'a fight between a guy in a white hat and a guy in a ski mask'.

In the weeks leading up to the bout, a dark cloud hovered over the Tyson camp. At times, it seemed as though people were ducking just to get out of the way of his words. Tyson's conduct decimated the pageantry that normally accompanies a heavyweight championship fight, stripped the occasion of its niceties, and reduced the event to its brutal essence: two men trying to inflict maximum physical damage upon one another.

Much of what leads up to a major fight is a dominance ritual. Purses, the colour of trunks, who enters the ring first. Here, in many respects, the entire promotion deferred to Tyson's peculiarities. It was more than a matter of keeping the fighters apart to avoid a pre-fight brawl like the one that occurred at their 22 January press conference. It was keeping Tyson away from everyone. During fight week, Showtime and HBO couldn't even get him to sit down and talk civilly with the media for ten minutes despite the fact that this was a $150,000,000 promotion.

Tyson's conduct engendered a near-unanimous rooting interest within the media against him. But the same reasons that led many people to feel that the fight shouldn't take place made it even more compelling drama. And underlying it all was the fear that Tyson would win.

Tyson has never gone to jail as champion. Were he to do so, some posited, it would wreak havoc with boxing. Hey; if Tyson won, street crime might rise by ten per cent. One got the impression that, if he'd thought of it, Iron Mike would have gone to Graceland and masturbated on the toilet where Elvis Presley died.

By contrast, the Lewis camp hosted an elaborate buffet luncheon for the media followed by a full press-conference and light workout by the champion. And no one talked about smearing brains on the canvas or called anyone a 'pussy bitch'.

'My mother brought me up a good boy,' said Lennox. 'It was important for me to grow up and be the best that I can to make her proud. You know, when she goes to the store and people say to her, "You've got a good son," that kind of thing makes her feel good.'

'I don't hold no hate for Mike Tyson,' Lewis continued. 'We're two competitors. The way I look at it, I'm going to be fighting within the rules. If he's coming in with something else, I'll deal with it. But I'll fight him within the rules of my sport because, for me, there's nothing in winning as a dirty fighter. I'm not interested in that. I'm a gentleman boxer. I fight with honour. I know there's people out there who love a train wreck. But sorry; I can't be a train wreck for them.'

All of this took place in Memphis, Tennessee. But once everyone got past the issue of whether Lewis–Tyson would happen at all, there were questions regarding how many people would be there to watch it. Initially, the promotion announced that all 19,185 tickets had been sold at prices ranging from $250 to $2,400. But soon, that pronouncement took on the look of a pyramid scam.

There's a time-honoured promotional tactic. Create a buzz that a particular sporting event or concert is where everyone wants to be; and suddenly, because of the buzz, everyone wants to be there. Lewis–Tyson fascinated the boxing community. Sports editors were in a frenzy over it. But ticket sales weren't exactly what they were reported to be.

Initially, it was announced that the fight had quickly sold out. Then came some interesting news. Several brokers who had been shut out of the ticket distribution were approached by other brokers with tickets to sell. Some brokers were even reported to have forfeited deposit money rather than pay full price for tickets that had been assigned to them. That led one broker who normally does a thriving business on big fights to acknowledge, 'The Lewis fans have always travelled well, but they're not travelling to Memphis the way we thought they would. And the other fans aren't travelling there either.'

Why not?

'It's a combination of things,' explained the broker. The tickets are unusually expensive. Twenty-four hundred dollars is a lot of money for a fight. There was a short lead time between when the tickets went on sale and the fight itself. Given Tyson's erratic behaviour, there's uncertainty as to whether the fight will actually take place. The World Cup is competing for customers. And Memphis isn't a particularly attractive destination.'

Suddenly modern-day Paul Reveres were shouting, 'The British aren't coming! The British aren't coming!' And the Lewis camp was particularly hard hit. It had purchased $4,000,000 worth of tickets with the intent of reselling them as part of tour packages. Three thousand sales were expected. But the number wound up at four hundred.

At one point, the Lewis camp went so far as to seek to return $1,000,000 worth of tickets that it had bought on a non-refundable basis. In so doing, it claimed that it had the exclusive right to sell fight tickets in the United Kingdom and that this right had been breached by various ticket brokers. But no such exclusivity existed and the request was denied. Meanwhile, rumours began circulating that local promoters had held back several thousand tickets in the hope of scalping them.

On 23 May, it was announced that one thousand previously unavailable tickets would go on sale to the general public. The official explanation was that additional seats had been freed up once the television production set-up in the arena was finalised. Then, on 29 May, the sell-out fantasy-bubble burst when 3,500 newly released tickets went on sale to the public at The Pyramid. As the fight approached, ducats were selling at discount. By noon on 8 June, $1,400 seats were available on the streets of Memphis for $500, and $900 tickets could be had for $300. The final announced paid attendance was 15,327. Almost 4,000 seats were empty. The reported live gate was $17,500,000, still a record, but well below the previously trumpeted total of $23,000,000.

Meanwhile, during fight week, things were getting dicey. Boxing in Tennessee is regulated by the Tennessee Board of Boxing and Racing, which is one of seven divisions within the Tennessee Department of Commerce and Insurance. But Tennessee has very little experience with big fights, and both camps felt that outside help was desirable. Thus, Larry Hazzard (commissioner of the New Jersey Board of Athletic Control) was brought in to deal with certain contingencies, and Eddie Cotton of New Jersey was designated as the referee.

Not everyone was comfortable with the choice of Hazzard. The last time he'd supervised a heavyweight 'title' fight was in Atlantic City in 1997, when Shannon Briggs was awarded a twelve-round decision over George Foreman in one of the most egregious examples of judicial indiscretion ever witnessed in boxing. Hazzard was also the final authority when Roy Jones Jr was disqualified for striking Montell Griffin, who was counted out by referee Tony Perez after taking a knee in their 1997 title bout. That ruling raised eyebrows because, under similar circumstances in 1994, referee Arthur Mercante had disqualified Riddick Bowe for whacking Buster Mathis Jr, who had taken a knee, but Hazzard then overruled Mercante and declared the bout 'no-contest'. Adding to the discontent was the fact that the referee for Foreman–Briggs had been Eddie Cotton.

The Lewis camp okayed Hazzard and Cotton in part because of the longtime relationship between Hazzard and Gary Shaw. Since October 1999, Shaw had been chief operating officer for Main Events (Lewis's American promoter). Prior to that, he had worked with Hazzard. But ten days before the fight, the Lewis camp learned that Shaw would be leaving Main Events after Lewis–Tyson and intended to set up his own promotional company. One of his first fighters, it was believed, could be Mike Tyson.

Once segments of the Lewis camp lost confidence in Shaw, Larry Hazzard was viewed with greater suspicion and it was decided that Greg Sirb (chairman of the Pennsylvania State Athletic Commission and former president of the Association of Boxing Commissioners) should be imported to help oversee the fight. The Tyson camp objected to Sirb's involvement because, after the Nevada State Athletic Commission denied Tyson a licence, Sirb had urged other states to follow suit. But the Lewis camp threatened a walkout, and Sirb came to Memphis.

Meanwhile, things had grown uglier in the Tyson camp with the addition of Stephen Fitch and Panama Lewis. Fitch goes by the name of 'Crocodile'. He wears combat fatigues, shouts a lot, and is basically a motivator.

Panama Lewis is something else. Once a successful trainer, he spent time in prison and is banned from boxing for life as a consequence of having tampered with a fighter's gloves, an act that led to permanently impaired vision for the fighter's opponent.

'Panama Lewis is famous for dirty,' acknowledged Zab Judah, a Tyson friend and confidant.

Some people felt that the presence of Fitch and Panama was par for the course. 'When you invite the circus to town,' said Lou DiBella, 'you shouldn't be surprised when wild animals and clowns appear.'

But Emanuel Steward was displeased. 'Crocodile is back from the swamp,' he told the media two days before the fight. 'And then they went to the swamp and got Panama Lewis. That's too bad because it brings things back in the direction of it being a freak show. We have a big enough problem with Mike's reputation and integrity without bringing in Panama Lewis. I don't want Panama Lewis or Crocodile anywhere near the ring on Saturday night because, when they realise that Mike is about to get knocked out, they could resort to anything.'

The fighters weighed in separately on Thursday. Tyson tipped the scales at 234$\frac{1}{2}$ pounds and Lewis at 246$\frac{1}{4}$. There was a school of thought that the scales were five pounds heavy, but neither camp made an issue of it. However, there was another matter that the Lewis camp saw as a big issue — drug testing.

Prior to the fight, Tyson's primary advisor, Shelly Finkel, and the rest of Team Tyson refused to answer questions from the media regarding drugs that Tyson might have been on during the preceding months, or was still on. Tyson's trainer Ronnie Shields said he was in the dark. And Tyson's previous trainer, Tommy Brooks, acknowledged, 'When I was working with Mike, I didn't know if he was on medication or not.'

However, it was known that one medication Tyson had been on in the past was neurontin.

Neurontin is commonly used to treat mood disorders. But it was originally developed as an anti-seizure drug and acts on the receptors along the spinal cord so that pain is not perceived as acutely as it otherwise would be. In other words, neurontin can help a fighter 'fight through pain' because there is less pain to deal with.

Tennessee doesn't have its own rules on drug testing so, after much debate, it was agreed that the state would follow standards set by the Association of Boxing Commissioners. That was significant because the ABC's rules require steroid testing, and there were those in the Lewis camp who suspected that Tyson was on steroids. Thus, if Tyson won and tested positive for steroids, he could be stripped of the title, which would have had enormous financial implications vis-à-vis a rematch.

As for neurontin, the subject was addressed in conversations with Tennessee authorities and at the World Boxing Council rules meeting the day before the fight. And it was ruled that there would be no test for neurontin. However, by then, the Lewis camp had done its medical homework and determined that, in addition to deadening pain, neurontin slows reflexes. 'I don't know if Tyson is on neurontin or not,' said Pat English, the attorney for Main Events. 'But if he is, we'll take that trade-off.'

Thus, only one medical battle remained to be fought. It was important to the Lewis camp that drug testing be conducted after the fight; not before it. Emanuel Steward was insistent on that point, and he prevailed. Part of his motivation was founded on reports that, when Aaron Pryor devastated Alexis Arguello in 1982, Panama Lewis had prepared a 'black bottle' for Pryor that contained a mixture of orange juice, honey and cocaine.

As the final hours ticked away, both camps expressed confidence. Normally, Tyson wears Everlast gloves. But for this fight, Lewis had demanded Reyes (which are known as 'punchers' gloves'). According to Shelly Finkel, 'The first time Mike tried a pair on, his eyes lit up.'

'I could kill him with these,' Tyson told Finkel.

'I fought on a lot of Mike's undercards,' Zab Judah added. 'And most times, he wasn't that interested in the fight. He was out shopping and going places. But here, Mike is living the fight. He's sleeping it; he's talking it; he wants it bad. Mike is looking to hurt this guy.'

Still, for all the talk, there was no hard evidence that Tyson had gotten himself into fighting shape. Thus, Emanuel Steward was concerned but confident.

'I haven't slept too good,' Steward admitted shortly before the fight. 'I'm more nervous about this fight than any fight I've ever been involved with. Mike didn't get to where he is being as small as he is without being a very good fighter. And I think that Mike will go to the top of his game and use whatever he has left in this fight. Either guy could land a big punch in the first ten or twenty seconds and this fight could be over. I worry about Tyson coldcocking Lennox. Anybody who fights Tyson and doesn't worry about that is crazy. So, yes, there's a possibility that Lennox will get hurt in this fight, and we've discussed that. You don't beat Mike Tyson easy.'

But Steward went on to say, 'Everyone is holding on to the image of Mike Tyson from ten or fifteen years ago. But that Mike Tyson is gone. The natural instinctive moves are gone. To be honest with you, I don't think that Mike Tyson deserves to be fighting for the heavyweight championship of the world. There's only one thing that Tyson can do based on his skills and physical structure; just come out and attack. And when a fighter rushes you from the opening bell, you have to fight with him. But if you look at the record: big fights, tough fights, dangerous fights – that's where Lennox is at his best. Plus, to beat Mike Tyson, you have to challenge him. You have to pressure Tyson and not give him time to set his traps; make him fight when he doesn't want to fight. And Lennox is prepared to do that. Lennox Lewis has not been intimidated by Mike Tyson. Never has been; never will be. Lennox went out of his way to make this fight. You don't go out of your way to make a fight with a guy you're afraid of. Lennox has no fear at all of Mike Tyson.'

Said Lewis, 'The talking is done; it's time for action. Lions don't run from hyenas.'

Still, there was the matter of those one-punch knockout losses to Oliver McCall and Hasim Rahman. Achilles had his heel, and Lennox has his chin. The prevailing view was that Tyson could afford to make a mistake and Lewis couldn't. By fight time, the Las Vegas odds in favour of the champion had dropped from 2 to 1 down to 8 to 5.

'Whatever happens,' Lewis's mother said shortly before the bout, 'Lennox will always be a champion to me.'

The fighters were scheduled to enter the ring on fight night at 10.15 p.m. But at nine o'clock, The Pyramid was two-thirds empty and long lines of ticketholders were backed up outside at security checkpoints. That raised the fear of lawsuits by fans who had paid thousands of dollars to come to Memphis and might miss the fight. There was also concern that civil disturbances could result. But delaying the start of the action would dramatically increase the cost of satellite time; and in some areas of the world, it was possible that the satellite feed would be lost altogether. Thus, at a hurried meeting attended by the mayor, police chief, security personnel, and representatives of both camps, it was decided that the settings on the checkpoint magnetometers should be changed. 'We're looking for guns, not nail files,' one attendee explained later.

Walking to the ring, Tyson looked like an unhappy child. Once, Iron Mike stood for the proposition, 'Don't go near that flame because you'll be badly burned.' But the smouldering fires that burned within have long since been replaced by a deadness inside. Waiting for Lewis to enter the squared circle, Tyson stood passively and stared down. It was a far cry from the young Mike Tyson, who snarled and paced angrily like a tiger eager for the kill.

By contrast, Lewis entered the ring looking belligerent and defiant.

A historic beating followed. Like Buster Douglas and Evander Holyfield, Lennox fought, not the myth, but the Mike Tyson he found in front of him. He kept Tyson at a distance, where he could fight and Tyson couldn't, and totally dominated him.

In round one, Lewis jabbed tentatively and let Tyson dictate the pace, tying up the smaller man when he got inside. Then, in the second stanza, Lewis began working his right hand and jab.

The Tyson camp had promised the Tyson of old; but instead, the world saw an old Tyson. A fighter can't disrespect his body for the better part of ten years and make it up in ten weeks. Tyson might have been in shape, but he wasn't in fighting shape. To get him into the ring, a lot of people lied to him. He showed no head movement, threw virtually no combinations, and landed an average of six punches per round. To the extent that he tried to get inside, he did so by lungeing forwards rather than working his way in behind a jab, slipping punches, and countering.

In round three, Lewis began landing straight right hands and Tyson started making silent compacts on the inside, allowing Lennox to tie him up. He looked very much like a man who understood that he was going to lose. By round four, Lewis was trading with abandon and Tyson was out of gas.

From that point on, Lewis beat up Tyson the way Tyson used to beat people up. In the vernacular of Memphis, he turned Tyson into 'wet ribs' – a slab of beef oozing red.

For most of round five, Tyson wasn't throwing punches any more; just catching them. Round six was more of the same. In round seven, Lewis turned it up a notch. And in round eight, he destroyed Tyson with a roundhouse right that left him stretched out on the canvas with blood streaming from his mouth, nose and cuts above both eyes.

All totalled, Lewis landed 191 punches (including 84 power shots) to Tyson's 49. And this was a night when the term 'power' punch was more than mere nomenclature. Against Lennox, Tyson was Joe Louis knocked through the ropes by Rocky Marciano, and Muhammad Ali taking a blow to the kidneys from Larry Holmes.

'That was one of the most thorough and systematic beatings a heavyweight champion has given to a legitimate challenger in the history of boxing,' Emanuel Steward said afterwards. 'Lennox just played with him. If Mike had been a sparring partner in camp, we would have gotten rid of him.'

The only sour note as far as Steward was concerned was the conduct of the fight by the referee, Eddie Cotton.

'I thought it was bad, and I thought it was obvious,' Steward said later. 'The whole night, Eddie Cotton was looking to protect Tyson and for an excuse to act against Lennox. He was a bigger threat to Lennox than Tyson ever was. It's like he was on a mission to give the title to Tyson from the opening bell. The warnings he gave Lennox early on for tying Mike up inside were ridiculous. Then he took a point away on what should have been called a knockdown for no good reason at all. He gave Mike time to recover a bit in the eighth round when he called a knockdown that wasn't; not that it made a difference. And on the final knockdown, when Lennox took Mike out with that big right hand, it looked like Cotton was getting ready to penalise Lennox again for pushing Mike down. All that talking I did in the corner – "He's dangerous; don't fool around; take him out now" – Mike wasn't dangerous. By that time, Tyson was gone. It's the referee who was dangerous. As long as Tyson was standing, I was afraid that Cotton would find a way to give him the fight. That's why I was so frantic. "Get him out of here, please!" I was afraid Cotton would find an excuse to take another point away from Lennox and disqualify him.'

'I agree with Emanuel,' concurred HBO commentator Larry Merchant. 'I thought that Cotton's misofficiating of the fight was blatant and brazen. What it amounted to, really, was a failed coup.'

Still, Lewis–Tyson was good for boxing. The fight engendered 1,800,000 pay-per-view buys, second only to Holyfield–Tyson II. The $105,000,000 pay-per-view gross was a record. And more significantly, the sport now has a dominant heavyweight champion.

Whether or not Lewis will continue in that role is subject to speculation. After the bout, he told reporters, 'Basically, I believe it's a good time for me to retire. I can see that, but preparing for Tyson was not the time to give it much thought. I didn't have time for saying "what if this?" or "what if that?" I have some more thinking to do. Nothing is going to happen in the next two weeks or so which can change anything. I'm still going to be the greatest boxer in the world for a little while. I know there could be no better time for me to go, after beating the man who overshadowed me for so long without fighting real fights for ten years. But then, I also think that maybe I don't need to go just yet. There's a lot of money to be earned out there, fighting people I know I can beat. The good thing is that I'm now free to retire any time. Beating Tyson has given me that option.'

Lewis is obligated by court order to defend his IBF title against Chris Byrd by December or relinquish the belt. But at this point, the belts are largely extraneous and he has other options. If Kirk Johnson beats John Ruiz for the WBA crown in July, Lewis and Johnson (both of whom grew up in Canada) could face off in a showdown north of the border. Alternatively, if Wladimir Klitschko triumphs over Ray Mercer in their WBO title bout later this month, Lennox could take on the Ukrainian giant and eliminate the one fighter who is seen as a legitimate potential successor to his throne.

And then there's the possibility of Lewis–Tyson II. After the fight, Tyson conceded, 'He was too big and too strong. I don't know if I could beat him if he fights like that. I'm just happy he didn't kill me.' But in the next breath, Iron Mike asked for a rematch, adding, 'If the price is right, I'll fight anybody.'

Then Tyson kissed Lennox's mum and wiped a smear of his own blood off Lewis's cheek. But before one gets carried away in praising his 'gracious' behaviour, it should be remembered that, after Holyfield–Tyson I, Tyson lavishly praised Holyfield and all but caressed his arm, saying, 'I just want to touch you.' Then, in Holyfield–Tyson II, he bit off part of Evander's ear.

One can only begin to imagine what the world would have heard if Tyson had done to Lewis what Lewis did to him – 'Every time I hit him, he cried like a woman...I tried to push the bone of his nose into his brain...How dare he challenge me with his primitive skills.'

Maybe now Tyson can threaten to eat Frans Botha's children.

But having said that, it should be noted that this is a dangerous time for Tyson. Prior to the fight, Tommy Brooks observed, 'Mike is a cat with nine lives, and he's on eight-and-a-half.'

Make that eight-and-three-quarters now.

Tyson's reign as the true heavyweight champion of the world was brutally sweet. It began in November 1986 when, at the age of twenty, he dismantled Trevor Berbick to win the WBC crown and ended in February 1990 when he lost to Buster Douglas. For those 39 months, he was the dominant heavyweight on the planet. It wasn't who he beat; it was how he beat them that was so impressive.

But Tyson has now been beaten, and beaten up, by three different fighters. And more damaging to his legacy, in boxing, the great ones hit back when hit; yet when Tyson is hit, he stops fighting. So, yes, Mike Tyson can still knock out a lot of heavyweights. And on a given night, he has a chance against anyone. But if Tyson keeps fighting, the toll on his body and mind will be considerable.

'I'm scared of some things Mike does,' Shelly Finkel admitted recently. 'I worry about him after boxing.'

But that time might be near. What will Tyson do next? He could easily make $500,000 a year from personal appearances and memorabilia signings. But that's not his style and might not be enough money to satisfy him. Thus, Tommy Brooks sounds a sombre note when he opines, 'I think Mike wants to go back to jail. He's not pressured there. He knows what he has to do. In jail, it's "do this" and "do that". No one will throw curve balls at Mike in jail; only fastballs down the middle. And in jail, he won't be taking punches. So as sad as it seems, I think, before too long, Mike will be in jail again or in the mortuary.'

Meanwhile, as for Lewis; the future looks bright. The past twelve months have been kind to him. A year ago, Lennox had been deposed by Hasim Rahman; he was being demeaned as a fighter; and Rahman was refusing to give him a rematch. But then he won a court battle that forced Rahman back into the ring with him and emerged victorious on a fourth-round knockout. Now he has beaten Mike Tyson.

Lewis is an unusual man. In public, he's controlled and never lets go of his emotions. Occasionally, he reveals a bit of his thinking. 'I have a rage to win,' he told reporters the day after dismantling Tyson. 'But for me, that should never replace the need to think deeply about what you're doing and trying to develop all your skills. Violence will always be a big part of boxing. But it has beauty too, and I like to bring that out a bit.'

Lewis–Tyson was Lennox's coronation. There were places where he would never have been regarded as number one until he beat Iron Mike. Now, for everyone, it truly feels as though Lennox Lewis is the undisputed heavyweight champion of the world.

Where does Lewis fit into the historical rankings? That's hard to say. His standing has been diminished by knockout losses to Oliver McCall and Hasim Rahman and the fact that he was unable to knock Evander Holyfield down over the course of 24 rounds of boxing. But to his credit, Lewis defeated McCall and Rahman in rematches. And as Tyson, Rahman, George Foreman, Ray Mercer and others have learned, Holyfield isn't so easy to put on the canvas.

Lewis has taken on all comers. He has never avoided the best available foe. He won an Olympic gold medal in 1988 and has been competing in the spotlight for fourteen years. But lest he grow too self-satisfied, Lennox should recall the thoughts of Mike Tyson, spoken less than two months ago.

'The title is like a woman,' said Tyson. 'It's like love. It doesn't care for anything but itself. It doesn't care who possesses it. It's always going to be loved. The title is going to be loved until the day it dies, so it doesn't care about me, about you. It's like a woman – "Fuck you; I'm so beautiful, I can get the next man with more money, with a better body. He has a prettier way for me to go."'

I explored 'the sweet side' of Lennox Lewis in conversations with the heavyweight champion and his mum.

Lennox's Mum

Lennox Lewis's father was never an active presence in his life. The formative influence on the man who is now heavyweight champion of the world was his mother, although Violet Blake is hardly a public figure. 'Mum doesn't talk to the media much,' Lennox acknowledges. 'She's afraid of saying the wrong thing. But there is no wrong thing. She's my mum.'

It's a loving relationship. Here's what Lennox Lewis and Violet Blake said recently about one another.

LENNOX LEWIS: I lived with my mum in England until I was nine. Then we took a trip to Canada, where my mum had friends. And after a while, she sent me back to England to live with my aunt. The separation was hard for me. I spent a lot of time at boarding school. There were two boarding schools, actually. I was always running away from the first one. I liked the second, but the government stopped paying for it and I needed someplace else to go. Mum's situation in Canada had gotten better by then. She'd found a job and saved some money and had a place to stay. So when I was twelve, I went back to Canada to live with my mum. And from then on, it was just her and me.

VIOLET BLAKE: When Lennox came to Canada, I met him at the airport and I told him, 'I'm not gonna ever leave you no more.' He was a good boy. The only problem I ever had with him was, the other children would tease him about his accent and sometimes he got into fights over it. But mostly, Lennox was a quiet child. The way you see him now is the way he always was. Very quiet most of the time. And he thinks a lot.

LENNOX LEWIS: When I was young, if I said I was going out, my mum would ask, 'Where are you going? Who are you going with? Be careful. How are you getting home?' And she'd always wait up until I got home. She'd breed worry into me before I went out, and that always made me more careful. Then I started boxing, and my mum didn't mind. After school every day, first there was basketball and then boxing. I wouldn't get home until eight o'clock at night. But mum knew where I was. She knew I was safe and doing something positive, and I wasn't home bugging her. And mum still doesn't mind my boxing. Every mother worries about her son getting hurt, but my mum knows I can defend myself.

VIOLET BLAKE: When Lennox is fighting, I worry about him, and I worry about his opponent too. But I tell myself, 'It's in God's hands.' I say, 'God, you gave me this child, and now I give him back to you to watch over him tonight.'

LENNOX LEWIS: My mum and I pray together in my hotel room before every fight. And when we pray, she prays for me and my opponent, that neither one of us gets hurt. Then she goes to the fight. She gets there early, because she likes to watch all the matches. It gets her ready for mine. And when I'm in the ring, she doesn't look away or cover her face with her hands. She focuses fully on the fight.

VIOLET BLAKE: I wouldn't change anything about Lennox. He's happy, which is all I ask for him, and he puts a lot of joy in my heart. I wake up every morning and thank God for Lennox. He's a wonderful son.

LENNOX LEWIS: It was always very important to me that I not disappoint my mother. I never had a police record. I never got a girl pregnant. Although now, I think my mum wishes I'd get married and get a girl pregnant so she could babysit. But you know, you can be married and have a bad life, and my life is good now. What it comes down to is, my mum wants me to be happy, and I want her to be happy. Sometimes mum calls me her baby. When your mum says 'my baby,' it's different from when your girl says it. When your mum says it, it's a much deeper feeling. It has more meaning. And I guess I'll always be her baby. It seems like, every year on my birthday, mum gives me underwear and socks. And it seems like, every year, I need them. And when mum's birthday is coming, I ask her what she wants. She'll never want for anything; I promise you that. But all she ever asks for is something like a winter coat.

VIOLET BLAKE: Lennox cares for me so well. He's so good that way, and it means I have more to give to other people.

LENNOX LEWIS: My mum is a warm, caring, loving, positive person, who has feelings and trusts them. And my respect for my mum has continued to grow as I've matured and come to understand what she's gone through. People ask me, 'What place do you consider home?' And I tell them, 'My mother's womb.' If they ask where I'm from, I tell them, 'I come from Violet.'

Round 2
Muhammad Ali

In October 1988, I was scheduled to meet with Muhammad Ali and his wife Lonnie to discuss writing the book that would eventually become Muhammad Ali: His Life and Times. *Writing a book is an extremely personal endeavour, and I wanted to make sure that, if the project went ahead, Muhammad and I would get along. I also wanted to make sure that I could capture Muhammad's voice; both the way he was when he was young, and the way he is now.*

In 1988, Mike Tyson was the undefeated undisputed heavyweight champion of the world. Some experts were even proclaiming that Tyson was better than Ali in his prime. Accordingly, before I met with Muhammad, I spent an afternoon writing 'I'm Coming Back to Whup Mike Tyson's Butt'. Then, when Ali and I met, I read the piece aloud and presented it to him. His response was to take a pen from his pocket and write across the front page, 'To Tom Hauser from Muhammad Ali – This is what I can still do to Tyson right now.'

Later, Muhammad and I made a few changes in the article and it was published in Boxing Illustrated, *the first of many collaborations between us.*

I'm Coming Back to Whup Mike Tyson's Butt

People are weeping and crying all the time these days, because Mike Tyson is heavyweight champion of the world. He's a bully, and no one can beat him. But that don't mean nuthin'. They said Sonny Liston was unbeatable, and I beat him. They said George Foreman was unbeatable, and I beat him. They say Tyson is unbeatable, but I'm coming back. I got a time machine, and I'm coming back to whup Mike Tyson.

Mike Tyson is too ugly to be champion. He's got gold teeth. He's got bald spots all over his head. I used to call Joe Frazier 'The Gorilla', but next to Tyson, Joe Frazier was like a beautiful woman. Everyone I fought, I had names for. Sonny Liston was 'The Bear'. George Chuvalo was 'The Washer Woman'. Floyd Patterson was 'The Rabbit'. George Foreman was 'The Mummy'. Mike Tyson is ugly; he's ugly like King Kong, so I'm calling him 'Kong'.

And Tyson is nuthin'. He never fought no one. He fought Larry Holmes when Holmes was an old man. He fought Trevor Berbick, and Berbick was a crazy old man. He fought Tyrell Biggs, and Biggs was an amateur. Michael Spinks was a light-heavyweight. Tony Tubbs; he was an embarrassment. Bonecrusher Smith; he lost the first nine rounds against Frank Bruno. Tyson never fought Sonny Liston; he never fought Joe Frazier; he never fought George Foreman; like I did, fighting all of them in their prime.

So I'm coming back to whup Mike Tyson. It's the biggest fight in the history of time. Bigger than David against Goliath; bigger than Napoleon against England and Russia. Too big for home television. Too big for closed circuit. They're putting this fight on special 3-D closed circuit with cameras and lenses like you ain't never seen before.

And the whole world is holding its breath. Everyone's rooting for me, but they're saying, Muhammad Ali, he's just a man and now he's fighting Kong. They're saying Mike Tyson is too strong, too mean. He hits too hard.

Here's how it goes.

Round One: It'll be all over in one; that's what they're saying. And Tyson comes out for the kill. Ali's dancing, jabbing. Pop-pop-pop-pop. Tyson swings – WHOOSH – hits nuthin' but air.

Pop-pop-pop-pop.

WHOOSH. Tyson hits nuthin' but air again.

Pop-pop-pop-pop. At the end of the round, the television people are adding up their punch-stats, and they can't believe it. Muhammad Ali: 107 jabs, 92 landed. Mike Tyson: 40 punches, and he didn't land one.

Round Two: It's just like round one.

Pop-pop-pop-pop.

WHOOSH.

Pop-pop-pop-pop.

WHOOSH.

Ali is pretty. The crowd's going wild. *Ali! Ali!*

Tyson lands a punch, but it don't do no harm.

Round Three: Ali's landing right hands. It's early in the fight, and already Tyson's left eye is starting to close. Women and children are holding their breath. Ali looks good. He's better than good. Muhammad Ali is the greatest, but there's nine more rounds to go, and Tyson is getting dirty now. He's butting and thumbing, throwing elbows and hitting low.

Round Four: Pop-pop-pop-pop. Ali is still dancing. Floats like a butterfly, but he stings like a bee. Pop-pop-pop-pop. Tyson is bleeding above the left eye. He's cut and the blood is flowing down. The experts is shaking their heads. Muhammad Ali is making Tyson look like a child.

Round Five: Tyson is taking a bad whuppin'. The crowd's going wild. Ali! Ali! Tyson's getting tired. Ali's talking to him, asking, 'Who's the greatest?' Tyson won't answer, so Ali hits him four-five-six right hands.

Round Six: It's the Ali Shuffle. Two billion people 'round the world, they're jumping up and down, hugging each other, weeping with joy. It's the real Ali. Not the Ali who lost to Larry Holmes; not the Ali you thought was old. This is Muhammad Ali, who destroyed Zora Folley; Muhammad Ali, who done in Cleveland Williams. Ali! Ali!

Round Seven: Tyson's gold teeth get knocked out into the crowd, and you can see his mother-in-law running after them. The crowd's in a state of histomania. Ali's punching so fast now, no one can hear the pops. It's p-p-p-p-p-p-p-p. Ali winds up for a bolo punch. The crowd is praying. They're pleading, don't take no chances; don't get careless with Tyson. But Ali's still winding up for the bolo, and Tyson's moving closer. Tyson is getting ready. He's gonna kill Ali. The crowd holds its breath. Tyson leaps with a left hook. But Muhammad Ali throws a right hand. It's faster than a speeding bullet. Faster than the punch that knocked down Sonny Liston. The eye can't see it, except with a super slo-mo replay camera.

TYSON IS DOWN ! ! !

Tyson gets up at seven.

Ding! There's the bell.

And now Tyson is mad. He's embarrassed. He's been humiliated. He's coming out for the next round, determined to put Muhammad Ali down.

Round Eight: Tyson charges out of his corner, throwing punches like wild. He's spitting blood. There's fire in his eyes. He's doing everything he can. And . . . . OH NO! Ali is tired. Ali has stopped dancing. After seven rounds with Kong, Ali's legs is gone. Ali's moving back. Tyson comes in for the kill. Ali's in a corner; he's in trouble. Tyson is ugly. He's a monster that has to be fed, and Muhammad Ali is the monster's meal.

Tyson with a left. Tyson with a right. The whole world is covering its eyes.

Wait a minute ! ! !

IT'S THE ROPE-A-DOPE ! ! !

Muhammad Ali tricked the monster, and now Ali is coming back strong.

Ali with a left. Ali with a right. It's Muhammad Ali; the greatest fighter of all time.

AND TYSON IS DOWN ! ! !

The count is one, two . . .

Tyson's eyes is closed!

Three, four . . .

He's not moving!

Five, six . . .

We have a brand new champion!

Seven, eight . . .

This is the greatest moment of all time!

Nine, ten . . .

It's all over! It's all over! The tyrant is dead! Long live the true King!

In November 1990, on the eve of the Gulf War, Muhammad Ali travelled to Iraq and met with Saddam Hussein in the hope that his presence would promote dialogue and forestall a wider conflict. Although his broader goal was not met, Muhammad did return to the United States with fifteen American hostages who had been held captive by the Iraqi government. At the request of the New York Times, *I elaborated upon Ali's motives.*

Why Muhammad Ali Went to Iraq

Last month in Baghdad, Muhammad Ali embraced Saddam Hussein and kissed him on the cheek. The moment was televised throughout the world and troubled many people. Ali isn't a diplomat. His actions aren't always wise. There was danger in the possibility that a visit from history's best-known fistic gladiator would feed Hussein's ego and stiffen his resolve. Regardless of what else happened, the meeting would be used for propaganda purposes in the Third World, where Ali is particularly loved.

Some of Ali's closest friends were also concerned that, in going to Iraq, he was being used for personal gain by one or more members of his entourage. Several of his associates, past and present, are the subject of a federal inquiry into alleged financial irregularities. While Ali was in Iraq, one of his attorneys was indicted on charges of conspiracy and tax fraud. And among those who accompanied Ali to Baghdad was Arthur Morrison, a self-described businessman who has traversed the United States leaving a trail of arrest warrants behind him.

As Ali's trip progressed, it became increasingly difficult for the world outside to distinguish between what he really said and what was reported by the Iraqi News Agency. There were self-appointed spokesmen purporting to act on 'hand signals' from the former champion. Others said, falsely, that Ali was unable to speak. But none of this is new to Ali. He has often dealt with con men and crazies. And the sideshow that accompanied him on his recent journey shouldn't be allowed to overshadow why Ali went to Iraq. It was an act of love in quest of peace. He hoped that his presence would promote dialogue and forestall war.

I've spent the past two years researching and writing about Muhammad Ali. For much of that time, I've lived with him, travelled with him and interviewed hundreds of his family members, associates and friends. I know him well. At least, I think I do. And one thing is certain: even though Muhammad's voice is not as clear as it used to be, his mind is alert and his heart is pure.

I've seen Ali get on a plane and fly to India because the children in an orphanage wanted to meet him. I've sat in his living room as he talked with sadness of hatred and racism in all of their virulent forms. He's a gentle man who will do almost anything to avoid hurting another person.

Ali was in Louisville visiting his mother, who had suffered a stroke, when he was asked to go to Iraq. He is on medication for Parkinson's syndrome. When he left that afternoon, he had enough medication with him to last for five days; yet he stayed in Iraq for two weeks. He quite literally endangered his health because he believed that what he was doing was right.

That, of course, has been a constant theme throughout Ali's life. He has always taken risks to uphold his principles. During the 1960s, he was stripped of his title and precluded from fighting for three and a half years because he acted upon his beliefs and refused induction into the United States Army during the height of the war in Vietnam. He now believes that all war is wrong. Ali is, and since Vietnam has been, a true conscientious objector.

Ali knows what many of us sometimes seem to forget – that people are killed in wars. Every life is precious to him. He understands that each of us has only one life to live. Many Americans now favour war with Iraq, although I'm not sure how many would feel that way if they personally had to fight. Ali, plainly and simply, values every other person's life as dearly as his own, regardless of nationality, religion or race. He is a man who finds it impossible to go hunting, let alone tolerate the horrors of war.

It may be that war with Iraq will become inevitable. If so, it will be fought. But that shouldn't cause us to lose sight of what Muhammad Ali tried to accomplish last month. Any war is a human tragedy, and we should always be thankful for the peacemakers among us. That's not a bad message for this holiday season or any other time of year. After all, it's not how loudly Ali speaks but what he says and does that counts.

On 19 July 1996, more than three billion people around the world watched as Muhammad Ali stepped from the shadows to light the cauldron signalling the start of the 1996 Olympics. It was a spectacular moment. And afterwards, quite a few people from NBC and the Atlanta Olympic Organizing Committee took credit for having originated the idea, with statements like, 'I thought it up a month before the Olympics ... No, it was my idea six weeks before the games.' Sorry, guys. I went on record in 1993 with the following article.

The Olympic Flame

The Atlanta Olympics are three years in the future, but elaborate groundwork has already been laid. Budweiser has agreed to become a national sponsor for a sum that might otherwise be used to retire the national debt. On-site construction has begun, and television planning is underway. Eventually, the Olympic torch will be transported to the United States. And the triumphal procession that follows will lead to the highlight of the Games' opening ceremonies – lighting the Olympic flame.

Traditionally, someone from the host country ignites the flame. At the 1984 Olympics in Los Angeles, Rafer Johnson received the torch and carried it up the Coliseum steps to rekindle the world's most celebrated fire. Last year in Barcelona, a Spanish archer shot an arrow into a cauldron, thereby reawakening the flame. The eyes of the world are always on this moment. And one wonders who will be chosen to fulfil the honour in Atlanta.

The view here is that the choice is obvious. One man embodies the Olympic spirit to perfection. He's a true American in every sense of the word and the foremost citizen of the world. At age eighteen, he won a gold medal in Rome fighting under the name 'Cassius Clay'. Since then, he has traversed the globe, spreading joy wherever he goes. Atlanta has special meaning for him. It was there, after three years of exile from boxing, that he returned to face Jerry Quarry in the ring. He loves the spotlight, and the spotlight loves him. Indeed, one can almost hear him saying, 'When I carry that Olympic torch, every person in the world will be watching. Babies in their mothers' tummies will be kicking and hollering for the TV to be turned on. It will be bigger than Michael Jackson. Bigger than Elvis. Bigger than the Pyramids. Bigger than me fighting Sonny Liston, George Foreman and Joe Frazier all at the same time. Bigger than the Olympics – '

Wait a minute, Muhammad. This *is* the Olympics.

Anyway, you get the point. So I have a simple proposal to make. I'd like the International Olympic Committee to announce that, as its gift to the world, Muhammad Ali has been chosen to light the Olympic flame in Atlanta. Muhammad has already given us one memorable Olympic moment as Cassius Clay. Now let him share another with the world as Muhammad Ali. That way, the 26th Olympiad will truly be 'the greatest'.

It has been said that one isn't truly a 'boxing writer' until one has written for The Ring. *Ergo, I penned the following anecdotal recollections and commentary for 'The Bible of Boxing'.*

Some Reflections on Time Spent With Muhammad Ali

Muhammad Ali: His Life and Times was published in 1991. Muhammad helped promote the book and, among other things, attended two book signings in New York. Each signing was enormously successful. Both stores reported that Ali had sold more books in a single session than any previous subject or author.

The final promotional event in New York was Muhammad's attendance at the annual Boxing Writers Association of America dinner. Muhammad spoke briefly, and told the audience about a slave named Omar. It was a parable that preached the message of humility and was met by sustained applause. Then Ali sat down and the program resumed. HBO's Jim Lampley was speaking, when suddenly Muhammad returned to the podium and announced, 'I forgot to tell you. I had two book signings this week, and I broke the all-time record at both stores.'

That left Lampley to wonder aloud, 'Muhammad, would Omar the slave brag about his book signings?'

'He would if he sold a thousand books,' Muhammad responded.

* * *

The Ali book was published in Great Britain by Robson Books and has become Robson's biggest boxing bestseller to date. But it's just as memorable for the bizarre promotional tour that accompanied its launch in England.

In September 1991, Howard Bingham (Muhammad's longtime friend) and I journeyed to London. Ali was supposed to meet us there. The problem was, he didn't. A week earlier, Herbert Muhammad (Ali's

former manager) had taken him to Abu Dhabi in an effort to raise funds
for a proposed Chicago mosque that was to be built with Herbert's
involvement. Herbert had promised to have Ali in London for the start
of our publicity tour. But Herbert didn't like the way I'd portrayed him
in the book. And once he had Ali in Abu Dhabi, things changed. The
result was a two-week publicity campaign replete with elaborate
dinners, book signings, and interviews that devolved into chaos.

The London media had a grand time with it. 'Ali Held in Abu
Dhabi', screamed one headline above the subtitle, 'Advisors Have
Poisoned His Mind'. The *Express* ran a page-one photo of Ali sitting
with four men in Abu Dhabi above the legend, 'Revealed: The Mystery
Men Behind Absent Ali'. Nor was the story confined to London. 'Ali
Mystery as Wife Pleads for Safe Return,' cried the *Manchester Post*.
The Times, Guardian, Independent, Observer, Evening Standard and
News of the World all weighed in. The British Press Association issued
repeated bulletins on the matter including quotes from someone named
Rashaad Mousoui, who described himself as a spokesperson for Ali
and declared, 'Muhammad Ali will not come to London. He does not
support the book any more.'

Of greater concern was the fact that Ali had gone to Abu Dhabi
with a limited supply of the medication he takes to control the symptoms of Parkinson's syndrome. Howard Bingham had brought more of
the medication to London, but there was no way to get it to Ali. He was
cut off from the rest of the world in Abu Dhabi. His own wife Lonnie
was unable to speak with him by telephone.

The following spring, Howard and I returned to England. This time,
Muhammad and Lonnie were both with us and the promotional tour
went as planned. Interviews and dinners that had been rescheduled
went off without a hitch. *Muhammad Ali: His Life and Times* reappeared on the bestseller list, where it had resided briefly the previous
autumn. One afternoon, I was sitting next to Muhammad at a book
signing in London when a woman in her forties passed through the line.
She looked at Muhammad; then at me. And in a thick Irish accent, she
asked, 'Excuse me; are you Ali's son?'

'No, ma'am,' I replied.

'Oh,' she said with obvious disappointment. 'You look just like him.'

My initial reaction was to dismiss her as daft. After all, I'm white and only four years younger than Muhammad. But then it occurred to me that this was one more example of how, when it comes to Ali, people are colourblind. And of course, it's a compliment of the highest order to be told that you look just like Muhammad Ali.

* * *

Another moment from that tour also stands out in my mind. A book signing had been scheduled for Harrods, and we were told that Mohamed al-Fayed would be at the main entrance to greet us. This was no small occurrence. The owner of Harrods rarely welcomed visitors in person.

In the car on the way to Harrods, Lonnie Ali and I engaged in a bit of fantasy. At most previous book signings, Muhammad and I had been given gifts. Pens were the most frequent offering.

'Wouldn't it be nice,' Lonnie said, 'if Mr al-Fayed brought me upstairs to women's fashions and suggested that I pick out a silk dress.' Never having owned a Rolex watch, I thought that one would look nice around my wrist. And if I recall the conversation correctly, Muhammad was too busy eating brownies to take part.

When our car arrived at Harrods, Mohamed al-Fayed was at the door to greet us. A half-dozen bagpipers led us in procession to the room where the book signing was to take place. During the course of the afternoon, twelve hundred people lined up to meet Muhammad. He kissed, hugged, shook hands, posed for photos and did just about everything else that anyone requested. I should add that Harrods made a handsome profit on the sale of twelve hundred books.

When the signing was over, the Harrods representative supervising the event brought us into a back room where some sandwiches and bottles of mineral water were set out on a table. 'Is there anything else I can do for you?' she queried.

'Yes,' I said. 'The other day, I was in your food hall, and you had the best lemon bars I've ever tasted.'

'Would you like some to take back to the hotel?'

'That would be great.'

An aide was dispatched with appropriate instructions. Ten minutes later, the Harrods representative placed a nicely wrapped box of lemon bars on the table in front of me.

'That will be nine pounds twenty pence,' she said.

They didn't give us pens either.

* * *

With considerable fanfare, our tour of England continued, until late one afternoon, we found ourselves in Nottingham. It had been a long day. That morning, we'd been in Leeds, where Muhammad had signed 900 books, posed for photographs, kissed babies and shaken hands with literally thousands of admirers. Now that scene was being repeated with 500 more people who had waited in line for hours for their hero to arrive.

Ali was tired. He'd been awake since 5 a.m., when he'd risen to pray and read from the Koran. His voice, already weak from the ravages of Parkinson's syndrome, was flagging. And the facial 'mask' which accompanies his medical condition was more pronounced than usual.

Most of the people in line were joyful. But one of them – a middle-aged woman with a kind face – wasn't. Muhammad's condition grieved her, and as she approached him, she burst into tears.

Ali leaned over, kissed her on the cheek, and told her, 'Don't feel bad. God has blessed me. I've had a good life, and it's still good. I'm having fun now.'

The woman walked away smiling. For the rest of her life, she would remember meeting Ali. Moments later, she turned to look back at him, but Muhammad's attention was already focused on the next person in line – a tall handsome black man. 'You're uglier than Joe Frazier,' Ali was saying.

* * *

And that, of course, brings us to Joe. It's no secret that, of all Muhammad's ring opponents, the one who still holds a grudge against him is Joe Frazier. Joe makes no secret of his dislike for Ali, and sometimes his antipathy extends to Muhammad's friends.

In 1991, I was in Atlantic City for a WBO heavyweight championship bout between Ray Mercer and Tommy Morrison. Frazier was in attendance, and I introduced him to a friend of mine named Neil Ragin.

Joe's response was a resounding, 'Grhummpf!'

'It's nothing against you,' I explained to Neil. 'Joe doesn't talk to me a whole lot.'

Which gave Neil a chance to ingratiate himself with Joe and keep the conversation going. 'Of course, Joe doesn't talk with you. You're Ali's man. Everybody knows you're Ali's man. Right, Joe?'

Whereupon Joe said simply, 'Right! And I ain't talking to you either, 'cause you the friend of Ali's man.'

Still, in recent years, Joe and I have gotten along fairly well. He's been a guest in my home. He's cordial when we meet. And in return, I have to say, I've always respected Joe as a fighter, and there's a lot about him that I admire as a person. I also believe that Muhammad went too far in labelling Joe a 'gorilla' and casting him as an 'Uncle Tom'.

Still, none of that justifies the venom that has been pouring recently from Joe Frazier's lips. Throughout his recent 'autobiography', Frazier repeatedly referred to Muhammad as 'Clay' and 'boy'. If a white person spoke those words, he'd be branded a racist, and with good reason. Even more troubling is the fact that Joe seems to take pleasure in Muhammad's current physical difficulties and pride in the thought that he might have contributed to them.

Joe Frazier doesn't get it. For starters, he doesn't understand that, without Muhammad Ali, his own career wouldn't have been as remarkable as it was. Joe was a great fighter. However, fighters are judged, not by bouts that are easy, but by bouts that are hard. Frazier won the heavyweight championship in pieces by beating Buster Mathis and Jimmy Ellis (both of whom also lost to Muhammad). After he beat Ali (which was when Joe truly became champion), his only successful title defences were against Terry Daniels and Ron Stander. Then he got knocked out by George Foreman, who knocked him out a second time three years later. Take away the three Ali–Frazier fights, two of which were won by Ali, and what have you got?

Like Frazier, George Foreman also fought Muhammad. And Ali was hard on Foreman before their fight, as he was with Joe. By the time they got into the ring in Zaire, Foreman was viewed by the citizens of

that nation as a virtual stand-in for the white imperialists who had once
ruled the Belgian Congo. But George understands what Joe Frazier
does not – the importance of Muhammad Ali. 'After the fight, for a
while I was bitter,' Foreman later said. 'But then I realised I'd lost to a
great champion; probably the greatest of all time. Now I'm proud just
to be part of the Ali legend. If people mention my name with his from
time to time, that's enough for me.'

People said and did horrible things to Ali during the course of his
career, but he forgave each and every one of them. His view of religion
and his personal nature both require that he be merciful. Few people are
as forgiving as Muhammad. Some might say that he's forgiving to a
fault. But Muhammad Ali continues to flower spiritually and grow as a
person. Joe Frazier would do well to learn from his example.

Meanwhile, when it comes to Joe Frazier, Muhammad still gives as
good as he gets. Several years ago, I was with Ali in New York for a
celebration at the United Nations. Muhammad's son, Asaad, who was
a year old at the time, was also there; as was Joe. And Joe was looking
for trouble. Smiling at Asaad, he told onlookers, 'Hmmm; that boy
looks just like me.'

Ali didn't miss a beat. 'Don't call my boy ugly,' he said.

The time I spent with Muhammad Ali has provided me with a treasure trove of memories to write about.

Muhammad Ali at Notre Dame:
A Night to Remember

Notre Dame versus Michigan, 1990. The first game of the season for two of college football's most fabled institutions. Notre Dame was the top-ranked team in the country. Michigan was rated as high as number two, depending on which poll you followed. The game had been sold out for months and was the hottest ticket in the nation.

Meanwhile, Howard Bingham and I were tired. Howard is Muhammad Ali's best friend. I was Ali's biographer. It was the day before the game, and we'd been reading aloud for five days. More specifically, we'd been reading the manuscript for *Muhammad Ali: His Life and Times* – all one thousand pages – with Muhammad and his wife Lonnie. I'd just finished the first draft of the book and wanted to make sure it was factually accurate. Also, I knew that reading it aloud would be the best way to elicit further thoughts from Muhammad.

Howard and I are sports fans. Since Notre Dame is only a twenty-minute drive from the Alis' home, we thought it would be fun to go to the game. Ali doesn't care a whole lot about football. But his presence opens doors; he likes big events; and he's a sweetheart when it comes to doing things for friends. Thus, my call to the Notre Dame Athletic Department: 'Would it be possible for Muhammad Ali to buy three tickets for tomorrow night's game?'

There was a long pause on the other end of the line. 'Let me call you back,' the woman said. Five minutes later, the telephone rang. 'How do we know the tickets are really for Mr Ali?'

'That's easy,' I told her. 'He'll pick them up in person.'

'All right; come by the Athletic Department today before five o'clock.'

'Do you want Muhammad to bring his driver's licence for identification?'

'That's not necessary. I think we'll recognise him.'

Shortly before noon, we drove to Notre Dame to pick up the tickets. The Athletic Department wanted to give them to us, but we insisted on paying; a small gesture given their open-market value. Then we went home, read *Muhammad Ali: His Life and Times* for another five hours; read some more on Saturday; and drove back to Notre Dame.

The game was scheduled for 8 p.m. Central Standard Time. We arrived around six o'clock. The weather was perfect, and the scene surrounding the stadium was quintessential bigtime college football. Tens of thousands of fans had set up grills and were barbecueing everything from hamburgers to shrimp. Many of them didn't even have tickets to the game. They just wanted to be near the action, and their reaction to Muhammad was as expected. As we walked around, we heard a lot of 'Omigod! It's Muhammad Ali.' And Muhammad has certain opportunities that aren't available to the rest of us. For example, he can walk around a tailgate party until he finds something that looks particularly good to eat, and what he invariably hears is, 'Muhammad Ali! Please join us.'

In other words, we ate quite well thanks to the generosity of strangers. Then we went inside the stadium to our seats, which happened to be on the fifty-yard line. That was nice for us; and I suspect, also good for Notre Dame recruiting since the folks around us were suitably impressed by Ali's presence.

Muhammad sat between Howard and myself. Notre Dame was coached by Lou Holtz. Its brightest star was Raghib Ismail, who was joined in the backfield by Rick Mirer, Tony Brooks, Ricky Watters and Rodney Culverhouse. Michigan was in its first year under new head coach Gary Moeller, who had the unenviable task of succeeding Bo Schembechler. But his job was made easier by the presence of Elvis Grbac, Jarrod Bunch, Jon Vaughn and Greg Skrepenak.

It was a great game. Notre Dame surged to a 14–3 lead, and it seemed as though everyone on earth was singing, 'Cheer, cheer for old Notre Dame.' Then Michigan began to roll and scored three unanswered touchdowns, whereupon 'Hail to the victors valiant' was very much in vogue.

Meanwhile, as the game progressed, I began to talk with an elderly woman sitting to my left. She was Ellen Stonebreaker, grandmother of the Notre Dame co-captain and middle-linebacker, Mike Stonebreaker. If I had to guess, I'd say she was about eighty. She was charming. And when Notre Dame was on defence, her eyes never left the field. Even Ali noticed the intensity with which she was watching. 'Look at that old lady,' he told me. 'She's like a hawk.'

Notre Dame won. Down ten points going into the fourth quarter, they rallied for two late touchdowns capped by an eighteen-yard scoring pass from Mirer to Adrian Jarrell with 1:40 left to play. But one moment in particular stands out in my mind.

It came in the second half. Ellen Stonebreaker had been sneaking glances at Muhammad for some time. Finally she said to me, 'You know something; that boxer is a good-looking fellow.'

'Tell her I don't fool around with white women,' Muhammad advised me. Which I duly reported to Mrs Stonebreaker, who seemed more bemused than disappointed. However, she did have one request.

'I haven't done this since I was a young girl,' she acknowledged. 'But could you get me that fellow's autograph?'

I asked how she'd like her name written. She said she'd prefer it if Muhammad used her maiden name. She spelled it for him. He wrote it out, drew a little heart, and signed 'Love, Muhammad Ali.'

Then he kissed her.

It was just another day for Muhammad; one that I'm sure he's long since forgotten. But as is often the case, whenever and wherever he travels, it was a memorable night for everyone around him.

I spent the last week of November 1996 in Los Angeles with Muhammad Ali to promote a book that we co-authored – Healing: A Journal of Tolerance and Understanding. *That led to a very special Thanksgiving.*

Muhammad Ali – Thanksgiving 1996 'I've Got a Lot to Be Thankful For'

As is his custom, Muhammad Ali awoke shortly after 5 a.m. on Thanksgiving Day 1996. He was in Los Angeles to pursue his latest mission; teaching people how to love. *Healing* is a cause that Ali can wrap himself around, and the people close to him feel good about it.

After washing himself with clear running water, Ali put on clean clothes and said the first of his five daily prayers. Then he moved behind his hotel-room desk and began signing bookplates that would be distributed to fans who attended one of several book signings in the days ahead. Ali's weight has been over 250 pounds for several years, and now he's decided to get down to 220. Accordingly, he skipped breakfast as part of his personalised brand of dieting and announced, 'This is my third day of not eating, except for one meal a day.' However, as the day progresses, Ali will eat pears, apples, and oranges from a large basket of fruit that has been sent to his room by the hotel management.

'And maybe a muffin,' Ali admits.

Correct that. Several muffins. And chocolate chip cookies, cheese and crackers; all before his 'one meal of the day' – a large Thanksgiving dinner.

'I'm losing weight because I'm planning a comeback,' Ali says. 'On my fifty-fifth birthday, I think I'll fight the top three heavyweights in the world, one round each, at Madison Square Garden.'

'You'd better get in shape fast,' Muhammad is cautioned. 'Your fifty-fifth birthday is in seven weeks.'

'Seven weeks? Maybe I'll do it when I'm sixty instead.'

At 9 a.m. Pacific Coast Time, Ali turns on the television to accommodate a guest who wants to watch the Kansas City Chiefs versus the Detroit Lions. 'In my whole life,' he admits, 'I've never watched a football game on television from beginning to end. Sometimes I go to the Super Bowl because the people around me want to go, and because of me, they can get in. But the only sports I'm interested in now are big fights. I like watching big fights to see how I'd do if I was in them.'

On the TV screen, Detroit's Barry Sanders is seen making a particularly shifty move, and Muhammad's eyes widen. 'How old is he?'

'Twenty-eight.'

'When I fought Sonny Liston, that man wasn't even born.'

The Detroit Lions score a touchdown, and the obligatory end-zone dance follows.

'You started that,' Ali is told. 'All the dancing and celebrating and showing off started with you.'

'I started the big salaries too. Big salaries started when me and Joe Frazier got $2,500,000 each the first time we fought.'

The Chiefs vanquish the Lions 28–24, at which point the Dallas Cowboys take the field against the Washington Redskins. Meanwhile, Ali has begun turning the pages of a Bible, pointing out contradictions.

'Look at Exodus 33:11. [And the Lord spake unto Moses face to face, as a man speaketh unto his friend.] Now look at Exodus 33:20. [And the Lord said, "Thou canst not see my face, for there shall be no man see me and live."] Some people think the Bible is the word of God,' Ali continues. 'But in one part of Exodus, it says Moses saw God's face. And in another part, it says no man can see God and live. How can the word of God be two different things? Here's another contradiction. John 5:31. [Jesus said, "If I bear witness of myself, my witness is not true."] Now read John 8:14. [Jesus answered and said unto them, "Though I bear record of myself, yet my record is true."] You're educated. You tell me, is Jesus's witness true or not true? Heavy, ain't it?'

Shortly after 2 p.m., Ali leaves the hotel to travel to the home of Connye Richardson, a longtime family friend. Richardson lives in Hancock Park, the section of Los Angeles that Ali lived in during his marriage to Veronica Porche. Ali has mixed feelings about his years in

Los Angeles. The period encompassed some of his greatest glories, but it was in Hancock Park that his fortunes began to turn. He was living there when he lost to Leon Spinks, Larry Holmes and Trevor Berbick. It was in Hancock Park that his health began to fail, his family life (now on solid foundation again) began to unravel, and he felt himself growing old.

Connye Richardson's home is spacious and comfortable. During the course of the day, twenty family members and friends will drop by. Ali is wearing tan slacks and a white short-sleeved shirt.

As he often does when he feels at home in someone else's living room, Muhammad turns on the television. A movie about Vietnam starring Gene Hackman is showing. The last twenty minutes are unremitting violence and gore. 'I made a wise decision when I didn't go to Vietnam,' Ali tells one of the other guests. 'All that killing was wrong.' Then he switches to CNN, which has a brief feature on a presidential pardon given by Bill Clinton to a 45-pound turkey. Instead of winding up on someone's dinner table, the turkey will spend the rest of its years on a petting farm in Virginia. Ali is asked if he thinks it's right for people to kill animals to eat when other types of food are available. He considers the issue and responds, 'Everything that God made, he made for a purpose. I don't believe in hunting just to kill an animal. That bothers me. But I think it's all right to eat animals like turkeys and fish and cows.'

Connye Richardson has been cooking for days, and it seems as though every one of God's foods is served. If Muhammad is truly planning to fight again in Madison Square Garden, this isn't the place to slim down. But it's a good Thanksgiving. And Ali is both happy and in a reflective mood as the day draws to a close.

'God has been good to me,' Muhammad says in the car going back to the hotel. 'I'm thankful I've got a good wife and nine healthy children. I'm thankful I was three-time heavyweight champion of the world. I'm thankful I live in a country like America. I'm thankful I've been able to travel and meet people all over the world. I'm thankful that, even though I haven't fought for fifteen years, people still remember me. I have a good life. I've got a lot to be thankful for.'

The Sanitisation of Muhammad Ali

Later this year, Sony Pictures is scheduled to begin principal photography on a feature film about Muhammad Ali.

Ali is an important figure in world history. In the 1960s, he stood as a beacon of hope, not only for black Americans, but also for oppressed people around the globe. Every time he looked in the mirror and preened, 'I'm so pretty,' he was saying 'black is beautiful' before it became fashionable to do so. When he refused induction into the United States Army during the height of the war in Vietnam, he stood up, not just to the United States government, but to armies around the world in support of the proposition that war is wrong.

But – and this is a big 'but' – one of the reasons Ali caused as much turmoil as he did was because there was an ugly edge to what he was saying. Part of his impact lay in the fact that he was pushing beyond, and in some cases against, the prevailing integrationist norm. And sadly, most of the recent tributes to Ali have failed to offer an honest exposition of his past.

An ABC made-for-television movie about Ali entitled *King of the World* that was broadcast earlier this year is a case in point. The film purported to follow young Cassius Clay from early in his professional career through his 1964 defeat of Sonny Liston to capture the heavyweight championship of the world.

There were several problems with the movie. First, the screenplay was awful. In addition to the usual distortions of fact that were deemed necessary 'for dramatic purposes', the story line was hopelessly convoluted. The movie also suffered from the hard reality that no one but Muhammad Ali can play Ali.

But the biggest problem with the film was that it sanitised Ali. In an effort to create a simple conflict between good and evil (with Ali being good), it ignored the fact that, during what might have been the most important fourteen years of his life, Ali adhered to the teachings of the Nation of Islam – a doctrine that Arthur Ashe later condemned as 'a racist ideology; a sort of American apartheid.'

Watching the movie, the uninformed viewer was left with the impression that Nation of Islam doctrine was, and still is, Islam as practised by more than one billion people around the world today. ABC depicted only that portion of Nation of Islam doctrine that taught black pride, black self-awareness and self-love. The movie showed a strong loving bond between Ali and Malcolm X. It gave no hint that, when Malcolm later broke with the Nation of Islam to pursue orthodox Islamic beliefs, Ali abandoned his former mentor.

The Nation of Islam taught Ali that white people were devils who had been genetically created by an evil scientist with a big head named Mr Yacub. It taught Ali that there was a wheel-shaped Mother of Planes one-half mile wide manned by black men in the sky, and that, on Allah's chosen day of retribution, fifteen hundred planes from the Mother of Planes would drop deadly explosives destroying all but the righteous on earth. Neither of these views are part of traditional Islamic thought or find justification in the Koran. Indeed, while the concepts of Heaven and Hell are central to traditional Islamic thought, the National of Islam rejected both. For much of the period from 1961 to 1975, Muhammad Ali was the Nation of Islam's most visible and vocal spokesman in America.

Unfortunately, when it comes to Ali, this sort of revisionism has become common. It began in 1977, when Ali himself starred in a feature film about his life entitled *The Greatest*. *The Greatest* was fictionalised and mediocre. Frank Deford summed it up when he wrote, 'Of all our sports heroes, Ali needs least to be sanitized. But *The Greatest* is just a big vapid valentine. It took a dive. A genuine film about this unique man and his times must wait until Ali can no longer indulge himself as star and censor.'

Yet even when Ali has relinquished control, the celluloid results have been questionable. In 1997, the Academy Award for 'best documentary feature' went to *When We Were Kings* – a film about Muhammad Ali recapturing the heavyweight championship of the world from George Foreman in Zaire. Much about *When We Were Kings* was laudable. But in 1974, when Ali and Foreman did battle, Ali still adhered to the teachings of the Nation of Islam. Did the film show that? No. Rather, in an effort to create a clear distinction between 'the good Negro' (Ali) and 'the bad Negro' (Foreman), a lot of footage of Ali extolling the virtues of Louis Farrakhan was left on the cutting-room floor.

Now comes Sony Pictures, with Will Smith reportedly set to play the role of Ali. One hopes that this movie will be more honest than its predecessors.

Ali's views on religion have changed considerably since he was young. In 1984, he publicly repudiated the separatist doctrine of Nation of Islam spokesman Louis Farrakhan, declaring, 'What he teaches is not at all what we believe in. He represents the time of our struggle in the dark and a time of confusion in us, and we don't want to be associated with that at all.' Later, Ali acknowledged, 'When I was young, I followed a teaching that disrespected other people and said that white people were "devils". I was wrong. Colour doesn't make a man a devil. It's the heart and soul and mind that count.'

Not everyone has been pleased with Ali's transformation. Football great Jim Brown, who was intricately involved with Ali's early career, later opined, 'The Ali that America ended up loving was not the Ali I loved most. I didn't feel the same about him any more, because the warrior I loved was gone. He became part of the establishment. And I suppose, in a sense, there's nothing wrong with that because, if you can make all people feel good, maybe that's greater than being a fighter for black people. But I didn't like it.'

Still, it's ironic that the same media forces that savaged Ali earlier in his life now seem determined to sanitise him. And it's also sad because, in the end, it's important that memories of the young Muhammad Ali be honestly preserved. Oftentimes, great men are considered great, not only because of what they achieve, but also because of the road they travel to reach their final destination. Sanitising Muhammad Ali and rounding off the rough edges of his journey is a disservice both to history and to Ali himself.

As the year 2000 progressed, members of Congress from both sides of the aisle were effusive in praising Ali. Much of that praise was genuine, but at times it seemed a bit hypocritical. Again, I ventured into the past.

Muhammad Ali and Congress Remembered

At long last, Congress has enacted the Muhammad Ali Boxing Reform Act. As a cure for what ails boxing, the proposed legislation leaves a lot to be desired. Still, it's a step in the right direction. Meanwhile, Senator Jim Bunning of Kentucky is sponsoring legislation that would authorise President Clinton to award Ali with a Congressional Gold Medal (the highest civilian honour that Congress can bestow upon an individual). Thus, it's worth remembering what an earlier generation of Congressmen had to say about Muhammad Ali at the height of the war in Vietnam.

On 17 February 1966, Ali was reclassified 1-A by his draft board and uttered the immortal words, 'I ain't got no quarrel with them Vietcong.' One month later, Congressman Frank Clark of Pennsylvania rose in Congress and called upon the American public to boycott Ali's upcoming bout against George Chuvalo:

> The heavyweight champion of the world turns my stomach. I am not a superpatriot. But I feel that each man, if he really is a man, owes to his country a willingness to protect it and serve it in time of need. From this standpoint, the heavyweight champion has been a complete and total disgrace. I urge the citizens of the nation as a whole to boycott any of his performances. To leave these theatre seats empty would be the finest tribute possible to that boy whose hearse may pass by the open doors of the theatre on Main Street USA.

In 1967, Ali refused induction into the United States Army at which point he was stripped of his title and denied a licence to box in all fifty states. That same year, he was indicted, tried, convicted and sentenced to five years in prison. Then, in October 1969 while the appeal of his conviction was pending, ABC announced plans to have Ali serve as a TV commentator for an upcoming amateur boxing competition between the United States and Soviet Union. Congressman Fletcher Thompson of Georgia objected:

> I take the floor today to protest the network that has announced it will use Cassius Clay as a commentator for these contests. I consider this an affront to loyal Americans everywhere, although it will obviously receive much applause in some of the hippie circles. Maybe the American Broadcasting System feels that it needs to appeal more to the hippies and yippies of America than to loyal Americans.

In December 1969, there were reports that Governor Claude Kirk of Florida would grant Ali a licence to fight Joe Frazier in Tampa. Congressman Robert Michel of Illinois took to the podium of the United States House of Representatives to protest:

> Clay has been stripped of his heavyweight title for dodging the draft. And I consider it an insult to patriotic Americans everywhere to permit his reentry into the respected ranks of boxing. It should be recalled that Mr Clay gave as one of his excuses for not wanting to be drafted that he is in reality a minister and that even boxing is antagonistic to his religion. But apparently, he is willing to fight anyone but the Vietcong.

Ultimately, the authorities in Florida refused to give Ali a licence to box. Then, in September 1970, it was announced that Ali would fight Jerry Quarry in Georgia. Once again, Congressman Michel had his say:

> I read with disgust today the article in the *Washington Post* concerning the upcoming fight of this country's most famous draft dodger, Cassius Clay. The article said that Mr Clay was out of shape, overweight and winded. No doubt, this comes from his desperate and concerted efforts to stay out of the military service while thousands of patriotic young men are fighting and dying in Vietnam. Apparently, Mr Clay feels himself entitled to the full protection of the law, yet does not feel he has to sacrifice anything to preserve the institutions that protect him. Cassius Clay cannot hold a candle to the average American boy who is willing to defend his country in perilous times.

Ali fought Jerry Quarry in Atlanta on 26 October 1970. Then a federal district court decision paved the way for him to fight Oscar Bonavena on 7 December (the anniversary of Pearl Harbor) in New York. After that, he signed to fight Joe Frazier at Madison Square Garden. Each fighter was to receive the previously unheard-of sum of $2,500,000. That outraged Congressman John Rarick of Louisiana, who spoke to his colleagues as follows:

> Veterans who have fought our nation's wars feel that any man unwilling to fight for his country is unworthy of making a profit or receiving public acclaim in it. Cassius Clay is a convicted draft dodger sentenced to a five-year prison term which he is not serving. What right has he to claim the privilege of appearing in a boxing match to be nationally televised? The Clay affair approaches a crisis in national indignation.

On 8 March 1971, Ali lost a hard-fought fifteen-round decision to Joe Frazier. Meanwhile, he remained free on bail while the United States Supreme Court considered the appeal of his criminal conviction. This was too much for Congressman George Andrews of Alabama, who spoke to his brethren and compared Ali to Lieutenant William Calley, who had been convicted of murder in the massacre of 22 South Vietnamese civilians at My Lai:

> Last night, I was sickened and sad when I heard about that poor little fellow who went down to Fort Benning. He had barely graduated from high school. He volunteered and offered his life for his country. He was taught to kill. He was sent to Vietnam. And he wound up back at Fort Benning, where he was indicted and convicted for murder in the first degree for carrying out orders. I also thought about another young man about his age; one Cassius Clay, alias Muhammad Ali, who several years ago defied the United States government, thumbed his nose at the flag, and is still walking the streets making millions of dollars fighting for pay, not for his country. That is an unequal distribution of justice.

On 28 June 1971, fifty months to the day after Ali had refused induction, the United States Supreme Court unanimously reversed his conviction, and all criminal charges pending against him were dismissed. The next day, Congressman William Nichols of Alabama expressed his outrage:

The United States Supreme Court has given another black eye to the United States Armed Forces. The decision overturning the draft evasion conviction of Cassius Clay is a stinging rebuke to the 240,000 Americans still serving in Vietnam and the 50,000 Americans who lost their lives there. I wish the members of the Supreme Court would assist me when I try to explain to a father why his son must serve in Vietnam or when I attempt to console a widow or the parents of a young man who has died in a war that Cassius Clay was exempted from.

Not to be outdone, Congressman Joe Waggonner of Louisiana echoed his fellow lawmaker's expression of contempt:

The United States Supreme Court has issued the edict that Cassius Clay does not have to be inducted because he does not believe in war. No draft-age young man believes in a war that he will have to fight, nor does any parent of a draft-age son believe in a war that their own flesh and blood will have to fight and possibly give his life in so doing. But our people have always heeded the call of their country when asked, not because they love war, but because their country has asked them to do so. And I feel strongly about this. If Cassius Clay does not have to be drafted because of questionable religious beliefs or punished for refusing induction simply because he is black or because he is a prizefighter – and I can see no other real justification for the Court's action – then all other young men who wish it should also be allowed a draft exemption. Cassius Clay is a phoney. He knows it, the Supreme Court knows it, and everyone else knows it.

Times change.

After a visit to the United States Holocaust Memorial Museum with Ali, I was left with a simple thought. If we can harness the energy and love that emanate from this man, maybe we can change the world.

A Day of Remembrance

On 24 June 1997, Muhammad Ali awoke in the nation's capital at 5 a.m. He said his prayers, ate a light breakfast, and read quietly from the Koran. Then, accompanied by his wife Lonnie and several friends, he left the Hay-Adams Hotel and drove to a unique destination – the United States Holocaust Memorial Museum.

The museum was not yet open to the public when Ali arrived at 7.45 a.m. He had come early because he feared his presence during normal visiting hours would cause a commotion unsuited to the decorum of his surroundings. Several staff members greeted Muhammad and his party when they arrived. There were introductions, and the tour began.

The mission of the United States Holocaust Memorial Museum is to inform, honour and inspire. More specifically, it is designed to present the history of the persecution and murder of six million Jews and millions of other victims of Nazi tyranny; to commemorate those who died; and to encourage visitors to contemplate the moral implications of their own civic responsibilities.

Ali began by assimilating facts as he walked through the museum...One-and-a-half million children were exterminated in the Holocaust...It wasn't just Jews...Gypsies, the physically disabled, mentally handicapped, and other 'undesirables' were also victims...Books were burned, synagogues destroyed...

As the tour progressed, Muhammad began to draw parallels between the Holocaust and the slavery that his own ancestors endured. Ali has spoken often about how black Americans were robbed of their African names and given slave names instead. Now he learned of people whose

Jewish names were replaced by numbers tattooed on their forearms. Standing in a boxcar used to transport Jews to death camps in Poland, he imagined himself in the cargo hold of a slaveship two centuries earlier.

Midway through the tour, Ali came to a glass wall bearing the names of thousands of communities eradicated during the Holocaust.

'Each of these names is a whole town?' Muhammad asked incredulously.

'Yes.'

'I never knew it was that bad.'

The tour went on...A pile of shoes taken from the dead at Majdanek...Bales of hair cut from the heads of concentration camp victims...A crude metal table where bodies were placed and gold teeth extracted with pliers...Grainy films of nude bodies piled high being bulldozed into trenches.

Ninety minutes after the tour began, Ali stopped to read a quotation in silver letters on a grey wall:

> First they came for the socialists.
> And I did not speak out because I was not a socialist.
> Then they came for the trade unionists.
> And I did not speak out because I was not a trade unionist.
> Then they came for the Jews.
> And I did not speak out because I was not a Jew.
> Then they came for me.
> And there was no one left to speak for me.

Finally, Ali entered the Hall of Remembrance and placed a white rose beside the museum's eternal flame.

During the course of his life, Muhammad Ali has taken many courageous stands. But his presence at the United States Holocaust Memorial Museum on 24 June 1997, is among his most important statements of principle.

The victims' faces on this particular morning were Jewish. But they could just as easily have been faces from Cambodia, Bosnia or Rwanda. By virtue of his presence, Ali demonstrated once again his solidarity with all victims of persecution. And he joined his spirit with millions of Holocaust victims and with the survivors who remember them.

I'm a big Ali fan. But there are limits to his talents.

Ali as Diplomat: 'No! No! No! Don't'

In 1980, in response to the Soviet Union's invasion of Afghanistan, the Carter Administration sought to organise a boycott of the Moscow Olympics. As part of that effort, it sent Muhammad Ali to five African nations to gather support for America's position.

Ali's trip was a disaster. *Time* magazine later called it, 'The most bizarre diplomatic mission in recent U.S. history.' Some African officials viewed Ali's presence as a racial insult. 'Would the United States send Chris Evert to negotiate with London?' one Tanzanian diplomat demanded. Ali himself seemed confused regarding the facts underlying his role and was unable to explain why African nations should boycott the Moscow Olympics when, four years earlier, the United States had refused to join 29 African countries in boycotting the Montreal Olympics over South Africa's place in the sporting world.

'Maybe I'm being used to do something that ain't right,' Ali conceded at one point. In Kenya, he announced that Jimmy Carter had put him 'on the spot' and sent him 'around the world to take the whupping over American policies', and said that, if he'd known the 'whole history of America and South Africa', he 'probably wouldn't have made the trip'.

That bit of history is relevant now because Jack Valenti (President of the Motion Picture Association of America) has unveiled tentative plans for a one-minute public service announcement featuring Ali that will be broadcast throughout the Muslim world. The thrust of the message is that America's war on terrorism is not a war against Islam. The public service spot would be prepared by Hollywood 9/11 – a group that was formed after movie industry executives met in November with Karl Rove (a senior political advisor to George Bush). In Valenti's words, Ali would be held out as 'the spokesman for Muslims in America'.

The proposed public service announcement might be good publicity for the movie industry, but it's dangerous politics.

Ali is universally respected and loved, but he isn't a diplomat. He doesn't understand the complexities of geopolitics. His heart is pure, but his judgments and actions are at times unwise. An example of this occurred recently at a fundraising event for the proposed Muhammad Ali Center. The centre is intended to be an educational facility designed to promote tolerance and understanding among all people. At the fundraiser, Ali rose to tell several jokes.

'No! No! No! Don't,' his wife Lonnie cried.

Despite her plea, Ali proceeded. 'What's the difference between a Jew and a canoe?' he asked. Then he supplied the answer: 'A canoe tips.' That was followed by, 'A black, a Puerto Rican and a Mexican are in a car. Who's driving?' The answer? 'The police.'

Afterwards, Sue Carls (a spokesperson for the Ali Center) sought to minimise the damage, explaining, 'These are not new jokes. Muhammad tells them all the time because he likes to make people laugh, and he shocks people to make a point.' Two days later, Lonnie Ali added, 'Even the Greatest can tell bad jokes.'

The problem is, this is a situation where misjudgments and bad jokes can cost lives.

Ali is not a bigot. He tells far more 'nigger' jokes than jokes about Hispanics and Jews. But Ali sometimes speaks and acts without considering the implications of his words and conduct. And he can be swayed by rhetoric; particularly when the speaker is a Muslim cleric with a following in some portion of the world.

What happens if, six months from now, Ali makes an intemperate statement about Israel? What happens if Ali calls for a halt to all American military action against terrorism in the heartfelt belief that a halt will save innocent lives? Will he then still be 'the spokesman for Muslims in America'.

Muhammad Ali leads best when he leads by example and by broad statements in support of tolerance and understanding among all people. To ask more of him in the current incendiary situation is looking for trouble.

More than two decades after his retirement from the ring, Muhammad Ali still stirs passions.

Ghosts of Manila

Albert Einstein once remarked, 'Nature, to be sure, distributes her gifts unevenly among her children. But it strikes me as unfair, and even in bad taste, to select a few of them for boundless admiration, attributing superhuman powers of mind and character to them.'

But society did just that with Muhammad Ali. Few people have ever received accolades equal to those that have been showered upon him. Indeed, Wilfred Sheed, who himself was sceptical of Ali's merit as a social figure, once observed that boxing's eras would be forever known as B.C. (before Clay) and A.D. (Ali Domini).

Enter Mark Kram. Kram is a very good writer. How else can one describe a man who refers to Chuck Wepner as having a face that looks as though it has been 'embroidered by a tipsy church lady', and likens Joe Frazier's visage after Ali–Frazier I to 'a frieze of a lab experiment that was a disaster'. Kram covered boxing for *Sports Illustrated* for eleven years. Now, a quarter of a century later, he has written *Ghosts of Manila: The Fateful Blood Feud Between Muhammad Ali and Joe Frazier.* The book, in the first instance, is the story of two men whose rivalry was ugly, glorious, brutal and enthralling. And secondarily, Kram declares, 'This book is intended to be a corrective to the years of stenography that have produced the Ali legend. Cheap myth coruscates the man. The wire scheme for his sculpture is too big.'

Thus, Kram seeks to raise Joe Frazier to a level virtually equal to that of Ali in the ring and perhaps above him in terms of character. And in so doing, he portrays what he believes to be the dark side of Ali.

Ghosts of Manila is divided into four parts. They cover, in order, Ali and Frazier in retirement; the emergence of both men as fighters and in the public consciousness; their three fights; and the two men, again, in retirement.

Kram concedes Ali's ring greatness. 'As a fighter,' Kram writes, 'he was the surface of a shield, unmalleable, made for mace and chain, flaring with light.' Describing Ali in the ring moments before Ali–Frazier I, he acknowledges, 'Whatever you might think of him, you were forced to look at him with honest lingering eyes, for there might never be his like again. Assessed by ring demands – punch, size, speed, intelligence, command, and imagination – he was an action poet, the equal of the best painting you could find.'

As for Frazier, Kram calls him 'the most skillful devastating inside puncher in boxing history,' and goes so far as to rank him among the top five heavyweights of all time. That seems a bit silly. Joe was a great fighter and every bit as noble a warrior as Ali. But there's a time-honoured axiom in boxing that styles make fights. And the list of fighters with the style to beat Joe Frazier numbers far more than five.

Kram is on more solid ground when he catalogues Frazier's hatred for Ali. The story of how Muhammad branded Joe an 'Uncle Tom' before their first fight, 'ignorant' before Ali–Frazier II, and a 'gorilla' before Ali–Frazier III is well known, but *Ghosts of Manila* makes it fresh and compelling. Thus, Kram writes, 'Muhammad Ali swam inside Joe Frazier like a determined bacillus... Ali has sat in Frazier's gut like a broken bottle.' And he quotes Frazier's one-time associate Bert Watson as saying, 'You don't do to a man what Ali did to Joe. Ali robbed him of who he is. To a lot of people, Joe is still ignorant, slow-speaking, dumb and ugly. That tag never leaves him. People have only seen one Joe; the one created by Ali. If you're a man, that's going to get to you in a big way.' And Kram quotes Frazier as saying of Ali, 'When a man gets in your blood like that, you can't never let go. Yesterday is today for me. He never die for me... If we were twins in the belly of our mama, I'd reach over and strangle him... I'll outlive him.'

Kram writes with grace and constructs his case against Ali's supervening greatness in a largely intelligent way. But his work is flawed. First, there are factual inaccuracies. For example, Kram is simply wrong when he discusses Ali's military draft reclassification and states, 'Had he not become a Muslim, chances are he would have remained unfit for duty.' That's not the case. In truth, Ali had been declared unfit for military duty by virtue of his scoring in the sixteenth percentile on an Army intelligence test. That left him well below the requirement of thirty. But two years after that, with the war in Vietnam expanding, the mental-aptitude percentile required by the military was lowered from thirty to fifteen. The change impacted upon hundreds of thousands of young men across the country. To suggest that Ali was somehow singled out and the standard changed because of his religion is ridiculous.

Also, there are times when Kram is overly mean-spirited. For example, Bryant Gumbel (who aroused Kram's ire with negative commentary on Joe Frazier) is referred to as 'a mediocre writer and thinker' with 'a shallow hard-worked ultra-sophistication and ego that not even a mother could love'. Ali in his current condition is labelled 'a billboard in decline', of whom Kram says uncharitably, 'Physical disaster of his own making has kept his fame intact. He would have become the bore dodged at the party. The future promised that there would be no more clothes with which to dress him up.' Indeed, Kram goes so far as to call the younger Ali 'a useful idiot' and 'near the moronic level'.

Kram's failure to distinguish fully between Nation of Islam doctrine and orthodox Islamic beliefs is also troubling. During what might have been the most important fourteen years of Ali's life, he adhered to the teachings of the Nation of Islam. Yet reading *Ghosts of Manila*, one might come away with the impression that Nation of Islam doctrine was, and still is, Islam as practised by more than one billion people around the world today. That's because Kram has the annoying habit of referring to Ali's early mentors as 'the Muslims', which is like lumping Billy Graham and the Ku Klux Klan together and calling them 'the Christians'.

Then there's the matter of Kram's sources; most notably, his reliance on two women named Aaisha Ali and Khaliah Ali.

Muhammad met Aaisha Ali in 1973 when he was 31 years old and she was a seventeen-year-old named Wanda Bolton. To his discredit, they had sexual relations and she became pregnant. Kram makes much of the fact that Wanda was 'on her way to becoming a doctor'. Given the fact that she was a high school junior at the time, that's rather speculative. Regardless, Ms Bolton subsequently claimed that she and Ali had been 'Islamically married' and changed her name to Aaisha Ali. Muhammad acknowledged paternity and accepted financial responsibility for their daughter, Khaliah.

Kram describes Aaisha several times as 'a mystery woman', which is a cheap theatrical trick. Her presence in Ali's past has been known and written about for years. More significantly, Kram uses Aaisha and Khaliah as his primary sources to trash Ali's current wife Lonnie (who Kram calls Ali's 'new boss'). Indeed, after describing Ali as 'a careless fighter who had his brain cells irradiated,' Kram quotes Lonnie as telling Khaliah, 'I am Muhammad Ali now.' Then, after referring to 'Lonnie and her tight circle of pushers,' he quotes Khaliah as saying of her father, 'It's about money. He's a substance; an item.' And after that, Kram recounts a scene when Ali and Lonnie were in a Louisville hospital visiting Ali's mother, who was being kept alive on a respirator. The final days of Odessa Clay's life were the saddest ever for Ali. Yet again relying wholly on Khaliah, Kram quotes Lonnie as saying, 'We can't afford this, Muhammad.'

The problem is, there are a lot of people who think that Aaisha Ali and Khaliah Ali aren't particularly reliable sources. I happen to have been present at one of the incidents regarding which Kram quotes Khaliah. It involved a championship belt that was given to Ali at a dinner commemorating the twentieth anniversary of the first Ali–Frazier fight. The dinner took place on the night of 14 April 1991, although Kram mistakenly reports it as occurring on an unspecified date five years later. Khaliah left Ali's hotel room that night with the belt. I experienced the incident very differently from the way Kram recounts it.

However, my biggest concern regarding *Ghosts of Manila* is its thesis that Ali's influence lay entirely in the sporting arena. Kram acknowledges that Ali 'did lead the way for black athletes out of the frustrating silence that Jackie Robinson had to endure.' However, even that concession is tempered by the claim that, 'Ali's influence in games today can be seen in the blaring unending marketing of self, the cheap acting out of performers, and the crassness of player interactions. His was an overwhelming presence that, if you care about such things, came at a high cost.'

And then Kram goes on to say, 'What was laughable, if you knew anything about Ali at all, was that the literati was certain that he was a serious voice, that he knew what he was doing. He didn't have a clue . . .

Seldom has a public figure of such superficial depth been more wrongly perceived.'

'Ali,' Kram says flatly, 'was not a social force.' And woe to those who say he was, because their utterances are dismissed as 'heavy breathing' from 'know-nothings' and 'trendy tasters of faux revolution'.

Apparently, I'm one of those heavy breathers. Kram refers to me as 'a lawyer-Boswell who seems intent on making the public believe that, next to Martin Luther King, Ali is the most important black figure in the last half century.' And in case anyone misses his point, Kram adds, 'Current hagiographers have tied themselves in knots trying to elevate Ali into a heroic defiant catalyst of the antiwar movement, a beacon of black independence. It's a legacy that evolves from the intellectually loose sixties, from those who were in school then and now write romance history.'

Actually, Kram has misquoted me. I believe he's referring to a statement in *Muhammad Ali: His Life and Times* in which I wrote, 'With the exception of Martin Luther King, no black man in America had more influence than Ali during the years when Ali was in his prime.' I still believe that to be true.

Was Ali as important as Nelson Mandela? No. Was Ali in the late 1960s more important than any other black person in America except for Dr King? I believe so. Indeed, Nelson Mandela himself said recently, 'Ali's refusal to go to Vietnam and the reasons he gave made him an international hero. The news could not be shut out even by prison walls. He became a real legend to us in prison.'

Kram's remarkable gift for words notwithstanding, Muhammad Ali in the 1960s stood as a beacon of hope for oppressed people all over the world. Every time he looked in the mirror and uttered the phrase, 'I'm so pretty,' he was saying 'black is beautiful' before it became fashionable. When he refused induction into the United States Army, regardless of his motives, he stood up to armies around the globe in support of the proposition that, unless you have a very good reason for killing people, war is wrong.

Dick Gregory once said, 'If you wanted to do a movie to depict Ali, it would just be a small light getting bigger and bigger and bigger and bigger. That was Ali in a sea of darkness.' One can imagine Kram gagging at imagery like that. But the truth is, Muhammad Ali found his way into the world's psyche.

Perhaps Reggie Jackson put it in perspective best. 'Do you have any idea what Ali meant to black people?' Jackson told me once. 'He was the leader of a nation; the leader of black America. As a young black, at times I was ashamed of my colour; I was ashamed of my hair. And Ali made me proud. I'm just as happy being black now as somebody else is being white, and Ali was part of that growing process. Think about it! Do you understand what it did for black Americans to know that the most physically gifted, possibly the most handsome, and one of the most charismatic men in the world was black? Ali helped raise black people in this country out of mental slavery. The entire experience of being black changed for millions of people because of Ali.'

In sum, Muhammad Ali might not have meant much to Mark Kram. But he meant a great deal to a lot of people. He made an enormous difference.

Round 3

Other Fighters

Sugar Ray Leonard retired from boxing and came back more times than anyone cares to remember. But the world knew he was through as a fighter when he lost to Terry Norris at Madison Square Garden on 9 February 1991.

Sugar Ray Leonard's Bittersweet End

The downfall of a great fighter is always sad to behold, and Sugar Ray Leonard was a great fighter. Ray Robinson would have beaten him at any weight, but it wouldn't have been a walk in the park. Leonard was a worthy successor to the original Sugar Ray's name.

Leonard fought Wilfred Benitez when Benitez was 39–0–1 and stopped him in the fifteenth round. He fought Thomas Hearns when Hearns was 32–0 and TKO'd Hearns in fourteen. He fought Ayub Kalule when Kalule was 36–0 and knocked out Kalule in nine. He fought Roberto Duran when Duran was 73–1 and forced Duran to plead 'no mas'. And he fought Marvin Hagler when Hagler was 62–2–2 and flurried his way to a twelve-round decision.

That's five wins against five opponents with a combined record of 242–3–3.

That's greatness.

But like all great fighters, Ray Leonard got old. The relevant numbers for his bout against Terry Norris weren't Ray's career mark of 36–1–1 or Norris's 26–3. They were 34 years 9 months versus 23 years 8 months. Indeed, in the eyes of many, Ray Leonard had long been semi-retired. He'd had 33 fights in his first five years as a professional. But in the nine years leading up to Norris, there'd been only five. And in four of those five, the erosion of Leonard's skills showed. Journeyman Kevin Howard knocked him down before succumbing in round nine. Donny Lalonde decked Ray and hurt him several times. Roberto Duran cut him badly. And Thomas Hearns 'dominated to a draw'. Only against Marvin Hagler was Leonard's greatness confirmed. No matter how one scored Hagler–Leonard, Sugar Ray shook up the world.

Like Leonard, Madison Square Garden has long had an aura of its own. Although it's no longer 'The Mecca of Boxing', it still enjoys a hallowed name. Leonard had never fought before as a professional in the Garden, and good story lines make for good boxing marriages. Hence, Leonard–Norris: a once-great fighter in a great arena against a very good young foe. Give Sugar Ray credit for going in tough. But almost always in that kind of match-up, the good young fighter prevails.

It was a sad night; for Leonard and the Garden. High ticket prices, the fading economy, a mediocre undercard and Showtime's live TV broadcast contributed to a disappointing turnout of 7,495. Before the bout, Ray talked like a young fighter; but in the ring he was old.

The first six rounds were competitive. The last six were one-sided to a fault. Ray Leonard got beaten up. His face was swollen; he was bleeding from the mouth. By night's end, he looked forty, not three months shy of 35. He fought with courage, but that was all he had. The moves that once made him great weren't there any more. The trademark flurries that intimidated Hagler were gone. In round two and then again in round seven, Leonard found himself on the canvas; an all too familiar venue lately in his career.

Sugar Ray Robinson might have pulled this one out. At age 36, the original Sugar Ray fought Gene Fullmer for the middleweight championship of the world. Trailing badly in round five, he knocked Fullmer out with a perfect left hook; possibly the best knockout punch ever thrown. But that was a different Sugar Ray. And against Norris, Ray Leonard no longer had what it takes. The best that can be said about Leonard–Norris is that Ray finished his career in Madison Square Garden on his feet; not face down on the Budweiser logo in some casino in Las Vegas or Atlantic City.

The judges' scoring was more one-sided than the fight. Bill Costello got it right at 116–110. Barbara Perez and Sid Rubenstein went overboard at 120–104 and 119–103. After the bout, Leonard announced his retirement. 'It took this kind of fight to prove to me that it's no longer my time,' he said.

And so Ray Leonard moves on, from an active fighter to the ranks of the immortals. He gave us all a lot of pleasure and bequeathed the world some truly great fights. Unfortunately, Leonard–Norris wasn't one of them.

On 11 July 1996, Riddick Bowe and Andrew Golota met in the ring for the first time. It was an ugly night. Golota pummelled Bowe for most of the bout, but was disqualified for low blows. A riot followed.

Bowe–Golota in Perspective

First the fight.

Riddick Bowe versus Andrew Golota was as one-sided as the experts thought it would be, except it was Golota who dominated. At 252 pounds, Bowe came in sloppy and out-of-shape; the heaviest of his ring career. By contrast, Golota, at 243 pounds, was focused and physically primed.

Golota is strong, tough and big. So big, in fact, that when he's backed up against the ropes, it's hard to see what's happening in the ring beyond him. When he gets hit, he does two things. He drops his hands (which is bad) and he fires back (which is good). To say Golota is a rough fighter is putting it politely. His biting and head-butting in past fights are a matter of record. If nothing else, Golota puts to rest the notion that all Eastern European fighters employ a straight-up 'amateur style' of boxing.

Still, against Bowe, except for the low blows, Golota fought a smart measured fight. Bowe might have won the second round, but that was it. Make no mistake about it; Riddick Bowe got beaten up. And looking back at the way manager Rock Newman has matched Big Daddy against weak opponents while studiously avoiding tougher foes, one has to wonder if Newman knows something about the limits of his fighter's ability that the rest of us don't. All that saved Bowe from defeat at the hands of Golota was a questionable disqualification at 2.33 of round seven.

The fouling began in round one, when, on several occasions, Bowe held Golota around the waist with his left arm and whacked him on the back of the head with hard rights. He did it twice more in round two, and then Golota went low on him. In round four, Bowe took a blow well below the waist and sank to the canvas. The punch was low, and referee Wayne Kelly's deduction of a point was appropriate. But when Bowe went down, he looked like a man thinking seriously about quitting. In round six, Kelly deducted a second point from Golota under dubious circumstances. The punch in question was near the border, and Bowe was wearing his trunks high. The third deduction, in round seven, was as debatable as the second. The final low blow, like the two that preceded it, was the kind of punch that most fighters fight through. But by that point, Bowe was looking for help. And it was here that Big Daddy went into an act worthy of Laurence Olivier. As fight maven Johnny Bos later noted, 'When you get hit in the proverbials, you go into a fetal position, but Bowe lay flat on his back.' Regardless, at that point, referee Wayne Kelly stopped the bout. My own view is that Kelly, who's a pretty good referee, overreacted.

The punch-stats told a part of the story. Golota landed one hundred more punches than Bowe. He outjabbed him 106 to 72, and scored 66 more power punches. But what those numbers don't fully show is that Andrew Golota gave Riddick Bowe the beating of his life. What Golota has to do now is learn to fight within the rules. He didn't bite Bowe (he didn't have to). But his history of biting and head-butting worked against him in this bout. He has huge potential, and he shouldn't waste it.

As for Bowe; he got off lucky. For much of the night, he fought like a man who didn't want to fight. And each time he was hit low, he acted like a man who didn't want to continue. In 1994, when Bowe fought Buster Mathis Jr, Big Daddy whacked Mathis while Buster was on the canvas and was immediately disqualified by referee Arthur Mercante. But that call was overturned and the bout declared 'no contest' because, before the foul, Mathis had acted like a man who didn't want to continue. Sound familiar? 'No contest' would have been a more equitable ending for Bowe–Golota.

However, 11 July 1996 will be remembered not so much for the fight itself as for what happened afterwards. There was a riot. And it came in waves. The first wave hit immediately after the disqualification, when Rock Newman and other members of Bowe's entourage (who were in the press section during the fight) stormed the ring.

Bernard Brooks Sr struck Golota from behind. Golota turned and confronted his assailant. Several would-be peacemakers held Golota back. And while the fighter was being restrained, Jason Harris (another member of Bowe's entourage) whacked him three times on top of the head with a walkie-talkie, opening an ugly gash. It was an unprovoked assault, with several members of Bowe's entourage looking very much like the thugs who beat Reginald Denny at a street intersection in Los Angeles and the cops who assaulted Rodney King.

Then came the second wave, with partisans of both sides storming the ring from outside of the press section. Bowe's 'fans' wanted to join the action. Golota's supporters saw their fighter being beaten by a mob. And because Madison Square Garden's security personnel weren't protecting him, they decided to do the job themselves. At this point, the riot was still limited to the ring and press section. But in the third wave, people in the crowd away from the ring began assaulting each other, and the disturbance became a racially motivated series of black–white confrontations.

The incident began at 10.43 p.m. Eighteen New York City police officers had been assigned to detail outside the Garden, but none were inside the building when the trouble started. MSG's fifty ushers and seventy security personnel were quickly overwhelmed, and five minutes passed before the police were notified. The cops arrived nine minutes later. At its peak, 150 police officers were assigned to the operation. Finally, at 11.19 p.m., the officer in charge of the site declared the disturbance 'under control'. Fifteen spectators and nine cops were treated for injuries at local hospitals. There were sixteen arrests.

As for who's responsible, there's plenty of blame to go around. The primary culprits were members of Riddick Bowe's entourage. Bowe himself seems like a basically decent person. His biggest vices appear to be undertraining and overeating, but too many of the people around him are thugs. The acted like thugs when they beat up a photographer after Bowe–Holyfield I in 1992. They did it again in 1993, when they employed brutally excessive force to subdue the idiot who parachuted into the ring during Bowe–Holyfield II. And Bowe himself has gone overboard in and out of the ring, sucker-punching Elijah Tillery, Buster Mathis and Larry Donald.

Inadequate control over the area immediately around the ring –
which was the shared domain of Spencer Promotions (Rock
Newman's promotional company), Madison Square Garden, and the
New York State Athletic Commission – was also a factor. The press
section is for the press. That's why it's called the 'press section'.
Properly set up and secured, it serves as a moat to protect against this
type of incident. It should be reserved for members of the media,
plus a small number of cornermen and working officials of the
NYSAC, but that wasn't the case on 11 July. Instead, an inordinate
number of Bowe partisans were given credentials and allowed to
hover inside the security net by the ring apron. And although their
behaviour grew more and more raucous as the fight progressed, nothing was done to put a lid on them.

And then there's the New York State Athletic Commission. The
NYSAC didn't cause the riot, but it certainly contributed to the
climate in which the riot occurred. In recent years, the NYSAC has
become a microcosm of governmental incompetence and corruption.
Its chairman, Floyd Patterson, was a courageous fighter. But
Patterson has serious memory problems, and is no more qualified to
head a governmental agency than Michael Katz is to be heavyweight
champion of the world. Patterson doesn't run the NYSAC. He's
being used as a cover by political operatives, who are filling most
commission jobs with people of questionable competence who know
next to nothing about boxing. It's the cruel cynical exploitation of a
man who deserves better. And the result is that no one in power is
protecting the fighters and no one in power is protecting the public,
because no one at the Commission knows what's going on.

The NYSAC has one referee who doesn't know how to stop a
fight when a fighter is in trouble. It has another referee who let a
fight continue when most of the lights in the arena went out in the
middle of a round. It has an inspector who let a fighter enter the ring
and begin a bout while wearing an earring. It has administrative
personnel who allow a manager's wife to take extra slices from his
fighters' purses in the form of 'booking fees'. And, oh yes! It also
has a lot of loyal Republicans on the public payroll, who are enjoying junkets and cashing cheques at taxpayer expense.

On the night of 11 July, 75 credentials were issued to the NYSAC. How many of those people actually worked that night? Didn't commission personnel know about Rock Newman and Lou Duva's reputation for incendiary behaviour? As the fight progressed, the people in Bowe's corner grew increasingly unruly. What did Commission officials do about it? The New York State Athletic Commission is a disaster waiting to happen. And unless there's a complete house-cleaning, things will get worse.

Meanwhile, 11 July isn't a reason to ban boxing. It's a reason to be more responsible in regulating it. And one can take heart from the conduct of fighters themselves.

There were a lot of professional boxers in the crowd at Madison Square Garden on 11 July. Black and white. And none of them were involved in the riot. Instead, they were telling others to 'cool it'. At one point, when the rioting was at its peak, I came face to face with Shannon Briggs, one of today's better young heavyweights. What followed was instructive. Shannon suggested that I walk with him to a corridor beneath the stands, so I wouldn't get hurt. And when we got there, I suggested he stay put because his size and dreadlocks would make him an obvious target for some nut with a bottle if he returned to the main arena. So we stood together, out of harm's way, and talked about the craziness that was going on around us. And I felt a lot in common with Shannon, who's a different colour and comes from a whole different world than I do. I think he felt the same way about me. And both of us were revulsed by the lunatics, black and white, who were screaming racial epithets and committing mayhem against one another.

After he knocked out Michael Moorer to regain the heavy-weight championship of the world, George Foreman was honoured by the Boxing Writers Association of America as its 'Fighter of the Year'. The following article was written for the programme distributed at the annual BWAA Dinner honouring 'Big George'.

George Foreman – Fighter of the Year

Boxing inspires wonderful fantasies.

During the course of my life, I've fantasised about getting in the ring and beating heavyweights from Sonny Liston to Mike Tyson. I've snapped my jab. My straight right has been on target. I've put all of my opponents on the canvas. And I'm sure I could give a great post-fight interview. The problem is, I don't have what it takes to get there. But on 5 November 1994, George Foreman blurred the lines between fantasy and reality when he knocked out Michael Moorer at 2.03 of the tenth round to capture the heavyweight championship of the world. For that achievement, he is honoured tonight as the BWAA's 'Fighter of the Year'.

Foreman's comeback might seem like a combination of miracle and luck, but he has worked long and hard to get here. To put things in perspective, his first pro bout was on 23 June 1969. Seven years and nine months later, he retired from boxing after losing to Jimmy Young. His comeback began against Steve Zouski on 9 March 1987. That was more than eight years ago. In other words, Foreman's second ring career has lasted longer than his first. And during the past eight years, he's suffered more than punches. He's been the butt of jokes and taken a lot of abuse.

When Foreman climbed into the ring against Zouski, he was ridiculed as 'a poster-boy for a Maidenform bra ad'. His early come-back opponents were a mix of has-beens and never-weres. George raised a few eyebrows in 1990 by demolishing Gerry Cooney. But common sense reminded us that Cooney had won only once during the previous five years. Then Foreman lost to Evander Holyfield, and the dream seemed at an end. After that, times got harder. There was a questionable majority decision over Alex Stewart in a bout that left George's face distorted beyond recognition. A lopsided loss to Tommy Morrison followed. And now –

Yeah; it was one punch. But so was Sugar Ray Robinson's fifth-round knockout of Gene Fullmer. Sure; George was way behind on points when he pulled it out. But so was Mike Weaver when he cold-cocked John Tate. So what if there are ten guys out there who'd be favoured over Foreman if they fought tomorrow? The Soviets were a better hockey team than the United States in 1980, but the Americans won at Lake Placid. Georgetown was a better basketball team than Villanova in 1985, but Villanova won the NCAA crown. Secretariat was a better horse than Onion. Ben Hogan was a better golfer than Jack Fleck. In sports, it's not who's 'better' that counts; it's who wins. That's why they play the games.

So what has George Foreman accomplished? For starters, he's the oldest man ever to capture a world boxing championship. For over a century, fighters have tried unsuccessfully to do what George has done. But more important, if one looks at the sweep of Foreman's career, it's apparent that he has become a fighter for the ages. When he prevailed at the 1968 Olympics, Lyndon Johnson was President of the United States and Michael Moorer was less than a year old. George has fought through the terms of seven presidents, touching on four decades. He's been a flag-waving Olympian, a menacing despot, a preacher, a joke, and finally, at age 46, a beloved champion.

For twenty years, this immense lumbering man was forced to endure memories of Zaire. He was the 'dope' in Muhammad Ali's 'rope-a-dope'. Now Zaire is in the past. Instead of 'rope-a-dope', we have 'munch-and-punch', 'eat-and-beat', 'snack-and-whack', and whatever else George wants. Twenty years ago, he was heavyweight champion of the world, and it wasn't much fun for the rest of us. Now the entire world can share in the enjoyment of this remarkable man's championship the second time around.

For two decades, George Foreman has been regarded as part of the Muhammad Ali legend. But in 1995, it's at long last clear that Muhammad Ali is part of the George Foreman legend as well.

Bad decisions are common in boxing. But Shannon Briggs over
George Foreman had all the earmarks of a corrupt one.

Fix?

On 22 November 1997, 48-year-old George Foreman and 25-year-old
Shannon Briggs did battle for what was loosely referred to as the linear
heavyweight championship of the world.

Foreman's credentials are self-explanatory. Explaining Briggs is a
bit more complicated.

Shannon is articulate, personable and bright. He's intellectually
curious, surfs the internet, and is interested, among other things, in
family genealogy. Indeed, he can trace his roots back to his great-great-
great-grandparents, who were slaves in Virginia before the Civil War.
While much of his adolescence was spent in relative comfort, there was
a time when he was forced to deal with a drug-addicted mother and a
stint of homelessness on the streets of New York.

Once upon a time, Briggs was touted as a rising star. He was an
amateur champion and a top prospect for the 1992 United States
Olympic boxing team until a hand injury took him out of the Olympic
trials. His manager Marc Roberts has invested a reported $1.4 million in
his career and done a good job of positioning him on the way to a 29–1
record with 24 knockouts. But the fact that Foreman was willing to fight
him was testament to the disappointing nature of Shannon's progress.
There were a lot of questions about him. The mediocre level of his opponents; his refusal to fight Joe Hipp on *HBO After Dark*; and the big
question mark – Briggs's third-round knockout loss at the hands of
Darroll Wilson in 1996 when, in the words of HBO's Jim Lampley,
Shannon 'folded like an accordion'. After the loss, the word was,
'Shannon Briggs doesn't take a very good punch, and he doesn't want
to.' Briggs said the loss to Wilson was due to an attack of asthma in the
ring. Briggs's trainer at the time, Teddy Atlas, said that Shannon had quit.

'I think Shannon has talent,' Atlas said recently. 'And I worked
very hard to give him a foundation, so he'd have the boxing mechanics

and mental strength necessary to face an opponent in the ring. But Shannon was always more interested in finding the easy way to do things. Physically, he worked hard, but mentally it was all a big con with him. He was great at schmoozing investors with Marc Roberts. You can con investors. But sooner or later in boxing, you meet an opponent who you can't con in the ring, like Darroll Wilson. I never said Shannon didn't have asthma. What I said was, Shannon didn't have an asthma attack that night. But a weak mind and panic can bring on a lot of things. I tried to help Shannon become a real fighter. Not a phoney; a real fighter. And the sad thing is, Shannon could have done all the stuff he wanted to do outside the ring and still become a fighter. I feel very betrayed by him.'

After Atlas made his comments, Briggs responded, saying, 'Teddy played an important role in my development as a boxer and as a person. I had a lot of love for Teddy and a lot of respect for Teddy, and some of the things he said hurt me a lot. You know what I'm talking about. That I quit against Darroll Wilson; that I lack character. If you look at the other side of things, I wasn't always happy with Teddy. Teddy talks a lot about character and discipline, but he isn't always as disciplined as he should be. If I did some of the things Teddy has done, if I'd gotten into some of the fights outside the ring that Teddy has gotten into, he would have been on me like a ton of bricks and I would have deserved it. There were lots of times when I thought Teddy was wrong about something. There were lots of times when I felt Teddy was much too into controlling other people and not enough into controlling himself. But whatever problems I had with Teddy, I didn't go public with them. And he did. He said a lot of very negative things about me to the media, and I felt betrayed. It hurt a lot; and it hurt more because he walked out on me after a loss when I was down. Teddy is still part of my thinking. I got some very good things from him, and you don't just break up with someone and forget about them completely. But I have to admit, I'm still bitter about some of the things Teddy said about me.'

No one other than Shannon Briggs knows what truly went on in his mind against Darroll Wilson. But everyone knew that Briggs had been handpicked by Foreman, because George felt he could break Shannon's will. If a fighter quits in the ring, one of two things happens afterwards.

Either quitting becomes part of his personality, like a circuit-breaker that trips whenever he's in trouble; or he hates having quit so much that he vows he will never quit again. That led to three very interesting questions:

1. Were Briggs's physical skills so superior to Foreman's at this point in their respective careers that Briggs's will would never be tested?
2. If Foreman tested Briggs's will, would Shannon quit?
3. If Briggs got Foreman in trouble, would he go for the win or would he lie back content to survive and let the win slip away?

In sum, while the promotion was about Foreman, the crucial questions regarding the fight revolved around Briggs.

'I'm not looking for a knockout,' Shannon said hours before the opening bell. 'If it happens, fine; but my mind isn't set on it. I envision using my jab, using my legs, fighting within my boundaries. If it turns into a test of brute strength, I'm in trouble, but that's not what the fight will be about. People say that George handpicked me as his opponent. But what they lose sight of is, I picked George too.' Then Briggs turned pensive. 'When George goes into the ring, he believes God is behind him, and that gives him strength. I have a different view of religion. I don't think God takes sides in sports contests. This is the biggest fight of my life, and I feel like it's all on me.'

At 9 p.m. on the night of the fight, there were sixteen people in Briggs's dressing room. An hour later, the number had dwindled to ten. By the time Shannon made his way to the ring, the following was down to his three cornermen. Then, finally, he stood alone with George Foreman. He'd watched Foreman on television, but had never seen him fight in person. After their press conference announcing the fight, he'd expressed surprise that George wasn't as big as he'd thought. Now he saw Foreman up close and personal; a massive presence who'd had 32 professional fights before Shannon was even born. And while George no longer enjoys the physical gifts he once possessed, he's far stronger mentally than when he was young.

As for the fight, Foreman moved purposefully and inexorably forward for twelve rounds. Shannon retreated as George advanced whether Foreman was punching or not, which allowed George to rest when he wanted to. There was no trademark Shannon Briggs 'swarm'. Briggs rarely threw his right hand with conviction. His jab was mostly a stay-away-from-me jab rather than a potent offensive weapon.

In round three, Shannon found himself on the receiving end of some punishment and it looked for a moment as though he might go down. In round eight, Foreman landed a series of sledgehammer blows, but again Briggs survived. Still, time was running out, and it appeared to virtually every onlooker that Shannon never did what he had to do to win the fight.

Then came the decision. When Steve Weisfeld's 114–114 score was announced, there was amazement at ringside. What fight had he been watching? Next, ring announcer Michael Buffer read the scores of Calvin Claxton and Lawrence Layton (116–112 and 117–113 respectively), and it appeared that sanity had been restored until Buffer intoned the words... 'For the *new*...'

The decision was inexplicable by any honest measure. Foreman dominated the fight. He outboxed Briggs. He outpunched Briggs. He landed 284 punches to Briggs's 223, and his were the harder blows. Those looking for a clue as to the scoring might take note of the fact that, subsequent to raising millions of dollars through a 1996 offering of Worldwide Entertainment & Sports stock, Marc Roberts has been involved with two major fights in New Jersey. Foreman–Briggs was the second of those fights. The first was the 14 December 1996 bout between Tim Witherspoon and Ray Mercer (another WWES fighter). That bout resulted in an absurdly lopsided decision for Mercer, and the most lopsided scorecard was turned in by Calvin Claxton.

Larry Hazzard (Chairman of the New Jersey State Athletic Commission) and several of his judges have a lot of questions to answer. Hopefully, those questions will be posed by law enforcement authorities in front of a grand jury.

Meanwhile, the Foreman camp was gracious in defeat. 'He's a good kid,' George said of Shannon after the fight. 'He just lost his mother. He stayed in there with me. I wish him well.' And Roy Foreman, Big George's brother, added, 'Shannon Briggs is a nice young man. The decision wasn't his fault. Shannon didn't score the fight.'

Briggs, for his part, was equally gracious. 'I was lucky,' he conceded in his dressing room shortly after the bout. 'The judges were nice to me.'

Mike Tyson was still on his honeymoon with the American public when I wrote the following cover story for Boxing Illustrated *in 1988. In the article, I gave Tyson credit – perhaps too much credit – for his ample ring skills. But I also raised questions that hadn't been previously raised regarding Tyson's character.*

Will Mike Tyson Become the Most Unpopular Athlete in America?

Mike Tyson lives to fight. There was a time when many families believed the noblest thing a person could do was become a priest. For Cus D'Amato, who brought Mike into the ring, being a fighter was the best way to serve God. More than any fighter practising his craft today, Tyson appears to believe in himself . . . No robe . . . Black trunks . . . The Tyson aura is that of a great white shark, an efficient killing machine. His opponents face instant annihilation for every second of every round. Fighters go into the ring against him scared; not the normal fear fighters endure, but something more. Tyson is there to hurt his opponents, and he knows how. To any foe who doesn't bail out early, he administers a beating. He never touches gloves with an adversary at the end of a round.

Tyson is one of those rare fighters who, more than money or glory, is fighting for a place in history. Much has been made of the fact that many of today's heavyweights think heavyweight means 'fat'. They fight like union members with seniority on featherbedding jobs. Any great heavyweight of the past would stand out among them, but Tyson is something more. His hand speed is superb; his power awesome; his defensive abilities on a par with the best. He can hurt an opponent with any punch in his arsenal at any point in a sequence, whether he gets off first or counters. He's thirty pounds heavier than Dempsey or Marciano; fifteen more than Joe Louis in his prime.

Right now, the only person who can beat Mike Tyson is Mike Tyson. If he gets bored, if personal problems rob him of discipline and motivation, if he loses control over his wilder side; it could happen. Meanwhile, unless Tyson changes course, in a few years he may well be the most unpopular athlete in America.

Wilt Chamberlain once complained, 'Nobody roots for Goliath,' but in boxing the contrary often is true. Seemingly unbeatable champions like Joe Louis have been revered by the public, and Tyson has been perfectly positioned for a love-in with the American people. Thanks to shrewd management and marketing, all America knows the heartwarming saga of 'Cus and the Kid' – an image reinforced by a series of television commercials for products ranging from Kodak to Diet Pepsi. It's hard to be unpopular when corporate America is pouring tens of millions of dollars worth of airtime into making you look good. Indeed, Tyson's visibility is such that, in one dizzying week last month, he appeared on the cover of *Life*, *Time*, *Sports Illustrated* and *People*.

Still, all along there have been rumblings that Mike Tyson is not a nice person. In the ring, there have been too many head-butts, elbows and punches after the bell. Comments about 'crying like a woman' and 'pushing the bone of his nose into his brain' have been cause for concern. In contrast to fighters like Muhammad Ali and Larry Holmes, who would beckon referees to stop fights against disabled foes, Tyson punches in the manner of Gerry Cooney versus Ken Norton, trying to destroy opponents who are already beaten and on their way down.

This ferocity is condoned because boxing is a brutal business and Tyson practises it well. However, Mike's conduct outside the ring is more difficult to excuse. More and more, he seems willing to go beyond the bounds of acceptable behaviour. There have been incidents of violence and ugly rumours of sexual misconduct that might land a lesser personage in jail. Someone who is rich and has skilled people looking out for him can often get things papered over. But it's becoming increasingly difficult these days to feel good about Mike Tyson. Yes, he came from hard surroundings. Yes, he has some good qualities in him. But too much ugliness is showing.

I write this now because Mike Tyson is at a crossroads in his development as a human being. In the ring, he appears like a Frankenstein creation who outstrips his opponents' worst nightmares. Future adversaries may well decide to bring paramedics with them instead of cutmen. But outside the ring, Tyson's future is less clear. His co-manager Jim Jacobs died on 23 March of this year, igniting a bitter struggle for control of the champion and his ring earnings. It's too early to predict the ultimate outcome of that battle. But looking at the dispute in terms of its major players, several things seem clear.

Don King: Don King is a man who kicks people in the groin and then wants to have sex with them. Bill Cayton and company have learned that the hard way this year. King, of course, wants to promote Tyson. 'Tyson don't need no manager,' is his present cry. 'Why give all that money to Bill Cayton when, with me as promoter, Tyson can keep it all.'

Anyone who wants to see how King looks after his fighters should sit down and listen to Muhammad Ali talk for five minutes. After that, they can speak with Tim Witherspoon. Out of a recent $700,000 purse, Witherspoon's 'manager', Carl King, took $350,000. Once various loans and miscellaneous expenses were paid, Witherspoon wound up with a reported $43,000.

If Tyson had signed with Don King when he turned pro, he'd be paying fifty per cent of his earnings to Carl King today, not one-third to Bill Cayton and company. And that would be after King took his cut off the top. Jacobs and Cayton had to do business with King to get Mike into the HBO tournament, and option requirements tied them together through the Tyson–Spinks bout. But Tyson is on top now, free to deal with whichever promoter he wants. And if he trusts Don King, he's making a big mistake.

Robin Givens and Ruth Roper: Givens, age twenty-three, was the only member of her class at Sarah Lawrence to be booed at graduation. On her first date with Tyson, her entourage included two publicists (love at first sight). Previous 'boyfriends' have included Michael Jordan and Eddie Murphy. In some circles, this is known as star-forni-cating. Her credentials as a Harvard Medical School student equal those of Rosie Ruiz as a Boston Marathon runner, and many people question whether she was ever really pregnant, which is reportedly why she and Tyson got married in the first place.

Momma Roper is a 'dignified, caring, honourable' woman, who says she contracted an unspecified venereal disease from Yankee slugger

Dave Winfield. Together, she and Robin have spent quite a bit of Mike's money; with his consent, of course. Robin has a Mike Tyson power of attorney (her most treasured autograph) among her belongings.

Not long ago, I asked Sugar Ray Leonard if he would give his own wife an unrestricted power of attorney. Ray's answer: 'First, let me say that I love my wife and I trust my wife. We've been together for a lot more years than Mike Tyson and Robin Givens. Would I give my wife a power of attorney? Man, you've got to be crazy.'

Robin and Ruth now want to take over Mike's financial dealings. In boxing, a fighter gets hit when he makes mistakes. At present, Mike Tyson is in the ring with his hands down and chin up, sharing space with two devious power punchers. Maybe the Tyson–Givens encounter will go the distance, but I doubt it.

Bill Cayton: This is where one starts to question Mike Tyson's decency and loyalty, not just his judgment. Jim Jacobs and Bill Cayton advanced Mike's career together. They invested literally hundreds of thousands of dollars and years of effort to help put him where he is today. So what do we hear now from Iron Mike: 'Bill Cayton caused all my marriage problems...Bill Cayton went to a priest to try to get us divorced...I hold Bill Cayton responsible for my wife's miscarriage.' Next, we'll hear that Bill Cayton gave Ruth Roper herpes.

Then there's the matter of Tyson and his wife claiming that Cayton hasn't been financially honest. Muhammad Ali and George Foreman fought in Zaire, one of the poorest countries in the world, Mike tells us, and each man got five million dollars. Yet when Iron Mike fought Tony Tubbs in Japan, one of the world's richest countries, he was paid less than either of his predecessors. This is the observation of a man who is not a great financial analyst. By Tyson's illogic (which sounds suspiciously like the babbling of a former numbers tsar turned fight promoter), Marvin Hagler should have been paid equal amounts for fighting Juan Domingo Roldon and Sugar Ray Leonard, since both bouts were held in Las Vegas. Who does Mike think made the deals that got him where he is today; the deals that made him richer at age twenty-one than Sugar Ray Leonard or Muhammad Ali.

Kevin Rooney: 'The one thing I wish Mike would remember,' says Kevin Rooney, 'is that he has an honest manager.' Kevin is a better trainer than a lot of people give him credit for. And unlike some people in this soap opera, Rooney hasn't forgotten the meaning of the word loyalty. Not long ago, Mike asked Kevin to discharge Steve Lott. Steve began working for Jim Jacobs and Bill Cayton in the 1970s. When Mike was getting started as a professional, he lived in Steve's apartment for almost two years. Steve talked with him, gave to him and shared with him. But Robin didn't like Steve, and rather than wield the axe himself, Iron Mike asked Rooney to do it (there's more than one way of showing cowardice, and this is one of them). Kevin's response was the proper one: 'No way, Mike. Do it yourself.'

In sum, it's time that Mike Tyson stopped feeling sorry for himself. It's time he stopped making ugly statements like, 'Bill Cayton will be dead and gone in ten years.' It's time he grew up. We already know that Mike Tyson is a great fighter, but the jury is still out on what kind of person he is. Can he grow and learn; can he exhibit loyalty and listen to criticism? If so, more power to him. But if Mike Tyson reverts to being a bully, if he gives in to his lesser instincts, then he will become the most unpopular athlete in America.

As 1988 progressed, Mike Tyson's image in the media began to change. Soon, getting product endorsements for Iron Mike was more difficult than beating him.

Selling a Troubled Champ

On Friday, 26 August of this year, Mike Tyson picked up the telephone and called his manager, Bill Cayton. Tyson and Cayton haven't been getting along lately. Cayton is regarded as one of the most honest businessmen in boxing, and the manner in which he and Jimmy Jacobs co-managed Tyson to superstardom is well known. However, when Tyson married actress Robin Givens, the Tyson–Cayton relationship fell on hard times. Thereafter, Tyson accused Cayton of causing his wife's miscarriage, stealing money from him, committing fraud, and more.

So how was their telephone conversation?

'It was very friendly,' Cayton reported. 'We chatted for a while, and then Mike asked, "When are you gonna start making some more [commercial endorsement] deals for me?" I told Mike I'd do my best, but it will be harder this time around than before.'

'Harder than before' is an understatement. In less than a year, Mike Tyson has gone from being a rising star with virtually unlimited commercial appeal to a superstar athlete whose commercial viability is on the skids. That's because the public is starting to see a side of Tyson that it doesn't like.

Why is Mike Tyson having image problems? Isn't this the man who was destined to star in the heartwarming true-life saga of *Cus and the Kid*?

Well, it turns out that life with Cus wasn't exactly like living with the Waltons, and the house in Catskill, New York, where Tyson trained, was far from the Little House on the Prairie. A young man named Teddy Atlas knows, because he was there. Atlas has become one of the most respected trainers in boxing. A street kid from Staten Island, he moved to Catskill in 1975 at age nineteen to live and train with Cus D'Amato. Fighting as a 139-pound amateur, Atlas won a Golden Gloves championship and planned to turn pro, but vertebrae and disc problems ended his career. That was when D'Amato convinced him to become a trainer. Atlas lived with Cus for six more years.

Tyson walked into Cus D'Amato's Catskill gym for the first time in 1978. A former fighter named Bobby Stewart was working with incorrigible youths at the state reformatory and wanted D'Amato to teach Tyson to box. Cus told Stewart and Tyson to get in the ring so he could see what Tyson had. Stewart was in his late twenties, overweight at 175 pounds, but still a former professional fighter. Tyson was twelve years old, 190 pounds.

'Bobby dominated,' Atlas recalls. 'Mike didn't have the technical skills to cope with him, but through raw strength and desire he forced Bobby to open up and punch hard just to control him. After the first round, Mike's nose was bleeding heavily, but he kept pressing, punching, furiously attacking, attacking, attacking, because that's all he could do.'

Looking back, one wonders if the experience wasn't a bit scary for Stewart; staring into the face of a foe who was battered and bruised but simply spat blood and kept coming. Perhaps inside he began to fear that, like a trainer in a cage with a wild animal, he wasn't really the stronger of the two, and if this beast could take away his jab or hook or whatever it was that kept him at bay, the beast would destroy him. From that day on, once a week, Stewart brought Tyson to the Catskill gym. A year later, Tyson was released into D'Amato's custody.

Tyson's first fight in the ring was at a 'smoker' – an unlicensed amateur bout – in the South Bronx. He still weighed 190 pounds, but now the weight was moulded solid. It was hard to believe he was only thirteen.

'The opponent was a seventeen-year-old Spanish kid who knew how to box,' Atlas recalls. 'It was a great fight, just about even. Then, in the third round, Mike caught him with a left hook and hurt him. The other guy was helpless. He couldn't go down, because he was tangled in the ropes, and the ref was slow coming in. That was when Mike flat-out destroyed him. He hit the Spanish guy again, and knocked his mouthpiece out so hard it splattered off the wall in the back of the room. The crowd didn't like it; most of them had bet on the other guy. But I think that night in the ring was the first time in his life that Mike heard people cheering for him.'

Tyson had twenty more smoker fights and won all of them, but outside the ring there were problems. 'Cus was a wonderful man,' says Atlas. 'But he failed to discipline Mike, which made it inevitable that Mike would have difficulties later on. When Mike started living with us, everything was "yes sir," and "no sir." He was polite in the institutionalised way prisoners are polite to prison guards; the way people are polite to other people who can help them. I think he was afraid that, if he did something wrong, he'd be sent back to the reformatory. But as he progressed as a fighter and started winning amateur titles, he got contemptuous of rules and authority all over again. Lots of young fighters lived with Cus, and over time there came to be two sets of rules: one for Mike, and one for everyone else. Outside the ring, if it didn't affect boxing, Cus's way of disciplining Mike was to not discipline him at all. If Mike's left hand dropped when he brought back his jab, Cus would have him throwing a thousand jabs a day until he got it right. But when it came to disciplining him around the house or for something that happened at school, Cus would say, "Let him alone. He's going to be heavyweight champion of the world."'

'After his workouts,' Atlas continues, 'Mike usually refused to shower. It was his way of defying authority. All he'd do was splash on a little cologne, but Cus let it go. When Mike got in trouble for assaulting a teacher at school, Cus told him, "Don't worry. If they expel you, I'll get you a tutor." I thought it was wrong. I felt, as long as we had Mike under our supervision, we had an obligation to develop him as a person as well as a fighter, but Cus wanted a champion. He felt Mike was his right. He wanted his monument at any cost. Cus put up with an incredible amount of crap from Mike, and do you know why? Because Mike punched harder than anyone else, and Cus was afraid that, if he tried to discipline Mike, to make him a better person as well as a better fighter, Mike wouldn't take well to that discipline. Cus didn't want to test those waters.'

Tyson's current trainer, Kevin Rooney, disputes Atlas's portrayal. Atlas and Rooney were boyhood friends on Staten Island, and later lived together with D'Amato. 'Cus disciplined all the boys,' says Rooney.

'Every day, if you did right, he praised you, and if you did wrong, he wouldn't talk to you. He never beat us. That wasn't his way. But if you loved Cus, the silent treatment drove you crazy. Cus didn't have special rules for Mike. The only exception he made was, Cus had a rule that, if you had trouble in school, you couldn't come to the gym. That's because he wanted to motivate everyone to do well in class, and he didn't want the parents of kids he was training to blame boxing for their children's problems. Mike sometimes had trouble in school because he came from such a different environment, but through it all, Cus kept him boxing. That was the only difference.'

Former light-heavyweight champion Jose Torres, another D'Amato protégé, stakes out a piece of middle ground. Torres, who watched Tyson grow up, acknowledges, 'Cus concentrated on boxing. That's because Cus felt that boxing discipline superseded everything; that if he could discipline Mike in the ring, eventually it would carry over outside. Mike was a bad kid. Because of Cus, he's a better person now, but I don't know how much better.'

Regardless of who one believes, third parties report that, in 1983, when Tyson was sixteen, he sought to impose himself sexually on a younger girl. For Teddy Atlas, it was the final straw. He confronted Tyson, the fighter got out of hand, and Atlas pulled a gun. In the aftermath of the incident, Cus found Mike in his bedroom packing a suitcase, ready to go. Forced to choose between his protégé trainer and his protégé fighter, D'Amato chose the latter. Atlas left and has refused to publicly acknowledge, confirm or deny the incident since then.

Meanwhile, in the ring, Tyson's needs continued to be met. Then, in 1985, he turned pro and an extraordinary marketing blitz was put in place by his co-managers, Bill Cayton and Jim Jacobs. After each Tyson fight, 'knockout highlight' cassettes were sent to a hundred sportswriters and television stations nationwide. Over 4,500 cassettes were distributed in this manner. The story of Cus and the Kid was told to countless media representatives again and again. ABC highlighted Tyson in its 1986 Statue of Liberty Centennial television extravaganza. And, of course, in the ring Tyson was awesome. By age 22, he had become undisputed heavyweight champion of the world. The next step was to turn that glory into cash.

Big purses in boxing are hardly new. Muhammad Ali, Sugar Ray Leonard, and many others have reaped extraordinary rewards for their ring skills. However, what separated Tyson from his predecessors was the money he stood poised to earn outside the ring. One month before Tyson's June 1988 bout against Michael Spinks, he had earned endorsement income of $2,675,000. But the best seemed yet to come. Just prior to the Spinks bout, Cayton negotiated a deal that guaranteed Tyson one million dollars for a series of Diet Pepsi commercials. Negotiations were underway with four more multinational corporations, and Pepsi was leaning towards a proposal to make Tyson its world spokesman for a fee of eight to ten million dollars.

So what happened?

'The second Pepsi deal fell through,' says Cayton. 'With the possible exception of Nintendo, none of the major contracts will be renewed, and no significant new deals are pending. Mike is still the top superstar athlete in the world, and I believe that some day, hopefully in the near future, he'll be commercially in demand again. But for the moment, the endorsements we would like to see simply aren't there.'

Why not?

'No one incident has been responsible for the drop,' explains Cayton. 'Rather, all of the incidents you've read about have had a cumulative effect. Mike's recent car accident [on 4 September in Catskill] was the last straw. But even before that, nothing major was in the works.'

The incidents, of course, are well catalogued:

- A scuffle in a Los Angeles parking lot that occurred when Tyson tried to kiss a woman parking attendant.
- Several bizarre automobile accidents.
- A curbside brawl with heavyweight boxer Mitch Green.
- A ruckus in an Albany department store.

Plus, the public at large is growing to dislike certain things about Mike Tyson, namely:

- His conspicuous consumption.
- His disloyalty towards those who helped develop him as a fighter.

- His sometimes dirty ring tactics.
- Whispers that Tyson's sexual conduct is beyond the pale of acceptability.
- The feeling that Tyson is excessively brutal; that he *needs* to beat people up, if not in the ring then somewhere else.

In sum, the public perception of Mike Tyson is becoming that of a man outside the boundaries of society. Is it an image problem?

'No,' says Teddy Atlas. 'Mike's problem isn't image. It's that the image is wearing off. All this stuff about what a sweet guy Mike is, the stories about how he became a generous, loving person because of Cus; that was image. Now the public is starting to see what Mike is really like, and they don't like what they see. People say, "This wouldn't have happened if Cus was alive; that wouldn't have happened if Cus was here." ' Atlas pauses, reflecting on the loss of his own father figure, mentor and friend. 'Believe me, it would have happened. Sometimes I think Cus died because he knew what was coming. If he'd been here to see what's going on with Mike now, who knows what it would have done to him. He would have been proud of what Mike has accomplished in the ring, but there's more to life than knocking other people out.'

Larry Holmes was once a great fighter with enormous heart, a deadly right hand and the most punishing jab in boxing. His time is now long gone, but Larry continues to do what he has done for decades.

I Saw Larry Holmes Fight

The truth is, I've always liked Larry Holmes. We met for the first time in 1984, at a press conference to announce his upcoming title bout against James 'Bonecrusher' Smith. I was just getting involved with boxing. When the press conference was over, we chatted briefly and I felt a fan's excitement at being in his presence.

Six years later, I was part of the boxing establishment. And after hearing Larry sing in Indonesia, I had the temerity to write a music review entitled 'Larry Holmes in Concert'. My critique of Larry's vocal ability was less than complimentary, which didn't exactly endear me to Larry. For the better part of a year, he refused to speak to me. Then he decided he would say hello but not shake hands. But beneath his gruff exterior, Larry Holmes is a softie at heart. Sooner or later, he forgives everyone. He's forgiven Don King a dozen times, and I'm not as bad as Don King. So eventually, Larry forgave me. The past few years, he's been downright friendly.

All of that history was very much on my mind when I saw Holmes at Madison Square Garden on 29 July 1997. This time, our interaction wasn't social. I was going to watch Larry fight. I'd seen fifteen heavyweight champions in the ring at various times in their respective careers. I saw Ali and Frazier do battle against each other twice. I watched Buster Douglas, Evander Holyfield and Floyd Patterson when they were at less than their best, witnessed Mike Tyson when he was young, and contemplated Riddick Bowe at his peak. And I've seen a host of alphabet-soup champions – Lennox Lewis, Tim Witherspoon, Ken Norton, Bonecrusher Smith, Michael Dokes, Pinklon Thomas, Tony Tubbs and Mike Weaver. But through it all, I'd never seen Larry Holmes in the ring and I wanted to experience that magic.

When Holmes was young, he was a great fighter. He's not anymore. His opponent was Maurice Harris who, to paraphrase, couldn't have carried Larry's jockstrap ten years ago. Harris has some skills but, prior to 29 July, he had won only nine of nineteen fights and been knocked out by the likes of Scott Lopeck, John Andrade, Dale Brown and Gerald Nobles.

It wasn't a very good fight. Holmes came into the ring at a career-high 248 pounds. Age has taken a toll on his reflexes, and whatever drama there was came not from the action but from the fact that we were watching Larry Holmes.

In the first round, Harris appeared in awe of his opponent and showed him too much respect. Then he caught on to the fact that Larry is a shell of his former self and swept rounds two through four. Round five was Harris's best. He started letting his punches go inside instead of tying up Larry when they got in close. Also, he started landing right hands, including one that shook Holmes at the bell. Then Harris got respectful again and Larry sucked it up, winning rounds six through eight by default. In boxing, ineffective aggression is better than no aggression at all. Harris came on strong at the end. The saddest thing about it all was that Harris actually outjabbed Holmes. That's like a house painter doing ceilings better than Michelangelo.

Outside of the Holmes entourage, only a handful of people in attendance at the Garden thought Larry won the fight. Unfortunately, two of those people were judges assigned to the bout by the New York State Athletic Commission. Thus, Holmes was awarded a split decision, even though Harris deserved a unanimous one. In the cosmic scheme of things, that makes up for Holmes–Spinks II when Larry got jobbed, although I suspect Harris feels differently about the matter.

Meanwhile, I don't regret going to the fight. Larry Holmes is old and Larry Holmes is fat, but he's still Larry Holmes. The people who heard Frank Sinatra sing when he was seventy years old knew he wasn't 'the real Sinatra' any more, but he was still Frank Sinatra. And for the rest of my life I can say to myself, 'Hey; I saw Larry Holmes fight.'

Evander Holyfield's upset of Mike Tyson in their first fight was one of those great moments in sports that it's a privilege to write about.

Holyfield–Tyson: What It Means

It ended the way most people thought it would – with Evander Holyfield sitting on a stool; a doctor at his side and his wife crying. Except the doctor was his wife. Her tears were tears of joy. And a lot of people who thought that Tyson–Holyfield shouldn't be allowed to happen (including yours truly) were exceedingly happy to have been wrong.

The fight was billed as a confrontation between Good and Evil, with the deck stacked in Evil's favour. Showtime was promoting the bout under the banner 'Finally', but phrases like 'Fatally' and 'The Execution' were being bandied about. Holyfield was considered damaged goods; a 34-year-old fighter whose time had passed. Too many beatings had taken their toll. His stamina was questionable; he got hit too much; and there was no way he could take Tyson's punch.

But Evander Holyfield was propelled by a religious fervour. Like Muhammad Ali before him, he found something larger than himself to flow into that enabled him to elevate his performance. Against Tyson, Holyfield was magnificent.

Holyfield always comes into his fights in shape, but this time he was in fighting shape. He has always taken a good punch, and when Tyson's landed, he survived. He has always been an aggressive fighter – just as aggressive as Tyson – and because he never took a round off, Tyson couldn't either. Plus Holyfield had more speed, skill and courage than any man Tyson had faced before. As the fight wore on, it became clear that Tyson had little in the way of a fight plan and virtually no help from his corner. And just as important, once Tyson's attempts at intimidation failed, the intimidator became the intimidated.

Give Tyson credit. A brutal body shot in round five took Holyfield out of the fight for a round. And credit Tyson for staying on his feet, except for a flash knockdown in round six. Holyfield whacked Iron Mike with eleven solid shots to the head in the last 22 seconds of round ten, and nine more at the start of round eleven. The hurt that Evander lay on Mike was 'vintage Tyson'. He beat Tyson up, but Tyson wouldn't go down. Thus, it was left to Mitch Halpern, who did an outstanding job of refereeing the bout, to stop the action at 37 seconds of the eleventh round.

An hour after the bout, Tyson was still dazed. But he was gracious in defeat; more so than he had ever been in victory. In defeat, perhaps for the first time, Mike carried himself like a champion. Meanwhile, the time has come to re-evaluate Evander Holyfield's place in history; and that of Mike Tyson.

Whatever Tyson's merits as a fighter – and they're considerable – it's now clear that his ring mystique has outpaced his growth as a boxer. Once, Tyson's name was mentioned with Muhammad Ali, Jack Johnson and Joe Louis as men who defined their era. Now he must battle in the years ahead simply to be included on the next plateau with warriors like Jack Dempsey, Gene Tunney, Rocky Marciano, Sonny Liston, Joe Frazier, George Foreman and Larry Holmes. Holyfield, too, will be a contender for acceptance on that level. And ironically, whether or not he achieves it will depend in part on Tyson. If Tyson flourishes in the years ahead, then Holyfield's reputation will grow with it. But regardless of his final ranking as a fighter, Holyfield's place in history is secure.

Boxing is not a gentleman's business. But every now and then, someone comes along and ennobles the sport in a way that elevates it above all others. Joe Louis did it against Max Schmeling. Muhammad Ali did it against George Foreman. And Evander Holyfield did it against Mike Tyson. Treasure the memory of 9 November 1996. Great action between two great fighters in a bout that transcends boxing equals a great fight. And Evander Holyfield versus Mike Tyson was a great fight; a glorious night for boxing.

Evander Holyfield brings a lot of positives to the table. But it was hard to overlook the negatives when he sought to have Lennox Lewis stripped of the WBA title and then claimed that beating John Ruiz would give him a legitimate claim to the heavyweight championship.

Evander Holyfield: A Tarnished Legacy

For sixteen years, ever since Evander Holyfield burst upon the scene at the 1984 Olympics, the key to his image has been the public's perception of his character. In the ring, Holyfield has been a warrior, giving his all in glorious bouts against Dwight Muhammad Qwai, Riddick Bowe and Mike Tyson. Outside the ring, he has become more confident and verbal, sharing his thoughts with humour and grace.

There have been problems along the way. As of last year, Holyfield had nine children: three by his first wife, one by his second wife, and five out of wedlock by four different women, including two during his second marriage. But people were willing to overlook this personal failing because of the belief that, when it came to boxing, Holyfield was a warrior who pursued the sport with a sense of absolute integrity. Because of our belief in his character, we forgave him the draw against Lennox Lewis. Evander would never be part of a rigged decision. All he did was fight.

But now, Holyfield's image is in jeopardy. On 12 August 2000, he'll enter the ring to do battle against John Ruiz for the WBA heavyweight crown. John Ruiz has never beaten a quality opponent. His main claim to fame is that he was knocked out in nineteen seconds by David Tua. He is in the tradition of the last New Englander to fight for the heavyweight title: Tom McNeeley. Meanwhile, Holyfield hasn't won a fight since 1998. However, none of this has kept Evander from proclaiming, 'A victory over Ruiz means I would be four-time heavyweight champion of the world.'

Right! And a victory over Brian Nielsen made Dickie Ryan heavyweight champion. Let a simple analogy suffice.

Suppose David Stern announced the match-ups for the final round of this year's NBA play-offs as follows: the Chicago Bulls versus the Los Angeles Clippers. Strange, you say. The Bulls are a once-proud franchise that lost 65 games this season and the Clippers lost 67. But that's the way things work in the convoluted world of professional boxing. Thus, Henry Akinwande, who was disqualified for cowardice in his 1997 bout against Lennox Lewis, was the WBA's mandatory challenger for Lewis's unified crown until it was determined that he was medically unfit to fight because of hepatitis. At that point, the WBA simply moved John Ruiz into the number-one slot and elevated Holyfield to number two.

Meanwhile, as the WBA was doing its thing, Lewis contracted to fight Michael Grant. Give Lennox credit. Once he won the title, he sought out the best available opponent. But there was a hitch. In order to get a rematch with Holyfield after their disputed draw, Lewis had been required to sign a contract that read in part, 'If Lewis wins the rematch, the parties understand and agree that Lewis's next bout after the rematch shall be against the WBA's mandatory challenger, or its leading available contender, pursuant to the rules and regulations of the WBA. Provided further that, if Lewis chooses not to fight such WBA mandatory challenger or leading available contender, Lewis shall vacate the WBA title.'

With the FBI breathing down its neck, the WBA chose to interpret its 'rules and regulations' in a manner that allowed Lewis to defend his title against Michael Grant before taking on Ruiz. However, by then, a series of ill-considered moves by Lewis's legal team had landed the matter in the United States District Court for the Southern District of New York before Judge Lewis Kaplan. Kaplan ordered Lewis to relinquish the WBA crown as a precondition to fighting Grant, despite Lewis's offer to fight Ruiz in July.

The most disappointing aspect of the whole mess is the role that Evander Holyfield played in it. Evander attended the court hearing and advocated stripping Lennox Lewis of the WBA title. Moreover, in late April, he issued a 2,000-word statement which boils down to one simple sentence: 'I believe that the rules of the sanctioning bodies should be consistently applied to all fighters.'

But the WBA rules are a sham. Its points-based ratings system was tailor-made to set up a title bout between Holyfield and Ruiz. The absurdity of it all is underlined by the fact that, under the system, Ruiz winning the so-called WBA Regional North American heavyweight title is worth more points than a fighter winning and unifying the heavyweight championship of the world. The system wasn't put into effect by the WBA until March of this year (on the eve of the Lennox Lewis versus Don King litigation hearing). And the WBA doesn't even apply its own system to every weight division.

The result? On 12 August, the two men Lewis refers to as 'The Mother Teresa of Boxing' and 'Johnny Louise' will fight for the WBA heavyweight championship.

And so it seems that, for Evander Holyfield, the Ten Commandments are dwindling to seven. We've lost 'Thou shalt not commit adultery' and 'Thou shalt not covet.' Quite possibly, 'Thou shalt not steal' will be the next commandment to go. Evander might not have stolen the WBA title, but one can make a pretty good argument that he was an accessory to the theft. And should he win on 12 August, he'll be in possession of stolen goods.

In sum, 'The Real Deal' is in danger of becoming 'The Real Steal'. There's right, and there's wrong. And for Evander to say, 'A victory over Ruiz means I would be four-time heavyweight champion of the world,' is just plain wrong. Whoever wins on 12 August will have as much legitimacy and credibility as Bruce Seldon did when he was WBA heavyweight champ.

It's in the best interests of boxing that the heavyweight championship be unified, with its crown resting upon the head of one man. Right now, that man is Lennox 'The Real Champ' Lewis. Thus, a word of advice to Evander Holyfield: when you beat John Ruiz on 12 August, you should take the WBA belt and present it to Lennox Lewis. If you do that, you'll be remembered in history with boxing immortals like Muhammad Ali, Joe Louis and Rocky Marciano. But if you keep the belt, you'll be linked for ever with Gilberto Mendoza and Jimmy Binns.

It's a test of character.

The first opportunity I had to write about Shane Mosley came when I saw him at Madison Square Garden against Eduardo Morales.

A New 'Sugar' Is Crowned

Every now and then, a fighter comes along who's just better than the rest. There are inklings of it in flashes of young brilliance and the way he finishes off opponents in four-round preliminary bouts. Then he moves on to tougher foes and pretty much dominates them too. When such a fighter grows into greatness, it's exciting to behold. And it happened at Madison Square Garden on 22 September 1998, when 'Sugar' Shane Mosley defended his IBF lightweight championship by knocking out Eduardo Morales at 2.06 of the fifth round.

Mosley is a three-time National Amateur champion, with an amateur record of 250 wins against ten losses. He won the IBF title from Phillip Holiday in August 1997 and has successfully defended it five times en route to a professional record of 29 wins and no losses with 27 knockouts.

Great athletes look different from the rest of the field in the way they go about their work, and Mosley has moved into that class. Morales was a credible opponent. He was undefeated coming into the bout, and had a fast left hook with good power. When hit, he fired back, but he was no match for Mosley. Mosley knocked him down in round three with a counter left that drove the challenger into the ropes followed by two hooks to the body. He decked him again in round five with a barrage of punches, and was pummelling him mercilessly when referee Arthur Mercante Jr stopped the contest. At bout's end, Mosley had landed 84 of 111 power punches and been hit by a meagre 21 blows.

Anyone who uses the moniker 'Sugar' had better be good. Correct that. Better than good; great. And Mosley is. He bears an uncanny facial resemblance to Sugar Ray Robinson and was born in 1971 (precisely fifty years after the original 'Sugar Ray'). But more to the point, Mosley has moved into that realm where his bouts are now part competition and part performing art.

Mosley is a complete fighter. He's fast, well schooled and punches with power. On those occasions when he suffers a defensive lapse, he takes his punishment well. Outside of Roy Jones, no one active in the sweet science today has more pure physical talent. Pound for pound, Mosley deserves to be ranked in the top five; possibly as high as number two, behind Jones. All he needs is the opponents to test him.

Shane Mosley has the right to use the name. A new 'Sugar' has been crowned.

When Michael Grant challenged Lennox Lewis for the heavy-weight crown in April 2000, I spent the entire day with Michael, including the hours in his locker room leading up to the fight.

The Heir Apparent

The 1960s gave birth to a new breed of athlete; men like Muhammad Ali and Jim Brown, who were big, well-coordinated and fast. Now, at the start of a new century, athletes have retained their speed and coordination and are even bigger than in the past.

On 8 February, a month into the new millennium, Michael Grant stepped before the assembled media at Madison Square Garden at a press conference called to announce his 29 April battle against Lennox Lewis for the heavyweight championship of the world. Grant is 27 years old, stands six feet seven inches tall, and weighs 250 pounds. Some observers call him the best pure athlete ever to come into boxing. Virtually everyone in the sport has marvelled at his strength, coordination and stamina. He has been viewed by many as a prototype athlete for the new millennium and the Heir Apparent to the heavyweight throne.

But on 8 February, there were also questions regarding Grant's skills. He had turned pro in 1994 with only twelve amateur bouts to his credit, and was a 'project' insofar as boxing was concerned. Thus, while he was praised by some, he was derided by others. Indeed, one week prior to the press conference, Michael had sat with his trainer, Donald Turner, in the living room of Turner's home and complained, 'D, they're dissing me. They don't take me seriously as a fighter, and they don't even treat me right as a person. Events are scheduled. I get there on time, and then I'm treated like a stand-by. I arrange my schedule; I stop whatever I'm doing so I don't keep other people waiting; and then when I get there, they make me wait for an hour.'

Turner had listened patiently and replied, 'That's because you're walking around thinking this fight is about you, and it isn't. Anytime there's a fight for the heavyweight championship of the world, it's about boxing. And you haven't made your imprint on boxing yet.'

At the press conference, there were the usual introductory speeches. Turner and advisors Craig Hamilton and Jim Thomas spoke for the Grant team. Promoter Panos Eliades, manager Frank Maloney, and trainer Emanuel Steward represented Lewis. In the middle of the speeches, Turner pumped his fists spontaneously into the air. Joy and anticipation were etched on his face.

There was an interesting energy. Most of the boxing intelligentsia had entered the room thinking Lewis would win. But now, there was a growing sense that maybe Michael Grant's time had come; that Holyfield–Lewis had been about boxing's past, and Lewis–Grant would be about boxing's future. Michael Katz, the dean of American boxing writers, had been sceptical about Grant for most of his pro career. Now Katz opined, 'One way or the other, one of them won't be standing at the end. I think Grant will win.' Lou DiBella of HBO was also present. On his way out of the Garden, with excitement and some surprise in his voice, DiBella said simply, 'I think we're in for a changing of the guard.'

The Next Great Heavyweight...The Heir Apparent... Expectations for Michael Grant were running high. But if the burden was enormous, so were the potential rewards. The heavyweight crown is the most coveted prize in sports. Its holder can trace his lineage to Jack Johnson, Jack Dempsey, Joe Louis, Rocky Marciano, Muhammad Ali and their brethren.

Thus it was that Michael Grant awoke in his room at the Grand Hyatt Hotel in Manhattan at 6 a.m. on the morning of 29 April. For two hours, he lay in bed listening to gospel music. Then he ordered breakfast – fruit salad, scrambled egg whites, and ham. At ten o'clock, Donald Turner came to the room and the two men talked for twenty minutes. That was followed by a light snack.

At 12.30, Grant went down to the hotel lobby and sat in a large cushioned chair surrounded by friends for an hour. 'There have been other fights where I was more relaxed than this one,' he acknowledged. 'But this is OK. I'm cool with it. I know this is for the heavyweight championship of the world; but I'm focusing on the fight; not the belt.'

This was the first time in his career that Grant had found himself an underdog in one of his fights. Lennox Lewis had been installed as a solid five to two favourite. The prevailing view was that Lewis's boxing skills gave him an edge. Also, Grant might be stronger, but Lennox was believed to be the harder puncher and he seemed to have an edge in hand speed as well.

Grant's edge was his stamina. In the past, Michael had worn his opponents down. And in the past, Lennox had shown stamina problems. The bottom line was, the longer the fight went, the better Michael's chances. Or phrased differently, the early rounds were expected to belong to Lewis and the late rounds to Grant. The outcome would hinge on what happened early; and if that wasn't dispositive, on how early it got late.

Thus, the objective of the Lewis camp was that there not be any late rounds. Emanuel Steward's plan was for Lennox to jump on Michael. But Craig Hamilton had a different view. Standing in the hotel lobby, Hamilton observed, 'When you're in the centre of the ring looking at Michael and the referee is giving final instructions, Michael can look very imposing. Lennox could be forgiven for asking himself at that moment, "Do I really want to jump on this guy? Maybe I should just use my superior boxing skills." Still,' Hamilton continued, 'there are times when Michael invites disaster. He backs up. He lowers his hands. He waits. He knows he shouldn't do any of those things. But he's won 31 fights in a row fighting that way, and I'm afraid there will be times when he does it again tonight.'

'It won't be easy,' Donald Turner added. 'Lennox has plenty of guts. He's not that good when he's backing up. Most fighters aren't. But he's very good coming forward. Michael has to fight a hungry fight. If Michael lays back, Lennox controls the fight and outboxes him. Michael has to back Lennox up and make it an action fight to win. He has to impose his will. Get off first. Initiate everything. Dictate the rhythm of the fight. If Michael does what he's capable of doing, he doesn't have to worry about what Lennox is doing. We know about Lennox. This fight is about Michael. I try to distance myself from the emotional part of it. I have to stay objective and level-headed; be a stabilising force for Michael and keep him in the real world. But Michael is adamant in believing he'll win this fight, and I believe with him. If Michael loses, I'll be the most surprised guy in the joint.'

At two o'clock, Grant went out for a walk. An hour later, Turner, Hamilton, Jim Thomas and associate trainer Bobby Miles walked over to

Madison Square Garden to arrange for last-minute ticket requests and check out the condition of the ring. Meanwhile, Michael returned to the hotel, had a three o'clock snack, took a nap, and spent the rest of the afternoon in his suite with his wife and a few friends. At 7 p.m., he ate his final pre-fight meal. Like every fighter who ever fought for the heavyweight championship of the world, he had dreams.

'I like Lennox,' Michael had said earlier. 'I think he's a gentleman. He's not an open person; he's very private. But if we were neighbours, there'd be a connection. We'd be in each other's homes from time to time.' Grant continued, 'Still, I know what I have to do when we fight. This is a wonderful opportunity for me, and it's about more than money and personal glory. Making other people happy is what makes me happiest, and there's a lot I can do if I'm heavyweight champion. People are starting to learn about me, and I want to learn about them too. I'm talking about the writers, the TV people, the fans; so we can be on the same page. I'm not just a piece of meat. Get to know me, and I'll get to know you. When I'm champion, I'll just say what's in my heart. I hope people will recognise the goodness in me. Not my position, but who I am. I won't change. My character won't change. But when I win the title, my life will.'

At 8.30 p.m., wearing a dark-blue jogging suit and grey peaked cap, Grant left his hotel with Don Turner, Jim Thomas and Bobby Miles. Fifteen minutes later, their limousine arrived at Madison Square Garden. Michael's assigned dressing room was 20 by 24 feet in size with scuffed grey linoleum underfoot and white cinderblock walls. A blue rubdown table stood in one corner of the room. Nine lilac-coloured folding chairs were scattered about. A TV monitor graced the wall by the door.

Michael crossed the room to the rubdown table and seated himself in an upright position with his legs dangling over the side. Then he lowered his head in contemplation. Following his lead, everyone else in the room remained silent.

'The most nervous I ever was before a fight was before my first amateur fight,' Michael Grant once said. 'I remember being in the locker room, banging the back of my head against my locker, saying, "I can't believe I'm doing this."'

He looked nervous now.

At 8.52 p.m., an inspector from the New York State Athletic Commission entered the room and gave a pair of plastic gloves to each of Grant's cornermen. A NYSAC physician who had come in with the inspector took Michael's blood pressure.

At 8.58, Grant lay down on the rubdown table with a half-dozen towels beneath his head and closed his eyes. Two minutes later, another Commission operative came in and asked for a urine sample. Michael got up, went into the adjacent lavatory, provided a sample, and returned to the rubdown table where, once again, he lay down and closed his eyes. The table was a foot too short. Michael's feet and then some dangled over the end.

The TVKO monitor on the wall heralded the start of the evening's live telecast. As several members of the Grant team watched, Wladimir Klitschko knocked out David Bostice in two rounds. Next up, Arturo Gatti KO'd Eric Jakubowski; also in two. Michael slept, or pretended to sleep, through it all.

At 9.43, the monitor showed Lennox Lewis arriving at Madison Square Garden. Three minutes later, someone from TVKO came into the room and asked if it would be possible to wake Michael for an interview. The answer was 'no'.

At ten o'clock, an hour after Michael lay down and closed his eyes, Donald Turner roused him gently. At 10.05, Keyshawn Johnson entered the room and approached Grant. 'You came this far,' the NFL star exhorted. 'You're gonna get it done, definitely.'

Paul Ingle versus Junior Jones, the next-to-last fight of the evening, appeared on the TV monitor.

At 10.15, Donald Turner began taping Michael's hands. Fifteen minutes later, he was done and a Commission inspector initialled the wraps.

At 10.30, Grant and Turner left the dressing room and walked to a nearby freight-loading area, where Michael jumped rope for three minutes. Four times, he missed a beat and the rope slid off his shoe against the floor. Then he returned to the dressing room and began a series of stretching exercises.

The number of people inside had grown to twelve, but the room was strangely silent. There was no aura of confidence and no crackle of electricity to signify that this was a fight for the heavyweight championship of the world. The atmosphere seemed more suited to an eight-round preliminary bout. And more significantly, the positive energy so abundant at the February kick-off press conference was gone.

As Grant began to loosen up, for the first time since he'd entered the room, his face seemed to transform into the face of a fighter. His eyes grew more focused, angry and intense.

Then the look receded.

Paul Ingle KO'd Junior Jones in the eleventh round.

At 10.50, the stretching exercises ended. Michael put on his protective cup and trunks and gloved up. Cutman Joe Souza applied Vaseline to his face. At eleven o'clock, referee Arthur Mercante Jr, who would preside over the title fight, came into the room and offered final pre-fight instructions. Mercante was brief and to the point. Two minutes later, he was gone.

For the first time, gospel music from a portable CD player sounded. Still, the room seemed strangely unalive.

At 11.02, Bobby Miles put on a pair of handpads. For the next six minutes, Grant hit the pads under Donald Turner's watchful eye with Miles shouting instructions: 'Jab, hook the body...Jab, hook the body, follow with a right.'

When the two men were done, Michael began to pace in a circle around the room. Now it was just a matter of time.

But something was missing.

Bobby Miles put the handpads on again and Grant pounded them for another two minutes. It was 11.15 p.m.

'Three minutes,' a voice from the doorway sounded.

Everyone in the room joined hands in a circle, readying for prayer.

'Be sincere, please,' Michael implored them.

They prayed together. Then Michael turned for a silent moment of his own. 'I always shed a tear before a fight,' Michael Grant had once said. Now he appeared to be shedding many of them.

The room still didn't feel right.

There would be no violent transfer of power tonight.

When Mike Tyson fights, inevitably the story goes beyond the boundaries of boxing. That was certainly the case before his October 2000 bout against Andrew Golota in Auburn Hills, Michigan.

Tyson, Michigan and Zoloft

Zoloft will be in the news a lot over the next two months. That's because Mike Tyson is expected to apply for a licence to fight in the State of Michigan.

Zoloft is an inhibitor that increases the availability of serotonin in the brain. Serotonin is a neuro-transmitter that transmits impulses and regulates mood. Zoloft blocks the reuptake of serotonin so more is available in the brain.

How important is Zoloft to Mike Tyson?

During an October 1999 hearing before the Nevada State Athletic Commission prior to Tyson being given a licence to fight Orlin Norris, doctors testifying on Tyson's behalf stated that he suffered from 'deficits in executive function that make him prone to impulsive behaviour.' However, the doctors voiced the belief that Tyson's condition could be controlled through psychotherapy and medication.

When Tyson was sentenced on 5 February 1999 for assaulting two motorists following a traffic accident in Maryland, his lawyers told the court that he needed Zoloft as part of his therapy. Tyson, the court was told, had begun taking Zoloft regularly and been taken off the drug only briefly, in January 1999, while preparing for his fight against Frans Botha. However, once in prison, Tyson refused to let a prison psychologist examine him and was denied access to Zoloft. The result was a violent temper tantrum during which Iron Mike became enraged and threw a television set, leading to his being placed in a five-by-eight-foot isolation cell as punishment.

Tyson is reported to have been taking Zoloft for about two years. During that period, he has had fights against Frans Botha, Orlin Norris,

Julius Francis and Lou Savarese. It is believed that he has gone off Zoloft prior to each of those bouts and, in them, he has: (1) tried to break Frans Botha's arm off at the elbow; (2) hit Orlin Norris on the break twice; the second time, after the bell; (3) fought foul-free against a human punching bag named Julius Francis; and (4) punched referee John Coyle, so he could punch Lou Savarese some more after Coyle had stopped the fight.

And of course, outside the ring without Zoloft, Iron Mike is reliably reported to have punched promoter Frank Warren. The prevailing view is that it wasn't Warren who initiated the fisticuffs.

Plus, Tyson exploded while his deposition was being taken in a civil lawsuit filed on his behalf against Don King. At that deposition, which was conducted at the law offices of Peter Fleming (King's attorney), Tyson became agitated and demanded to know why King was staring at him. He then threw a sheaf of papers at his former promoter. Another of King's attorney's, Michael Murphy, demanded that Dale Kinsella (who represents Tyson) control his client, at which point Tyson threw a glass of water at Murphy, attacked him, and had to be restrained by security personnel who were in the room.

Also, let's not forget that Iron Mike has been convicted of rape and bit Evander Holyfield twice.

Thus, it seems logical to ask, 'If Mike Tyson is licensed to fight in Michigan, will he be on or off Zoloft for the fight?'

'I can't comment on that,' says Tyson advisor Shelly Finkel.

'Is there anyone who can?'

'No,' Finkel answers.

So let's present the dilemma plain and simple. There's not a lot of medical literature on the issue of whether or not Zoloft affects world-class athletic performance. Certainly, being on the drug does nothing to increase strength or reflexes. If anything, it hampers aggression. But a person taken off Zoloft is likely to suffer from withdrawal symptoms for several weeks. That means, during the initial period without Zoloft, a patient is likely to experience more anxiety and rage than would be the case if he, or she, had never been on the drug to begin with.

In other words, the State of Michigan is about to import a man who, while within its borders, will be denied the medication that keeps him from acting like a psychopath.

The Michigan State Athletic Board of Control has nine members, all of whom have been appointed by Governor John Engler. Its chairman is Dave Sebastian, who said last month that Tyson wouldn't be licensed to fight in Michigan without a hearing. However, in reality, boxing in Michigan is regulated by the Department of Consumer and Industry Services. The Athletic Board of Control is only an advisory body.

Moreover, according to David Mayo of the *Grand Rapids Press*, the Michigan Athletic Board of Control is a 'spurious governing group' whose nine members are all political appointees. Michigan law requires that six of the nine board members be 'license-holding professional boxing workers'. The rationale for this requirement is that boxing should be run by people who know something about boxing. However, Mayo reports that three of the 'professional' board members, including Chairman Sebastian, have fulfilled their requirement by simply acquiring a timekeeper's licence at the time of their appointment. 'Anyone can become a licensed timekeeper,' writes Mayo. 'You pay 35 dollars per year, and you get a license. If you need someone to stare at a stopwatch for three minutes and then ring a bell, you've got the right group.'

I happen to be among the small group of boxing commentators who think that Mike Tyson is still one of the best heavyweights in the world. I also think that the people who are supposedly looking out for Tyson's best interests should ask themselves whether Iron Mike would be better off if he avoided high-stress situations like prizefighting without Zoloft.

'I think it's crazy,' says Dr William Hoffmann, a psychiatrist with experience in the athletic arena. 'If you go on and off Zoloft, you're messing around with a patient's neuro-transmitters. To get the maximum benefit from Zoloft, you have to go on it and stay on it long-term. To put a patient on Zoloft and take him off Zoloft and put him on and take him off is abusive.'

'This is an ongoing issue for boxing, not just because of Mike Tyson but also because of Ike Ibeabuche and a number of other fighters,' adds Flip Homansky. Homansky served as Chairman of the Medical Advisory Board to the Nevada State Athletic Commission until recently, when he was appointed to the commission itself. 'My view,' Homansky continues, 'is that, if someone needs a drug like Zoloft, then they shouldn't be taken off it to get them into the ring or make them better in the ring or make them more aggressive in the ring. That's simply not the right thing to do in terms of the welfare of the individual.'

Also, putting aside Mike Tyson's best interests for the moment, the interests of society at large must also be considered.

In opposing Tyson's request for a visa to fight Lou Savarese in Scotland this past June, Roseanna Cunningham told fellow members of Parliament, 'With Tyson, the message is that no matter what the crime, the level of violence, the fact that your behaviour has included rape, you can go on, live your life, make megabucks, be a hero, be surrounded with all the trappings of success, and gain preferential treatment from officialdom. If we do not challenge that image head-on in every way we can, then we collude by default in that image.'

The primary reason Mike Tyson will be allowed to fight in Michigan is because millions of dollars are involved. That means the State of Michigan, like too many of our governmental entities these days, has one set of rules for the very rich and another set of rules for the rest of us.

It seems as though every time I write something critical about Mike Tyson, I get a spate of E-mails calling me a racist motherfucker. But if one is serious about writing on boxing, some things have to be said.

The Intimidation Factor

With all the talk about Mike Tyson's bizarre behaviour at his recent (October 2000) press conference in Los Angeles, one moment has been all but lost in the shuffle. Talking about Lennox Lewis, Tyson raged, 'He tried to bully me once, and he's kind of big. He makes me kind of nervous without his gloves and shorts on, so if he ever tries to intimidate me again, I'm gonna plant a bullet in the back of his motherfucking skull.'

Lennox Lewis bullying Tyson? 'If he ever tries to intimidate me again...?'

And something in my mind clicked. The same day that Tyson had his meltdown in Los Angeles, I spent some time alone with Lewis while he was in New York to promote his 11 November championship bout against David Tua. Inevitably, our conversation turned to Tyson, and Lennox said he'd had a confrontation with the ex-champ recently in Las Vegas. 'He called me a bitch,' Lewis said. 'I thought about going after him, and then I figured, "Why bother?" But next time, I might do it.'

At that point, we were interrupted by the scheduling demands of an HBO photo shoot. I wasn't sure how seriously to take Lennox's remarks. Now, judging by Tyson's rant, it appears that I should have taken them very seriously. For the moment at least, Lennox Lewis seems to be winning the war of intimidation against Mike Tyson.

Fear is a funny subject among fighters. Cus D'Amato, who did more than anyone else to mould Tyson as a fighter, often waxed eloquent on the subject. 'Heroes and cowards feel exactly the same fear,' D'Amato said once. 'Heroes just react differently to it.'

Once upon a time, Tyson was a master intimidator. He's still awfully good at it. But Buster Douglas took a large chunk out of Iron Mike's aura of invincibility, and Evander Holyfield destroyed it. Now Tyson might actually be intimidated by Lennox Lewis rather than the other way around.

None of this is to prejudge the outcome of Lewis–Tyson, which would be a competitive fight. Also, it's worth noting that, before we get there, Tyson has to beat Andrew Golota; Lewis has to beat David Tua; HBO and Showtime have to work out a deal – and at least one more important question has to be revisited: should Mike Tyson be allowed to fight?

Tyson's conduct, in and out of the ring, is a matter of public record. But even veteran Tyson-watchers found his comments in Los Angeles to be chilling: 'I don't care about living or dying. I'm a dysfunctional motherfucker... Bring on Golota; bring on Lewis. They can keep their titles. I don't want to strip them of their titles, I want to strip them of their fucking health... I'm in pain, so I want them to be in pain. I want their kids to see pain... I don't care about his [Lewis's] children, if he has any. Fuck 'em... You don't know me; you can't define me. I'm a convicted rapist, a hell-raiser, a father, a semi-good husband. I raise hell. I know it's going to get me in trouble or killed one day, but that's just who I am. I can't help it... Listen, I'm a nigger. No, really, really, listen to me. I'm a street person. I don't even want to be a street person; I don't like typical street people. But your grandchildren will know about me. They'll be like, "Wow, wasn't that a bizarre individual?"'

Greg Garrison is a former prosecutor who was retained by Marion County, Indiana, authorities to serve as lead counsel in the 1992 prosecution of Mike Tyson for rape. Garrison tried the case and won a 'guilty' verdict that led to Tyson being incarcerated for three years.

Garrison has been fairly silent on the subject of Mike Tyson as of late, but that doesn't mean he's without opinions on the subject.

'I don't care if Tyson is allowed to fight again or not,' Garrison said last week. 'He's made such a complete fool of himself, it doesn't really matter. But the way people are talking about him, it's as though you have some racehorse or gamecock and you're giving it whatever it needs to compete. Zoloft is supposed to be what keeps Tyson from going completely nuts. At least, that's what the doctors who give it to him say. I'm not sure if he's a psycho or if he's just no damn good. But if they're going to take him off Zoloft to get him ready to fight, it seems to me that, if he has to be that nutty to be in the ring, then he shouldn't fight.'

When the subject of Zoloft was raised at Tyson's press conference in Los Angeles, Tyson told the assembled media, 'I'm on it to keep from killing you all.' He then added, 'I don't want to be on it. I'm jacked up. My sex life is jacked up. My dick don't work.'

Garrison had this to say in response: 'The last thing that's going to quit working on Mike Tyson is his dick. So if his dick isn't working any more, he's in really bad shape.'

There are rumours that Garrison has been contacted in recent years with regard to several sexual assaults that Tyson is alleged to have committed after the Desiree Washington incident, and also with regard to another rape that Tyson is alleged to have committed prior to his encounter with Washington. At least one of these cases has reportedly been settled for a substantial amount. 'I'm familiar with a couple of those incidents,' Garrison acknowledges. 'Some I can talk about; some I can't. In fact, it's probably better if I don't talk about any of them.'

'I just wish he'd go away,' Garrison says about Tyson in closing. 'He's not worthy of all the attention. All he is, really, is another ex-con who can't stay on the right side of the law. But I suppose, the way things are, for the time being, we'll keep seeing pictures of Mike Tyson mowing his lawn, Mike Tyson playing with his children, Mike Tyson shooting his neighbours, or whatever else Mike Tyson feels like doing on any given day.'

Meanwhile, the self-described 'baddest man on the planet' – the fighter who once denigrated opponents with the taunt, 'How dare they challenge me with their primitive skills?' – has been reduced to threatening to sneak up behind Lennox Lewis and 'plant a bullet in the back of his motherfucking skull'.

The Nevada State Athletic Commission hearing at which Mike Tyson was denied a licence to fight Lennox Lewis was as dramatic in its own way as the chaotic press conference that preceded it.

Nevada Says 'No' to Mike Tyson

The Nevada State Athletic Commission has denied Mike Tyson's request for a licence. The decision came after a two-and-a-half-hour hearing with Tyson present and was by a four to one vote. The sole dissenter was commission chairman Luther Mack.

The decision came after days of intense lobbying. During the past week, pro-Tyson forces repeatedly made the argument that the Las Vegas economy needs the proposed championship bout between Tyson and Lennox Lewis. Sources close to the NSAC report that Jesse Jackson was even called upon to do some last-minute lobbying on the questionable grounds that Tyson's civil rights would be violated if he were denied a licence. But Tyson's history of antisocial behaviour, past and present, was too much to overcome.

The rallying point for those opposed to licensing Tyson was a 22 January press conference in New York intended to announce the fight. According to the Lewis camp, Tyson and Lewis were to stand on platforms on opposite sides of the stage at the Hudson Theater and glare at one another. Because of the uniform black-curtain background, split-screen television technology would make it look as though they were engaged in a staredown in close proximity to each other.

Tyson was introduced first. Dressed in black, he strode on to the stage and took his place, as planned, on a small platform. Lewis was introduced next. At that point, Tyson left his platform and walked in a menacing fashion towards Lewis.

'He definitely was coming to sucker-punch me,' Lewis said later. 'I could see it in the way he was moving and in his eyes.'

Lewis's bodyguard stepped between the two men. Tyson threw a left hook at the bodyguard, and Lewis retaliated with an overhand right. During the scuffle, Tyson bit through Lewis's pants and into his thigh, causing significant bleeding. At the instruction of Lewis's attorney, the wound was later photographed and Lewis was given a tetanus shot.

After the combatants were separated, Tyson moved to the front of the stage, grabbed his crotch, thrust his hips back and forth, and began screaming obscenities. Someone in the crowd hollered, 'Get him a strait-jacket.' Tyson shouted back, 'Fuck you, you white faggot. I'll fuck you up the ass, white boy. I'll fuck you till you love me,' and other obscenities.

The press conference was terminated. An hour later, Lewis issued a statement that read, 'As a result of today's events, I will re-evaluate my options after the relevant boxing commission has ruled.'

The commission referred to, of course, was Nevada. Tyson's licence had been revoked by the NSAC after he bit Evander Holyfield twice during their 1997 rematch. Fifteen months later, it was reinstated. Thereafter, Tyson fought in Las Vegas against Frans Botha and Orlin Norris. In the Botha fight, he tried to break Botha's arm off at the elbow. Against Norris, Tyson hit his opponent on the break twice; the second time, clearly after the bell. Norris fell to the canvas and injured his right knee. The bout was ruled a no-contest. The NSAC then held a hearing on the matter and decided that Tyson should be allowed to receive his purse. At that hearing, then-commissioner Lorenzo Fertitta told Tyson's promoter to, 'pack Mr Tyson's bags up and take this act on the road. I'm not so sure we need him here in the State of Nevada.'

Last weekend, Larry Merchant of HBO framed the core issue. Noting that the Nevada State Athletic Commission had told Tyson to clean up his act before reapplying for a licence, Merchant cited a long list of subsequent transgressions and queried, 'Is this a serious discussion of whether Mike Tyson abided by the terms of their mandate to clean up his act? Because, clearly, he didn't. So either they condone his behaviour or they punish him for it. There's perfect clarity to the issue.'

There are five commissioners on the NSAC. Luther Mack (who owns several McDonald's franchises), Flip Homansky (a physician), Amy Ayoub (a political consultant), Tony Alamo Jr (also a physician) and John Bailey (an attorney). Since Tyson's meltdown, two of them –

Homansky and Ayoub – were believed to be leaning 'no'. Mack was considered a 'yes' vote. Fairly or unfairly, the public perception was that Alamo would vote whichever way his father told him to. Tony Alamo Sr is a vice president at Mandalay Bay. And even though Lewis–Tyson was to take place at the MGM Grand, all of the Las Vegas casinos stood to benefit from the bout. That left John Bailey as the likely swing vote.

Surprisingly, a number of major Nevada media players opposed Tyson's licence request. An editorial in the *Las Vegas Review-Journal* declared, 'Even if the MGM or some other Nevada venue is desperate enough to risk its reputation in the hopes of cashing in on a Tyson fight, now is the time for the Nevada Athletic Commission to do its job. Mike Tyson is not mentally fit to step in the ring. He should never again be licensed to fight in this State.'

A strongly worded column by Royce Feour, the most influential boxing writer in Nevada, followed. 'Why shouldn't Tyson be licensed?' Feour asked. And then he answered, 'The health and safety of his opponent and the referee, for starters. And the safety of the spectators, should he start a riot. How much more evidence does the commission need? There is only one proper thing to do: deny Tyson's application. If that means the Lewis–Tyson fight goes to another state or country, so be it. That would be the new site's problem.'

Other sports columnists followed suit. And behind the scenes, HBO also reportedly weighed in. HBO, of course, is tied to Lewis, while Showtime is tied to Tyson. The two cable giants had agreed to finance, publicise and televise the fight as a joint venture. But after Tyson's press conference behaviour, HBO higher-ups are believed to have decided that they wanted out. How to get out legally and gracefully was the issue. HBO didn't want to do anything that would render it liable for breach of contract. But a clause in one of the many bout contracts relieves HBO of certain obligations if Tyson can't get a licence to fight in one of several specified states. Accordingly, HBO discreetly let it be known to the powers that be in Las Vegas that it wouldn't be displeased if Tyson's request for a licence were denied by the commission. That would make Tyson exclusively Showtime's problem.

The hearing on Tyson's licence application began at 1.35 p.m. Tyson was represented by Las Vegas attorney Bob Faiss. Also present on his behalf were attorney Elizabeth Brennan, business manager Matthew Johnson, physical conditioner Keith Kleven and advisor Shelly Finkel.

Faiss coordinated Tyson's presentation, which consisted largely of videotapes and expository argument. The attorney began by telling the commissioners that Lewis–Tyson would take place whether it took place in Nevada or somewhere else. He also criticised the 'unceasing media pressure' on his client, and said he would forbid questions regarding allegations of rape and other criminal conduct currently pending against Tyson in order to 'preserve Mr Tyson's constitutional rights'. He then likened Iron Mike's obscenity-laced press conference tirade to John L Sullivan's boast, 'I can lick any son-of-a-bitch in the house.' And he drew an analogy between Jack Dempsey's ring savagery and Tyson biting off part of Evander Holyfield's ear.

Faiss's explanation regarding the press conference debacle was as follows. At the last minute, Tyson was advised by a member of his team that the Lewis camp had agreed to a face-to-face staredown. Indeed, Faiss claimed that 'Mr Tyson's intent was to play an assigned role in another production of boxing theatre.' Thus, Tyson crossed the stage and was surprised when he was shoved by Lennox's bodyguard. Thinking that they were 'play-acting', Iron Mike threw a left hook in response, deliberately missing his target. Then Lewis 'sucker-punched' Tyson. In other words, Tyson was 'a powerless non-participant'. He was 'shaken, beaten and bloodied', and believed he had been 'doublecrossed'. Furthermore, Feiss said in closing, 'Mr Tyson states he did not bite anyone.'

Returning to the obscenities, Faiss likened Tyson's use of what he referred to as 'the "F" word' to *The Sopranos* and added that it was constitutionally protected speech. He also claimed that none of the offensive language would have been uttered but for the fact that Tyson had been provoked by a reporter. This overlooked the reality that the reporter's insult was occasioned by the fact that Tyson was standing on the stage, already screaming obscenities and simulating masturbation.

Faiss's presentation ended at 2.40 p.m. Then the statements and questioning by commissioners began.

Tyson had an answer for every allegation. To hear him talk, none of the chaos that has marked his life has been his fault. Referee John

Coyle got punched in the Savarese fight because 'he didn't stop the fight in an appropriate way.' Tyson tried to break Frans Botha's arm in a clinch because Botha was 'fighting dirty'. The Lewis–Tyson press conference fisticuffs were the result of Lennox's camp not following the agreed-upon script. The obscene diatribe that followed occurred because, 'After the mayhem, a gentleman said something humiliating and embarrassing to me, and I tried to inflict similar pain on him. He violated me as an individual, and I violated him. He was at liberty to say what he wanted to say to me, and I was at liberty to say what I wanted to say to him.'

Tyson also stated that he was not on medication, hadn't been for six months, and that his psychiatric therapy ended last spring. 'I'm no longer in need of treatment,' he said in response to a question. That seemed to trouble the commissioners. 'How are you controlling your tendency toward violence without medication?' Amy Ayoub wondered. 'Whatever the [psychiatric] plan was,' John Bailey offered, 'it didn't work.'

There was also one moment of pathos, when Tyson was asked if he had any friends (as opposed to business associates) who he could sit down and talk things out with.

'I don't have one friend in my entire life,' Tyson answered. 'I was never successful with friends.'

The questioning ended at 3.25 p.m. Then, after a seven-minute break, each commissioner made a statement and the pattern of votes became clear:

AMY AYOUB: 'We respect the presumption of innocence until proven guilty, but there's also guilty when proven guilty. Why have laws if we're not going to enforce them?'

FLIP HOMANSKY: 'From the bottom of my heart, I wish things had gone better. We're all losers here.'

JOHN BAILEY: 'When everything is at stake, you're unpredictable and capable of the very worst conduct. When you have uncontrolled rage, you put peoples' lives in jeopardy. And ultimately, you're the one who is responsible.'

Bailey was articulate and thoughtful. His statement was a moment of high drama, and it sealed Tyson's fate.

At 3.55 p.m., Faiss asked for a ten-minute recess. When the hearing resumed, Tyson, Shelly Finkel and Matthew Johnson were no longer present. Faiss sought to withdraw the licence application, but his request was denied. At 4.05 p.m., the vote was taken and Mike Tyson went down to defeat.

So what comes next?

For starters, Madison Square Garden is out as a possible site. Previously, MSG pushed hard for the fight, and Garden officials had discussions with New York State Athletic Commission personnel that left them confident Tyson would be licensed to fight in New York. But a New York licence is far less likely now. And in any event, MSG chief operating officer Seth Abraham says, 'Madison Square Garden will no longer take the fight. We closed the book on Lewis–Tyson as of Monday, January 21st [when Abraham learned that the fight was slated for the MGM Grand].' Also, Abraham acknowledged, 'When the Garden was putting together its bid, we contacted our biggest sponsors and had difficulty getting sponsor support. Our sponsors were concerned about participating in a Tyson fight, and that was before January 22nd.'

Also, it's unclear that Lewis still wants the fight. Last Saturday at Madison Square Garden for Shane Mosley versus Vernon Forrest, Lennox was non-committal when asked on-camera. Off-camera, he was slightly more revealing.

'Do you still want to fight Tyson?' someone queried.

'We already fought,' Lewis answered. 'Although I only hit him a glancing shot. He didn't feel my full power.'

But then Lennox grew more serious.

'There are rules of conduct that all people are supposed to follow,' he said. 'I follow those rules. I follow them outside the ring, and I follow them as a boxer. I try to beat a man down fairly with my hands. Not bite him, not head-butt him, not try to break his elbow.'

'Lennox genuinely has not made up his mind yet as to whether or not he will fight Tyson,' Adrian Ogun (Lewis's business manager) said that night.

The ambiguity remains; although shortly after the NSAC vote, Lewis issued a statement that read in part, 'Prior to today, I've made no public statements concerning the events of January 22nd. I remained silent at the direct instruction and insistence of my attorneys, who advised me that revealing the truth about what occurred would have undoubtedly led to a lawsuit by Mike Tyson claiming that I interfered with the licensing process. However, now that the licensing proceedings are over and a licence has been denied, I am no longer bound to remain silent. The fact is that Mike Tyson bit through my trousers and took a significant piece of flesh out of my thigh. I was particularly disturbed by the fact that he went before the commission today and did not tell the truth by denying what he knows occurred. I have made no decision yet about the possibility of fighting Mike Tyson in another jurisdiction that may license him because I want to consider carefully the reasons expressed by the commission in denying the licence. I know that all of my fans were looking forward to the Lewis–Tyson fight, as was I. I am sorry that the situation has not yet been resolved.'

None of this means that the chaos is over. Unless Mike Tyson is indicted for sexual assault, he'll be licensed somewhere. Maybe he'll even get a title shot. Jose Sulaiman will most likely rule that Iron Mike is still the WBC's mandatory challenger; or Tyson could wind up in the ring with WBA 'champ' John Ruiz. But no one fight or athletic contest makes or breaks a sport. And the Nevada State Athletic Commission sent a crucial message today. The way to dispose of Mike Tyson isn't to beat him up in a boxing ring. It's to resolve his fate as a matter of law.

The day after this article appeared online, my telephone rang at 5.55 a.m. It was Bernard Hopkins. Prior to doing his road-work, he'd checked the internet for stories about himself, read this one, and was calling to thank me. The thought crossed my mind that he could have called after his roadwork. But the truth is, I always enjoy talking with Bernard; and he's easy to write about. All that's necessary is to listen and take notes.

Bernard Hopkins – Y4145

Felix Trinidad is the box-office star of the ongoing middleweight championship series. But the most compelling personality to emerge from the tournament is Bernard Hopkins.

Hopkins minces no words when it comes to boxing. 'In the ring,' he says, 'all fights are grudge matches. I'm a dangerous guy. I destroy careers. I ruin other people's dreams. There's a time to be humble and a time for war. Boxing is war. Boxing is serious. It ain't no joke; it ain't no show. You have to think violent. Don't cry and complain to the referee, "Bernard is hurting me." We're not in church; we're fighting. If you want to not get a bruise, then go play golf.'

Hopkins grew up on the mean streets of Philadelphia; one of eight children, four boys and four girls, born to Bernard Hopkins Sr and his wife Shirley. 'I always had leadership qualities,' he reminisces. 'Fifth grade, sixth grade; if someone was messing with another kid, he'd come to me for protection. It wasn't free. Maybe it was just a peanut butter sandwich with bananas, which was my favourite sandwich, but I always charged something. Later on, I was the guy that girls came to for protection if their boyfriend was beating up on them. But the truth is, I was ignorant; I was a thug. You have two kinds of people, lambs and wolves; and I was a wolf.'

Hopkins's story is best told by the perpetrator himself, so let him continue.

'Most of the people I preyed on were tough, but I was tougher. I never stole anything from a woman, and I didn't use a weapon. Mostly, I took things by intimidation. I'd see someone with a chain I liked and it was, "Nice chain. Can I see it?...I said I want to see the chain...Let me see the chain...Give me the fucking chain now." They weren't going to fight me. I had the reputation. Sometimes, I'd just look at a guy and he'd take his chain off without my even asking. My reputation preceded me..."Like those shoes, man...Give me the shoes...Give me those shoes now!" I was tired of wearing hand-me-down clothes and looking like I'd been dressed by Jehovah's Witnesses. I thought respect was having chains and nice clothes and money to spend. I'd go out gambling and, whether I lost or won, I'd be the one who went home with the money. I'd lose, beat someone up, and take it all back again. None of the situations were big money. It was all petty stuff, but it gave me an adrenalin rush. One time, I was wearing nine gold chains.'

'At home, I'd hide what I stole,' Hopkins continues. 'If my mother or father caught me with a chain, I'd lie and say I borrowed it from a friend. After a while, they knew. You could have taken the police administration desk and put it on our front porch. My mother used to say to me, "You know, some day, you're going to jail." And she was right. I don't know how many times I was suspended from school. I didn't respect life; I put myself in a lot of positions to be six feet under. My teachers used to tell me that I wouldn't live to be eighteen, and I believed them. When I was fourteen years old, I got stabbed with an ice pick over a craps game. My lung was punctured inches from my heart. I spent thirty days in the hospital. A year later, I got stabbed again, this time in the back. The guy who did it; I know I did something wrong to him. But I did so much wrong to so many people that I don't know what it was. I have teethmarks all over my hands from the street fights I was in. Why was I spared? I don't know.'

At age seventeen, Hopkins was sentenced to prison for multiple offences. One sentence was five to twelve years. The second, which ran consecutively, was three to six. In other words, at age seventeen, Bernard Hopkins was facing up to eighteen years in prison. He had just finished eleventh grade.

'I don't blame the judge,' Hopkins says reflectively. 'I'd been in court thirty times in two years. What else was he supposed to do? The truth is, I had to go to the penitentiary to be saved from the graveyard. I'm not happy about the things I did back then, but the way I turned my life around speaks for itself.'

For 56 months, from 1984 through 1989, Hopkins was one of 3,000 inmates in Graterford State Penitentiary in Pennsylvania. 'In prison, the sharks are waiting for any fear you might show from the moment you walk in,' he remembers. 'You get off a big blue bus, shackled from your ankles to your waist to your wrists. You can't even spread your legs, so you sort of shuffle forward. The inmates who are already there are checking you out in the receiving room like you're a fresh young chicken. Y4145 was the number they gave me. That was my name in prison. I'll never forget that number.

'I saw a lot of things in prison that aren't clean or nice to talk about,' Hopkins continues. 'I was seventeen years old. I didn't consider myself dangerous, but I was surrounded by killers, rapists, child molesters, skinheads, mafia types, so I was in a dangerous situation. I saw a guy stabbed to death with a makeshift ice pick in an argument over a pack of cigarettes. You see rapes. You don't go in the shower with no clothes on. You take a shower wearing your shorts because, no matter how tough you are, it's not enough if you're up against four or five people. That HBO show *Oz* is like cartoons compared to what I saw in prison.'

Not long after Hopkins was imprisoned, his brother Michael was shot in the back and killed in a street fight over a girl. 'I was on the phone,' he remembers. 'The way it works in prison is, you make your calls collect and you're allowed ten minutes before it's the next person's turn. So I'm talking with my mother, and I can hear in her voice that something is wrong. I said to her, "Mom, I know something is wrong. What is it?" So she passed the phone to my sister Bernadette who passed it to my sister Marcy, and finally my mother got back on the phone and said, "Michael got shot last night. He died." And the guy behind me is saying, "Come on, man! Your ten minutes is up. It's my turn."'

Twice a week, every week for 56 months, Shirley Hopkins journeyed to Graterford State Penitentiary to visit her son. 'Twice a week is all you're allowed,' Hopkins explains. 'I don't think she missed more than three or four visits ever in a year. My girlfriend left me. My friends wouldn't accept collect calls. But my mother was always there; in the rain, in the snow, going through the indignity of having her body touched when they searched her everywhere from her pocketbook to her bra.'

Whose fault was it?

'I'm not blaming anyone but Bernard Hopkins for putting myself and my family in that situation,' Hopkins continues. 'Maybe society put the traps there for me to fall into. But if you fall into them, it's your own fault. There's not a day that goes by that I don't remember those 56 months in prison. It was all I could do to maintain my sanity. I did the best I could to mind my own business. I put a front on; I tried to look tough. But I hated it. I wanted to get out as soon as possible. In 56 months, I never had a write-up. And I told myself, I promised myself every day, "If I ever get out of here, I'm not coming back again." But I also had to get ready for when I got out. I was seventeen years old; couldn't spell, could barely read. If I said a word, I didn't know if I was using it right. I said to myself, "I've got to fix this." So I started studying in prison and got my graduation equivalency diploma. And I started thinking more about what I'd done. When you commit a crime, you're not thinking about anyone but yourself. Then, after a while, you start to think about all the people that you let down, like your mother. But you haven't really started thinking right until you realise that the person you put in fear when you robbed them is a person too; that they're someone else's son or brother or father. And I also learned in prison that you don't have to be bad to be tough.'

Boxing also played a role in Hopkins's rehabilitation. Graterford was one of six prisons that participated in a joint boxing programme. While in prison, he won four national middleweight penitentiary boxing championships. 'Boxing was my best therapy,' he remembers. 'It saved my sanity. I'd boxed when I was young; started when I was seven years old and had some amateur fights. In prison, they said I was punch-drunk. They said I was crazy. I used to run the prison yard like a gerbil on a wheel, around and around, around and around, saying over and over to myself, "Some day, I'm gonna get out of here. Some day, I'm gonna be a champion."'

Hopkins was released from prison in 1989 with nine years of parole facing him. He had to be good to stay free. He was 22 years old at the time and, in his own words, 'I haven't spit on the ground since then.' It wasn't easy being on the outside. 'A lot of the guys I'd known when I was younger were dead,' he remembers. But some were dealers; had the big cars, fancy jewellery, and all that. I was a convicted felon with a GED [General Equivalency Diploma], working at an unskilled job and fighting four-round preliminary fights. I wasn't allowed to vote because I'd been in prison, but you better believe I was allowed to pay taxes. And some of the prison habits died hard. Like people would say to me, "Bernard, you're not in the penitentiary any more. Why are you covering your plate with your left hand when you eat?"'

Hopkins lost a four-round decision in his first pro fight when he was overmatched against a more experienced foe. Then he hooked up with trainer Bouie Fisher. In 41 fights since then, only Roy Jones has beaten him, and Bernard has held the IBF middleweight crown since 1994. But the road has been far from smooth. Or, as Hopkins says philosophically, 'We reap what we sow. When I started to get good in the ring, Butch Lewis, who was my promoter, took advantage of me. He did to me what I did to other people when I was taking chains, only he did it by deception instead of intimidation.'

Outside the ring, Hopkins is genuinely devoted to his family, particularly the three women in his life: his mother, his wife, and his daughter.

Shirley Hopkins is now 55 and battling cancer. Bernard has been with her every step of the way, driving her to and from each of the chemotherapy sessions that ended this past April.

Regarding his wife, Hopkins says forcefully, 'I'm 36; Jeanette is 31. We've been together for twelve years; been married for eight; and she's as strong as I am. When we started living together, she had a job with Community Legal Services in Philadelphia making $25,000 a year while I was struggling as a fighter. We slept on the floor. There were no shortcuts to get to where we are today. And you can write this; I want you to write this. I love my wife, and I'm one hundred per cent faithful to my wife. I don't hang out at clubs. I don't have groupies. Sometimes, someone will start coming on to me, and I'll tell her, "I'm married."

Then maybe she'll ask, "Are you happily married?" But I love my wife enough not to hurt her like that, and I hope she feels the same way about me.'

'And I have one child,' Hopkins continues. 'Absolutely only one child; our daughter, Latress Gerney Hopkins. Most of my friends had babies early on and, after a while, my wife and I were getting strange looks. We were trying; we were doing all the right things; but I was firing blanks. I guess it wasn't time for me to be a father.'

Latress was born on 28 June 1999.

'I'd never been in an operating room and seen a baby delivered,' Hopkins reminisces. 'But I was there that day. It was a C-section. I was looking through a curtain; my wife was sedated. Then I saw this bloody head come out, and the nurse asked me, "Do you want to hold her, Mr Hopkins?" She gave me the baby all wrapped up. I held my daughter thirty seconds after she was born. And I made a promise to myself right then; I told myself, "This baby is going to have a father." People ask me sometimes if I think I'm a role model. Yes, I'm a role model. When I talk with young people, being a champion gives me more leverage. Automatically, it gets me respect so I have more influence with them. And the most important thing I can show other people is how a man should feel about his wife and children and his responsibilities to them.

'I've done wrong,' Hopkins acknowledges, 'and it shouldn't be forgotten. But good things can happen if you decide to truly turn your life around. Sometimes I think about how maybe my life would have been different if I'd had someone like Bernard Hopkins to talk to me when I was young. You know, I missed out on so much when I was young. I never went to a high school prom. I was in jail when my class graduated from high school. Some day, I'd like to take my wife back to the high school I went to and chaperone at the senior prom.'

Bernard Hopkins used to take other people's gold chains. Now he's into taking other guys' belts. But he's doing it the honest way; in the ring. The middleweight championship series that he's participating in was consummated for numbers that he deserves but had never seen before. First there was a $200,000 signing bonus plus $50,000 in training expenses and a purse of $1,000,000 to fight Keith Holmes. That bout took place on 14 April 2001, and Bernard was dominant, although he was booed for what some in the crowd perceived as a lacklustre performance. But as Hopkins said after a similar experience last year against Syd Vanderpool, 'The boos don't bother me. I'm from Philadelphia. I've heard people boo Santa Claus.'

Next up, of course, is Hopkins versus Felix Trinidad on 15 September at Madison Square Garden. For that one, Bernard will receive another $50,000 in training expenses and a purse of $2,750,000. Once Bouie Fisher and miscellaneous items such as the cost of sparring partners are paid, all of the rest will go to Bernard. Lou DiBella, who guided Hopkins to the tournament, will be compensated directly by Don King out of other revenue sources. DiBella and Hopkins have a handshake agreement, not a written contract. That's also the case with Bernard and Bouie Fisher.

Trinidad–Hopkins has the potential to measure up to Hagler–Hearns. 'This fight is my future,' Hopkins said recently. 'It's the last fight before they open the vault for me and let me pick out anything I want. After I beat Trinidad, just give me everything he has. The big money, the covers on magazines, pound for pound. Everything Trinidad has, I want it.'

But he has to beat Trinidad first.

'I'm the champion,' Hopkins told the media when the championship series was first announced. 'Holmes and Joppy are only beltholders.'

That might have been true. But like Hopkins, Felix Trinidad is a legitimate champion. Like Hopkins, he has a strong sense of pride and enjoys testing his opponent's will. He too believes in himself and is a true warrior. Indeed, Hopkins himself recently acknowledged, 'Trinidad's greatest asset is his heart and willingness to get up and his determination not to lose.'

If there's a lingering question about Trinidad, it's that he hasn't beaten a great fighter in his prime. Pernell Whitaker was over the hill; David Reid and Fernando Vargas seem to have been overrated; and the scoring of the judges in Trinidad versus De La Hoya was questionable. But if De La Hoya gave Trinidad a boxing lesson, it's a lesson that he learned well. Not only is Felix better at 160 pounds than he was at 147; he's better pound for pound at 160 than he was at 147. It wasn't just that he beat William Joppy; it's the way he beat him that was so impressive. With every fight, Trinidad looks more and more like the real thing and the greatest in a line of champions from Puerto Rico that includes Jose Torres, Wilfred Benitez and Wilfredo Gomez. He's also the first Puerto Rican with a legitimate claim to boxing's pound-for-pound title.

Handicapping Trinidad–Hopkins, one has to acknowledge that Trinidad is now a full-blown middleweight. Indeed, he walks around between fights at a weight ten to fifteen pounds heavier than Hopkins.

Speed? Felix went up to 160 pounds with no apparent loss here. There's a school of thought that he might simply be too fast for Hopkins.

Power? Trinidad appears to have brought his power with him. And unlike Felix, Hopkins doesn't have one-punch knockout power.

So how does Bernard Hopkins beat Felix Trinidad? Oscar De La Hoya showed what a skilled boxer with enough power to keep Felix honest can do against him. To beat Trinidad, Hopkins will have to give him angles, not stay in front of him, punch, grab, maul, pick his spots, tie him up, take things step by small step, and otherwise disrupt Trinidad's offensive flow. In other words, to win, Hopkins will have to win ugly. Or as he says, 'There's a difference between being a rough tough fighter who's using all his skills and a fighter that's being dirty. I plan to fight Trinidad rough and tough. There's punishment that's going to be laid out on me, and I'm going to lay out punishment on him.' But then, almost in the same breath, Hopkins adds, 'You know, you can say I'll fight this way or I'll fight that way. But once that leather starts getting thrown, no one knows what will happen.'

And last, there's the age factor. 'What is age?' Hopkins asks rhetorically. 'You judge a guy by his performance; not his age. I'm 36; Arturo Gatti is 28. From a fighting point of view, who's older?'

But the fact remains that Hopkins is 36 and Trinidad is 28. So yes; Bernard is in the best shape that a 36-year-old can be in. And yes; he's fuelled by a powerful rage backed by a will of iron. But has his opportunity for superstardom come too late?

There are occasions when an ageing fighter has a great and inspired night. Bernard Hopkins hopes that 15 September will be one of them.

'I know the odds,' he says in closing. 'I hear what people are saying. But I was born black in America on 15 January 1965. I was an underdog the day I was born.'

Author's Note: The Hopkins–Trinidad bout was later rescheduled for 29 September due to the 11 September terrorist attack on the World Trade Center.

When Bernard Hopkins and Felix Trinidad finally met in the ring, I watched the fight sitting next to Lou DiBella.

Hopkins–Trinidad and Lou DiBella

Shortly before eleven o'clock on the night of 29 September, Lou DiBella settled into his fifth-row seat at Madison Square Garden. DiBella was tired. Nerves and excitement had kept him from sleeping the night before. Now, the same nerves and excitement had him on edge. The Garden was jammed. Nineteen thousand spectators had gathered for the fight of the year. Bernard Hopkins versus Felix Trinidad had stirred passions beyond anything in recent memory in boxing. The bout was also a milestone in DiBella's transition from HBO to the present.

Last year, DiBella left the number-two slot at HBO Sports to form DiBella Entertainment, Inc. While his long-term goals are many, his primary business to date has been packaging bouts for a select group of fighters.

DiBella is one of the good guys in boxing. He was fair with the fighters when he was at HBO, and he's doing right by them now. He has a sense of justice, and his frustration-slash-anger is apparent when discussing the inequities of life for those less fortunate than himself.

Then there's the matter of DiBella's relationship with Bernard Hopkins. Hopkins marches to the beat of his own drummer. He has strong views, and acts upon them regardless of the consequences. 'I have self-esteem,' Bernard tells anyone who will listen. 'I am what I want to be. It's hard to beat me down.'

Hopkins is also the most verbally gifted champion since Muhammad Ali and, in some ways, even more verbally gifted than Ali. He's a walking quote-machine; extraordinarily articulate and expressive. The same can be said of DiBella, although Hopkins recently noted a significant difference between them with the observation, 'I didn't go to Harvard; I went to prison.'

Sitting in his seat at Madison Square Garden, DiBella reflected on the moment at hand and acknowledged, 'Tonight is far beyond anything I've done before. It's important to my company financially, but it's hugely important to me personally because Bernard will always be hugely important to me. I cherish the relationship I have with Bernard. The first guy to come to me after I left HBO and say "I'm with you" was Bernard. Most people have no idea what a good person Bernard is, and this is the most important night of Bernard's life.

'I think Bernard will win this fight,' DiBella continued. 'He believes with everything that's in him that he's going to win, and his confidence has me confident. But Bernard said something the other day. He told me, "Lou, I know there's nothing certain in a fight, but I have the opportunity and that satisfies me." If they steal this fight, if Bernard wins and they take it away from him, Bernard will be the angriest man on Earth.' DiBella's voice trailed off, then picked up again. 'And I'll be the second angriest.'

The night was the culmination of a mad-cap, often horrifying month for everyone involved. Hopkins had been incredibly focused and intense, walking around like a man with nitroglycerine in his veins. He looked like an empty frying pan that had been put on a stove over a high flame. It might seem harmless, but don't touch it.

There was a flag controversy that erupted after two ugly press conference incidents. To Hopkins, his impending fight was a fist fight between two men; not an ethnic war. But many saw him as 'anti-Puerto Rican'.

There was a referee controversy, spurred in part by Bernard's past conduct in fights and his declaration, 'There's no such thing as a clean fight. Fighting is always dirty.'

And there was controversy about Trinidad's personal life with the revelation that a young woman named Brenda Colon was five months pregnant with the fighter's child, to which Hopkins responded, 'I don't care about Trinidad's situation. I don't care if his cat got hit by a car. I don't care if his fish died because he didn't feed them. I don't care nothing about his personal life right now.'

The controversies dimmed following the horrifying events of September 11. In the aftermath of the nation's loss, Hopkins followed the fortunes of several firehouses and developed a particular affinity for the Ninth Battalion, located on Eighth Avenue and 48th Street, which had lost fifteen men in the World Trade Center bombing. His concern would carry over to fight night when, for the first time in eleven years, he entered the ring without two self-styled 'executioners' leading the way. Instead, two men dressed in dark suits carrying the hats of an NYC policeman and firefighter accompanied him to the fray.

'I'm sensitive to what happened,' Hopkins said three days before the fight. 'But I have no control over what happens around the world. I have a personal war to take care of, and I'm not going to link the two. Don't mix the war that's going on for America with the war that's going on for Bernard Hopkins. I separate what happened at the World Trade Center from Saturday night. For me, there's no love in the air, because I'm getting ready to put physical pain on someone. It's going to be him or me that feels the pain, and I want it to be him. I'm not in a mourning stage right now.'

As for the fight itself, the inclination of most observers going in was to give the physical edge to Trinidad. Hopkins took issue with that view, proclaiming, 'This is the first time Trinidad has been in the ring with a man who's bigger than he is. I'm too much man for Trinidad. Styles make fights, and easy fights come with styles that are made for other fighters. This fight will be easy for me.'

Hopkins also noted, 'Trinidad only knows one way to fight. He hasn't had to go to a Plan B in his entire career.'

Still, Trinidad was seen as younger, stronger and faster than Hopkins, whose body had seemed increasingly fragile in recent bouts. If Bernard had an edge, it was believed to be in the area of will, where his was perceived as made of iron. 'I beat up guys who have heart,' he said days before the fight. 'I never think about a way out. I'm always looking for a way to win.'

The fight was a reality check for both men. Hopkins was ready, but Trinidad was ready too. No one had ever broken Bernard's spirit, but no one had broken Tito's spirit either. It would be champion against champion; the best fighting the best. To many, the determining factor seemed to be, 'Would the difference in physical talent between the two men outweigh the difference in will between them?'

In the end, as is always the case in boxing, actions spoke louder than words. Hopkins has always wanted the spotlight. Now he had it. And in the brightest glare possible, he imposed both his will and skill on Trinidad, fighting a brilliant, magnificent, disciplined fight.

For a long time, Bernard has been known for 'winning ugly'. Nothing in his career foreshadowed a performance as artistically beautiful as this.

Rounds one through six were a tactical fight. Both men fought cautiously and respectfully of one another, with Hopkins employing lateral movement and fighting Trinidad the way Oscar De La Hoya fought him two years ago. Meanwhile, Trinidad moved inexorably forward, and one had the impression that Tito wanted to fight while Bernard wanted to box. Then, in rounds six through nine, the exchanges grew more heated. And in round ten, Hopkins began to beat Trinidad up.

The final rounds were supposed to belong to Trinidad, but Hopkins dominated. He staggered Felix at the bell ending round ten; brutalised him in round eleven; and put him down with a chopping right hand to the jaw a minute into round twelve.

Trinidad rose at the count of nine on unsteady legs. 'Given the magnitude of the fight,' referee Steve Smoger said later, 'I was going to make a careful assessment. It's possible I would have let him continue.'

That would have made for an interesting situation, since Hopkins was already lying on his back in ring centre in euphoric celebration, and one of his cornermen was entering the ring to congratulate him. Fortunately, Papa Trinidad was also entering the ring to embrace his son and stop the fight.

There are no easy roads to greatness in boxing. Great fights make fighters great. And in boxing, more than any other sport, the way in which a man wins is factored into the equation. Winning alone is not enough.

Bernard Hopkins has now earned the right to be called 'great'. As he said before the bout, 'This is my opportunity to show my greatness. This is the fight where I settle a lot of things that people have said about me. This is the fight that sets me apart.'

For a long time, what Hopkins heard was, 'Yes, Bernard; you're the best, but the middleweight division isn't what it used to be.'

That might have been true. But Hopkins has now thoroughly dominated Felix Trinidad; a great fighter in his own right. And more significantly, he has tied Carlos Monzon's record of fourteen consecutive middleweight title defences. In that regard, a look at opponents is instructive.

The best fighters Monzon fought during his reign were Nino Benvenuti (twice), Emile Griffith (twice) and Jose Napoles. But Benvenuti was on the downside of his career when the two men met and won only five of his last eleven fights. Griffith won only fifteen of his last thirty fights, starting with his first loss to Monzon. And Napoles was a 34-year-old welterweight who weighed in against Monzon at 153 pounds. Hopkins would have been competitive against Monzon. And Hopkins versus Marvin Hagler is a fantasy fight of the highest order.

I'm not sure a fighter can go where Hopkins has gone these past few months more than once in a lifetime. Bernard spent the weeks leading up to the fight trying to transform himself into a force of nature, imperious to blows and pain. That sort of mindset is hard to achieve and will be harder to duplicate in the future. But for now, all of that is irrelevant. The important thing for the moment is that, on 29 September 2001, Bernard Hopkins gave us all something special to savour. It was a performance for the ages.

The best fighting the best often makes for a great fight.

Mosley–Forrest:
A Good Fight Becomes a Great One

When Shane Mosley versus Vernon Forrest first appeared on boxing's radar screen several years ago, the assumption was that, when it happened, it would be a blockbuster fight. Things didn't turn out that way. Mosley–Forrest never became a megafight, but it was a great one.

The two men entered the ring at Madison Square Garden on 26 January as the best welterweights in boxing; undefeated champions in their prime; one of them arguably pound for pound the best fighter in the world. That was Mosley, who held the WBC crown. Actually, technically speaking, Forrest was no longer a 'champion'. The IBF stripped him of his belt for not making a mandatory defence against Michele Piccirillo of Italy. But once Forrest decided he wanted to fight Mosley, giving up the IBF title was a no-brainer. If he lost to Mosley, he'd lose the IBF title anyway. And if he won, he'd be the WBC welterweight champion and a boxing superstar.

Meanwhile, 'no brains' was the more appropriate nomenclature for everyone who contributed to the IBF stripping Forrest. That included Forrest's management team, which didn't ask the IBF for an extension of his mandatory defence so he could engage in a title unification bout until it was too late; and also the IBF, which will wind up with the winner of Piccirillo versus Corey Spinks as its 147-pound champion. But as Joe Dwyer (Chairman of the IBF Championship Committee) noted several weeks ago, 'At least you know we acted on principle, because we would have gotten a much bigger sanctioning fee for Mosley–Forrest.'

Regardless, even before he was stripped of his title, Forrest was cast in the role of challenger against Mosley and a six to one underdog. That irked him.

'I'm no second fiddle for Shane,' Forrest said before the fight. 'There's three belts. He has one and I have one, and his is no bigger

than mine. He knows I'm coming for him, and I know he's coming
for me. I was better than he was last time, and I'll be better on
January 26th too.'

'Last time' was a reference to the one previous time that the two
men met in the ring. Forrest defeated Mosley in the 139-pound division
at the 1992 Olympic trials, and much of the pre-fight build-up focused
on that bout. Vernon Forrest, the story line went, was the last man to
beat Shane Mosley.

'He came out doing what he still does, trying to be aggressive,'
Forrest said of that bout. 'But I outboxed him and took him to school.
It was Boxing 101. We're both older, smarter and more experienced
now. This fight isn't about what happened ten years ago. This fight is
about who's the best welterweight in the world today. Shane has gotten
a lot better, but it's not like I've been sitting in a time capsule. I've
gotten better too. Both of us are punching harder now. That comes with
maturity. But I'm bigger than Shane and I'm stronger than Shane. This
fight will be like Hopkins–Trinidad.'

Meanwhile, Mosley had his own recollections of their 1992
encounter. 'It was a close fight, but it was an amateur fight,' he said.
'And it was ten years ago. When they raised his hand, I lost. That was
it. After that, I put all that behind me. We were boys then, and we're
men now.'

Mosley also noted that, having lost to Forrest at the 1992 Olympic
trials, he became Forrest's sparring partner as the latter prepared for
Barcelona. 'We sparred about three times,' Mosley remembered. 'And I
really lit into him in those sessions. I was steadily tattooing him with
right hands and jabs. I just picked up on his style. When I sparred with
him, I learned him; so he's going to be very easy for me to take care of.

'This is a fight I've wanted for a long time,' Mosley continued.
'This man is the reason why I fight as hard as I do every fight. I'm
already the best. Now I want to redeem myself. I don't have any grudge
or gripe with Vernon. I just want to go ahead and take care of business.
I'm going to do a lot of damage. I don't want to just beat Vernon
Forrest. I want to knock him out. I'm going to show him how much
I've learned and how great a fighter I really am. Power, speed, agility.
I'm going to put everything into one fight and that's for Vernon Forrest.

I'm so sharp and I've trained so hard. I've prepared to the utmost. I can't see him standing in the ring with me for six rounds. What I possess now is too much for Vernon, and he doesn't realise that yet. I don't think it's going to be too pretty for him.'

So that was the setting. And 26 January was a memorable night. The Theater at Madison Square Garden was sold out. The place was alive. Arturo Gatti and Terron Millet set the stage for the main event with a slugfest that looked like a fantasy movie and ended with Gatti reviving his career via a brutal fourth-round knockout.

Then it was time for Mosley–Forrest. And all of a sudden, as Forrest had pledged, Bernard Hopkins versus Felix Trinidad seemed to be echoing through the Garden. For the second time in as many MSG fight cards, a fighter with a legitimate claim to the 'pound for pound' crown went down.

Mosley started strong in round one, throwing lead right hands and going upstairs with a pretty good left hook. But two minutes into the fight, Forrest began to establish his jab. Mosley won the round. Clearly though, his hands were full.

In round two, they got fuller. Twenty seconds into the round, the two men clashed heads. Initially, Forrest seemed more stunned by the collision, but Mosley suffered a cut on the hairline above his left eye. The cut wasn't in a bad place, but it seemed to throw Shane off a bit. Then, with 1.20 left in the round, a huge overhand right staggered Mosley and backed him against the ropes, where a six-punch barrage punctuated by a hook to the body, a right uppercut, and an overhand right, all of which landed flush, put him down. Mosley was up at the count of four but badly hurt with 1.04 left in the round. At that point, Forrest was all over him. And suddenly the Garden was consumed by the kind of chaos that reigns when a seemingly invincible fighter is reeling and on the verge of defeat. Mosley survived, but barely, as Forrest administered a fierce beating and a second knockdown just before the bell.

Thereafter, the drama never ceased. In round three, Mosley moved away from his foe, buying time to collect himself. In four and five, his strength returned. But each time he seemed to be getting back into the fight, Forrest took things up a notch and fired back harder. Still, Mosley persevered, showing enormous heart and courage. And by round seven, miraculously, he was back in the fight. Yes, he was way behind on points. But Vernon was tiring and holding whenever Shane got in close. Mosley won rounds seven, eight and nine. If he ran the table, anything was possible.

Midway through round ten, the possibilities changed. At 1.30 of the round, Forrest landed a hellacious hook to the body, and an involuntary scream escaped Mosley's lips. After the fight, Shane would acknowledge, 'The left hook to the body got me. I said to myself, "Wow; that really hurt!" But my will and my pride wouldn't let me go down. I said to myself, "He'll have to hit me again on the jaw to put me down."'

Forrest did just that, following with a vicious right uppercut and an overhand right that sent Mosley's mouthpiece flying. The next thirty seconds might have been the worst half-minute of Shane Mosley's life, but he wouldn't succumb. Finally, there was a break in the action and referee Steve Smoger called time to put Mosley's mouthpiece back in. But for all practical purposes, the fight was over.

In rounds eleven and twelve, Mosley survived on courage. Great fighters don't crumble; and he didn't, but he lost. The scoring of the judges was anti-climactic: 115–110, 117–108 and 118–108. This observer had it 116–109.

One can look at the fight in one of two ways. The first is that a very good fighter had a great night, while a great fighter had a less-than-good one. The other possibility is that, when a great fighter meets a very good one, it can turn out that the very good fighter is great.

Either way, Forrest earned a lot of respect. He did things in the ring better than he'd ever done them before. He shut Mosley down, limiting him to single-digit connections in nine of twelve rounds. And he hit Mosley with more solid blows than Shane had experienced in all of his previous outings combined. Forrest hadn't been regarded as a particularly hard puncher in the pros. But against a pretty big puncher, he consistently landed the harder blows.

Afterwards, Mosley said he wanted a rematch. Forrest promised he'd give him one.

'It was basic boxing,' Forrest said at night's end. 'I beat him before because I was a better fighter, and I beat him tonight because I'm a better fighter. Everybody was talking about his speed, but I've got speed too and power to go with it.'

Mosley's take on things was a bit different. 'I fought it all wrong,' he posited. 'I should have done more boxing instead of attacking. And Vernon fought a perfect fight; he beat me. But my heart goes deep. I always said, if I lost a fight, I'd leave it all in the ring and put myself out one hundred per cent. That's what I did tonight, and that's what I'll do if we fight again. My goal is still to beat Vernon Forrest.'

Meanwhile, Vernon Forrest is still the last man to have beaten Shane Mosley.

Round 4

Issues and Curiosities

Hello, Joe: A Letter to Joe Louis

Hello, Joe. 26 October 2001 is coming up. That's the fiftieth anniversary of the last fight of your career; the one against Rocky Marciano. I remember what you said after you fought Jersey Joe Walcott in 1947: 'I saw openings I couldn't use. A man gets old, he don't take advantage of those things as fast as he used to.' This from a man whose fists were once weapons that seemed to fire automatically.

When you fought Marciano, you were older. There's a photograph of you, knocked through the ropes, lying on the ring apron with your bald spot showing. KO by, eight. From then on, things weren't good for you. Americans have a gift for creating heroes, but we tend to discard them once they're used up. Anyway, I thought I'd drop you a line and bring you up to date on what's happening here.

I was too young to see you fight. I've only watched films and read about you. I know that you were born in 1914 in a sharecropper's shack in Alabama. Your family moved north to Detroit, and you had your first pro fight in Chicago against Jack Kracken on 4 July 1934. KO one. Three years later, you were the first black man since Jack Johnson to challenge for the heavyweight championship. KO eight over James Braddock. Afterwards, Braddock said your jab felt like someone jammed an electric light bulb in his face and busted it. He was courageous. After the umpteenth knockdown, when one of his cornermen said he was going to stop it, Braddock told him, 'If you do, I'll never speak to you again.' So they let you finish the job, and Braddock said of those final punches, 'I couldn't have got up if they'd offered me a million dollars.'

That night launched your twelve-year reign as heavyweight champion of the world. I'm told that fighting you when you were in your prime was like staying in the casino too long. Eventually, anyone foolish enough to try was going to lose. Johnny Paycheck said it best: 'God, how the man can punch!' And along the way, you became the first black man to be viewed as a hero by Americans of all colours. Your fight against Max Schmeling in 1938 was deemed the clearest confrontation between good and evil in the history of sports. It was the first time that many people heard a black man referred to simply as 'the American'. On that night, you were the greatest fighter who ever lived. KO one.

When World War II broke out, Franklin Roosevelt felt your biceps and proclaimed, 'We need muscles like yours to beat Germany.' You had your own say at a 1942 armed forces benefit at Madison Square Garden. 'We'll win,' you told the overflow crowd, 'because we're on God's side.' Later, Jimmy Cannon wrote, 'Joe Louis is a credit to his race; the human race.'

Anyway, here we are in 2001 and a lot of things about boxing have changed. The top fighters today are virtually all black and Hispanic. And you can't duck them. I mention that only because, in your first 54 bouts, the only black men you fought were Wille Davies and John Henry Lewis. Then, at the end, there were Jersey Joe Walcott, Ezzard Charles and Jimmy Bivens.

When you fought, there was one heavyweight champion of the world. Now, at any given time, there can be up to four claimants. In fact, five years ago, boxing suffered the indignity of dividing its greatest prize among Frank Bruno, Bruce Seldon and Frans Botha. The world sanctioning bodies that control the sport today are as bad as the mob ever was.

Overall, the heavyweights aren't as good as they used to be. That's because a lot of guys who would have been heavyweights in your day are going to college now on football and basketball scholarships. And heavyweight champions today seldom get off the canvas to win. When guys like Mike Tyson and Lennox Lewis go down, they lose.

Championship fights are twelve rounds now instead of fifteen, which could have meant trouble for you the first time around against Billy Conn.

The fighters are bigger now than they used to be. These days, 210 pounds is a 'small' heavyweight. Fighters in the other weight classes are larger too. For example, welterweights in championship bouts usually enter the ring somewhere between 154 and 160 pounds because they're allowed to weigh in thirty hours before they fight.

You defended your title seven times at Yankee Stadium and twice at the Polo Grounds. The Polo Grounds was torn down in the 1960s, and the last fight at Yankee Stadium was a quarter-century ago. Live ticket sales are now a secondary consideration for promoters. The big money comes from site fees and cable television.

The print media is of secondary importance as far as publicising fights is concerned. TV exposure is considered far more valuable, and a new communications outlet called the internet is gaining ground.

Superstar fighters make more money today than you would have dreamed possible. A featherweight named Naseem Hamed was paid more for one fight earlier this year than you earned in your entire career.

Incidentally, speaking of Hamed, his ring entrances are bizarre. 'Ring entrance' is a term you might not be familar with. In your day, fighters simply walked to the ring before a fight. Suffice it to say, I was watching television not long ago and one of the fighters delayed his entrance because the CD player that was supposed to play his ring-walk music malfunctioned. Some other time, I'll explain CD players to you.

These days, ring canvases are blue, and fighters generally wear red gloves. But sometimes the gloves are green, black, white or yellow. This past July, a pugilist named Hector Camacho Jr opted for pink.

At the big fights, you see almost as many women as men in the expensive seats. And this will throw you for a loop, Joe. Nowadays, they've got women fighters. Most of them aren't very good, but a few are for real.

Some things, though, haven't changed. There's still the thrill of a great fight. And the glory. We have a fighter in 2001 named 'Sugar' Shane, who looks a lot like the original Sugar Ray. Fights like him too.

You had a bum-of-the-month club. There's another extra-ordinarily talented fighter named Roy Jones Jr, who fights a bum every six months.

There's a fighter named Mike Tyson, who never fulfilled his promise as a boxer but he's still awfully good. All fighters, in a manner of speaking, come to hurt their opponents. But some are more fervent about it than others, and Mike seems to derive more pleasure from that aspect of the game than his brethren.

Fighters still lose their money. A lot of them end up in debt to the government for back taxes.

And the great ones still never quit when they're on top. Virtually all of them fight too long. A fellow named George Foreman came back at an advanced age and made it work to his advantage. But not many champions get out in time on their own terms.

Quite a few fighters have drug problems. Like you, some have been hospitalised for psychiatric difficulties.

And then there's Muhammad Ali.

Ali has slowed down some. I remember how you spent your last four years wheelchair-bound after a heart attack and stroke. You had trouble speaking at the end. Ali now has difficulty with words too. The young Ali threw punches faster than most people could think them. But the hands that once flicked out jabs in four-hundredths of a second tremble a lot these days. I know there were harsh words between you and Ali way back when. But Muhammad now has more appreciation for what you went through than he did when he was young. We all get wiser as we get older.

Most fans love roundcard girls. A few aficionados think they're out of place. But like them or not, the women who carry placards around the ring between rounds have become a fixture in boxing.

Roundcard Girls

In recent years, the business of boxing has been bisected, dissected and commented upon at length. Savvy fans know all about Don King's monopoly power and fighters' multimillion-dollar purses. They're familiar with Mike Tyson's troubles and the role television plays in determining who, when, and where champions fight. However, one aspect of the sport has been left unstudied – roundcard girls.

Roundcard girls weren't always with us. They first came out of the Nevada desert in the late 1950s, when Las Vegas casinos began promoting fights. And while the country as a whole has moved toward feminism, boxing has gone in the opposite direction. Today, roundcard girls are a fixture in fight clubs across the nation. Las Vegas and Atlantic City are reputed to have the prettiest because they draw on casino showroom talent. But beautiful flowers bloom everywhere.

'People don't come to the fights to see the roundcard girls,' says Steve Griffith, Director of Marketing and Public Relations for Madison Square Garden Boxing. 'But there's no doubt that fans have a better time because the girls are there, and good times translate into ticket sales.'

Thus, when the Michael Spinks versus Gerry Cooney promotion was going badly, promoter Butch Lewis sought to boost the event by offering Fawn Hall and Donna Rice $25,000 apiece to serve as roundcard girls. Neither accepted, but Lewis got what he wanted: lots of free press. Smalltown promoters frequently hype fights by holding roundcard girl contests several days before a bout, with local media representatives acting as judges. Back in the 1970s, a Harlem nightclub-turned-fight-club used topless roundcard girls to attract customers until the New York State Athletic Commission intervened.

What are the qualifications for being a roundcard girl?
Looks.
Looks.
Looks.
And rapport with the crowd.
Using these assets, their functions are threefold:

1. Entertain the audience, particularly during slow-moving preliminary fights when fans tend to get restless. This function, of course,
   is limited to male members of the crowd, although Graciella
   Casillas, the California women's lightweight champion, once
   demanded unsuccessfully that her promoter use roundcard boys
   during a fight.
2. Carry advertising around the ring. Roundcard ads are as diverse as
   the family of man. Once, in Akron, Ohio, a candidate for local
   office paid a promoter one hundred dollars to put campaign bumper
   stickers on the roundcards.
3. Advise fans which round it is. This is fairly straightforward, since
   the round number is printed on each card. However, Caesar's
   Palace complicates the matter by making the girls carry cards
   inscribed with Roman numerals.

The prototype of a roundcard girl is Pamela Sue Medeiros, who
plies her trade regularly at Madison Square Garden. 'The lovely
Pamela Sue' (as ring announcer Ed Derrien calls her) is 24 years old,
tall, blonde and beautiful. A native of Cranston, Rhode Island,
Pamela Sue came to New York six years ago to pursue a modelling
career, and has appeared in such publications as *Glamour* and
Harper's Bazaar. However, most of her printwork has been for
lingerie and swimwear catalogues.

'Being a roundcard girl is something I always wanted to do,' says
Pamela Sue. 'I don't know why. It just always seemed like fun. Two
years ago, the Vanderveer Agency called and said, "Pam, don't get
insulted, but we have this offer for you." I jumped at the chance.'

As far as Pamela Sue is concerned, the Garden job is ideal. Her
costume consists of a black leotard and white tuxedo jacket; not the
more revealing lowcut dresses required by casinos. The pay is good;

one hundred dollars a night. The Garden is a class operation, and she gets a good seat for the fights. 'I have a boyfriend,' she acknowledges, 'but when I'm in the ring, he's not jealous. He figures he has what everybody else wants, so let the guys in the crowd be jealous of him.'

Pamela Sue's evening begins at 6.30, when she appears in the Madison Square Garden lobby to hand out programmes. Then, once the fights start, she and another roundcard girl ('the beautiful Sahara') work their magic. Broken down in sequence, it unfolds as follows:

1. With ten seconds left in every round, the timekeeper raps his microphone four times to warn the referee that the round is about to end. This is Pamela Sue's wake-up call.
2. The bell rings, and she walks up the ring stairs.
3. A young man designated as the 'rope-splitter' parts the strands, and Pamela Sue steps into the ring.
4. Once she's in the ring, the rope-splitter hands her a roundcard.
5. Pamela Sue examines the card to make sure it's not upside down, raises it above her head, and moves counterclockwise around the ring. 'I don't count the seconds,' she reports. 'I just make a complete circle, wave to the crowd, and leave.'
6. The rope-splitter parts the strands, helping Pamela Sue out of the ring and down the stairs.

Pamela Sue's closest brush with celebrity status came when Iran Barkley and Michael Olijade did battle at Madison Square Garden. A show called *Muppet Babies* was playing the Garden at the same time, and someone at NBC, which was televising the fight, got the bright idea that Miss Piggy should do a stint as a roundcard girl. Thus, by prearrangement, after the second round, Pamela Sue stepped into the ring followed by Miss Piggy, who knocked Pamela Sue on the head, grabbed the roundcard, and strutted around. However, Barkley had knocked Olijade down during the previous round, and NBC kept its cameras focused on the fighters' corners, not on the charade in mid-ring. Also, coming as it did at a particularly tense moment, the comedy was out of place.

Indeed, some purists feel that way about all roundcard girls. 'I hate them,' says Mickey Duff, one of Great Britain's premier managers and promoters. 'Two men are fighting their hearts out, and there's no reason for some woman to be wandering around wiggling her bloomin' arse. It's an affront to the fighters and an insult to boxing.'

Still, the practice goes on, and roundcard girls have spawned some of boxing's finest legends.

Don Elbaum began promoting fights in 1958, and has made the rounds of hundreds of arenas, including a five-year stint as promoter-matchmaker for the Tropicana in Atlantic City. Roundcard girls at the Tropicana are cocktail waitresses employed by the hotel and paid fifty dollars a night. But some of Elbaum's roundcard girls in other locales have practised different professions.

'I used to promote fights in Steubensville, Ohio,' Elbaum remembers. 'It was a wild town with some of the best-run whorehouses in the country, and the guys who ran them would give me professional hookers to use as roundcard girls for free. From my point of view, it was great. I didn't have to pay the girls, and I sold extra tickets to boot because the people who ran the whorehouses bought seats for their customers in order to display their wares.'

Another time, Elbaum recalls, a roundcard girl saved one of his fighters from defeat. 'I had a light-heavyweight named Tom Girardi; a prospect, a good kid. Another fighter pulled out, and Tom took the fight on short notice against some guy whose record was two-and-six. I figured it was safe, but Tom had gone to bed with his girlfriend the night before, not realising he was going to fight, and he got tired. It was a six-rounder, and after round three, Tom came back to the corner and said he didn't think he could go six. Anyway, the referee had been staring at the roundcard girl all night; she was a doll. After round four, I handed the girl a card that said "6" instead of "5". Then I started shouting, "Last round, Tommy; you can do it." Well, of course, the referee is staring at the girl. He thinks it's round six, makes the fighters touch gloves, and says the fight is over after what's really only round five. I cut the gloves off real quick, and Tom, who was completely out of gas, won a split decision.'

Asked for more, Elbaum goes on. 'In Uniontown, Pennsylvania, I had two roundcard girls working a show in a high school gym. Somehow, during the night, they discovered they were going out with the same guy. I gotta tell you, those two girls put on the best fight of the night; a real knockdown, drag-out, hair-pulling battle. If I'd known in advance, I would have billed it as a co-feature. Another time, in McKeevesport, Pennsylvania, I promoted a kid named Jack Rogers; a good fighter and as handsome as a kid could be. During the middle of the fight, the roundcard girl sashayed by. Jack pushed his cornerman aside, and said to the girl, "I'd like to see you after the fight." She nodded. And you better believe, after the fight she was there.'

Those who consider Elbaum a sexist will be pleased to know he got his comeuppance at Brooklyn's Rollerama Arena in 1977. 'Don and I were sitting together that night,' recalls fellow matchmaker Johnny Bos, 'and the roundcard girl was particularly flirtatious. She winked; she wiggled. Halfway through the show, Don turned to me and said, "That's a hell of a broad; I wonder who's taking her home tonight." Then, during the last fight, the girl reached up and pulled off her wig. It was a guy!'

So, there you have it. Roundcard girls sell tickets, carry advertising, entertain the crowd, and, on occasion, even determine the outcome of fights.

And you thought they were just another pretty face.

Given his conduct in and out of the ring, Mike Tyson is fertile soil for the imagination and for satire.

Tyson–Golota: The Whole Story

It's over now; the biggest-grossing fight in boxing history. Finding a site for the bout was more difficult than first imagined. The Nevada State Athletic Commission refused to grant Tyson a licence, and there were similar problems with the Michigan Department of Consumer and Industry Services. The British Home Secretary announced that Iron Mike was no longer welcome in England; and the Polish Ministry of Sports said 'nyet' to the contest. There was momentary hope when the New York State Athletic Commission agreed to the bout on the condition that the fighters donate five per cent of their respective purses to the New York State Republican Party, but then Madison Square Garden declined to bid on the venture. Finally, Tyson–Golota landed in Atlantic City under the sponsorship of Donald Trump.

Now let us revisit the highlights of Mike Tyson versus Andrew Golota.

12 September 2000: At a kick-off press conference, America Presents announces that it will promote the bout. At the same time, Tyson–Golota is formally titled in accordance with the results of internet voting. 'The balloting was quite close,' Dan Goossen tells the assembled media. '"Anything Goes", "Disgusting", "Protect Yourself At All Times", "Gory Glory", and "Yuk!" all received considerable support. But the top vote-getter was "Psycho".' At the close of the press conference, Tyson throws Donald Trump through a plate-glass window.

19 September 2000: A fight-promotion poster shows a grinning New Jersey Governor Christie Todd Whitman frisking Mike Tyson for drugs while two New Jersey state troopers look on. Meanwhile, Showtime reports that pay-per-view orders are running ahead of any fight ever.

2 October 2000: Tyson visits a children's petting zoo in New Jersey and bites the head off a baby duck. 'Mike has been under a lot of pressure lately,' explains his advisor Shelly Finkel. Meanwhile, Larry Hazzard (Chairman of the New Jersey Board of Athletic Control) tells reporters, 'There's nothing to worry about. Both fighters will be muzzled during the fight.'

6 October 2000: Showtime announces that Howard Stern will team with Steve Albert and Bobby Czyz as a guest commentator for the bout.

9 October 2000: Tyson stops taking his Zoloft in preparation for the fight. Later in the day, witnesses report that Iron Mike has driven his motorcycle down the middle of the Boardwalk in Atlantic City, run over seventeen tourists, and snatched the purse of an 85-year-old woman who had just won 37 dollars at the slot machines. Shelly Finkel tells reporters, 'Mike is upset because he feels that the media focuses on the negative aspects of his life and overlooks the positive.' Challenged to name one positive aspect of Tyson's life, Finkel responds, 'Mike has done so many positive things, I can't begin to name all of them.'

13 October 2000: Showtime announces that two exotic dancers named Busty Dusty and Wendy Whoppers have been recruited as roundcard girls for the fight.

16 October 2000: At the final pre-fight press conference, Tyson tells Golota, 'I'm going to push your nose bone into your brain, punch your testicles into your stomach, rip out your kidneys, cut open your chest, masturbate on your heart, and eat your children. Then my pigeons will peck out your eyeballs.' Shortly thereafter, Shelly Finkel explains to reporters, 'Mike was upset because last night he was watching television and saw a documentary about a poor baby seal that was clubbed to death for its fur in Alaska.'

17 October 2000: Shaken by Tyson's savagery, Andrew Golota falls into a deep depression and starts taking Zoloft. Meanwhile, Larry Hazzard announces that, in addition to the regular ringside physicians, the State of New Jersey will provide a psychiatrist for each corner.

18 October 2000: Tyson is photographed with George W Bush and his mother, Barbara, who are campaigning in New Jersey. Later in the day, Barbara Bush files sexual molestation charges against Tyson, claiming that Iron Mike fondled her breasts and whispered, 'I want to suck your pussy.' Shelly Finkel tells reporters, 'Mike is very upset by these unfounded allegations, which he feels are nothing but an attempt to set him up for a civil lawsuit. If Barbara Bush wants to get rich, she should buy a lottery ticket.'

19 October 2000: Larry Hazzard acknowledges that he's having difficulty finding a referee for the fight, and assures prospective candidates, 'There will be no danger to the referee. Security personnel armed with stun-guns will be stationed in each corner in case either fighter gets out of control during the bout.'

20 October 2000: Mike Tyson versus Andrew Golota lives up to its billing. Neither fighter can bite because of the muzzles, but the bout is replete with head-butts, low blows, punches after the bell, arm-twisting, and knees to the groin. Midway through round five, Tyson leaves the ring and charges into the press section to slug a reporter he doesn't like. After a quick conference with Larry Hazzard, the referee orders that two points be deducted from Iron Mike's score. Hazzard will later explain, 'There was no disqualification because Mike got back into the ring within the time allotted under New Jersey rules for a fighter who has been knocked from the ring.' At the end of round nine, Tyson is bleeding badly from both eyes, his nose is broken, and he's helpless against the ropes. At this point, Golota tells the referee, 'I think I quit now.' At the post-fight press conference, Tyson tells the assembled media, 'I'm the baddest man on the planet. Tell Lennox Lewis that I'm going to eat his children, beat up his mother, and split his head open like a baby seal.'

Gentleman Mike Tyson

Mike Tyson's advisor, Shelly Finkel, has just received a comprehensive report from a public relations agency hired to rehabilitate Iron Mike's image. I've acquired a copy of the report (which is highly confidential) and am pleased to share it with our readers:

MEMORANDUM FOR SHELLY FINKEL
FROM PR ASSOCIATES
23 OCTOBER 2000

As you know, Mike Tyson versus Lennox Lewis is starting to have an inevitable feel to it. As you are also aware, the folks at Showtime were enormously impressed by the fact that, in six minutes of ring action last Friday night, Mike threw only four elbows and head-butted Andrew Golota only twice. Steve Albert waxed eloquent for a national television audience about how Mike 'never did anything in a misconduct way', and added, 'I was impressed by his deference to the referee.' Bobby Czyz, who was so busy talking about himself that he didn't hear Golota tell Al Certo to stop the fight, was equally impressed, noting, 'Mike, to his credit, didn't respond to any of the things that annoyed him.' And, Shelly, you put it best when you told Showtime's Jim Gray, 'The thing I was most happy about was, every time the ref said "break", Mike went out of his way to break clean.'

Shelly, we have a wonderful opportunity in the aftermath of the Golota fight to reshape Mike's image for Tyson–Lewis.

The American public has a short memory. The fact that Mike has been convicted of rape, bitten off part of Evander Holyfield's ear, announced to the world that his male organ isn't functioning properly, says he wants to kill people, and last week addressed reporters as 'white boy' and 'nigger' is old news.

Meanwhile, Lennox Lewis has been outspoken in calling Mike ' an imbecile...a misfit...a disturbed person...a madman... and a moron.'

The American people don't like ugly. Let's blast Lennox for going negative. And then, let's implement the following nine-step programme:

1. Bring Barney to the introductory press conference announcing Tyson–Lewis. He can replace the guy in Mike's entourage who wears camouflage fatigues, shouts at people, and goes by the name of 'Crocodile'. Mike can lead everyone at the press conference in singing the Barney theme song ('I love you; you love me; we're a happy family'). Then he can remove his cap and show everyone a tattoo of Barney on his head. The beauty of this is, if Mike ever feels silly walking around with a Barney tattoo on his head, he can grow his hair long to cover it up.
2. It's important that Mike evince a more enlightened and respectful attitude toward women. I want you to leak a story to *USA Today*, saying Mike loves the way Joyce Carol Oates writes and has requested that she serve as a roundcard girl for Tyson–Lewis.
3. To further emphasise Mike's sensitive side, let's arrange for him to have tea with some old people and read poetry to them. I recommend 'Ode to a Nightingale' by John Keats. And, Shelly, make sure the tea-cups are china, not plastic. Some lace doilies would also be nice.
4. 'Iron Mike' has a forbidding ring to it. Midway through the promotion, let's announce that Mike has decided to change his nickname to 'Happy Mike'.
5. See if you can track down one of the old ladies that Mike mugged when he was twelve years old and arrange for a touching photo-op reunion.
6. While we're on the subject of reunions; let's do our best to effectuate a reconciliation between Mike and Greg Garrison, who prosecuted Mike for raping Desiree Washington.

7. Ask Kellogg's if they're willing to market a Mike Tyson cereal; something along the lines of ear-shaped bites promoted by the slogan, 'If you can't beat 'em, eat 'em.' It will give Mike a jollier image and could make some money for all of us. After all, it worked for George Foreman with cheeseburgers and that 'lean mean grilling machine'.

8. Start airing a televised community service message from Mike Tyson to the youth of America. Shelly, you have a background in music, so you understand the power of song. Mike should rap the following lyrics:

> I love white people
> They're so cool
> Boys and girls,
> Stay in school.

9. On fight night, have Mike enter the ring to more soothing music than in the past. Mozart's Symphony Number 39 in E Flat Major would be a good choice.

Once the bell rings, you'll have done everything possible to help Mike reshape his image. From that point on, he'll be on his own.

This was the first article I wrote for the Showime Boxing website.

The Always-Exciting, Perpetually Scintillating, Kick-Off Boxing Press Conference

Boxing's kick-off press conferences have one purpose: to get media coverage. In many respects, they're analogous to Hollywood's annual Academy Awards show, which offers four hours of mediocrity followed by everything interesting being crammed into the final twenty minutes. Kick-off press conferences give the media ninety minutes of self-important corporate executives followed by the main-event fighters talking for two minutes each. But in boxing, instead of Whoopi Goldberg and Billy Crystal moving things along, we get Don King, Murad Muhammad and Gary Shaw.

In the old days, newspaper reporters and photographers watched dutifully at press conferences as fighters signed contracts to do battle. Then Joe Louis, Rocky Marciano, or whoever would lean over, shake hands with his opponent, and say, 'I'm looking forward to a good fight. May the best man win.'

Then Muhammad Ali arrived on the scene and turned what was basically a non-event into an occasion of considerable magnitude. Ali dubbed George Foreman 'The Mummy' and Leon Spinks 'The Vampire' at kick-off press conferences. At the start of publicity for Ali–Holmes, Ali appeared with a moustache and told the media, 'You're looking at Dark Gable.' Holmes was unimpressed and responded, 'His ass is grass, and I'm the lawnmower.'

There were times when Ali press conferences had an ugly edge. His 'what's my name' torture of Ernie Terrell had its origins in an inadvertent comment by Terrell on the day their bout was announced. And bad feelings still exist from Ali pummelling a black rubber gorilla at the kick-off for Ali–Frazier III and telling the world, 'It will be a chilla and a thrilla when I get The Gorilla in Manila.' Still, when all was said and done, Ali presided over the glory years for kick-off press conferences. Or as longtime boxing scribe Ed Schuyler notes, 'They should have gotten rid of them when Ali retired.'

The main problem with contemporary kick-off press conferences is that, although carefully scripted, they're rarely entertaining or clever. 'Maybe they're amusing the first time,' says Teddy Atlas. 'But once you've been through it two or three times, you realise it's the same old BS. First the promoter gets up and talks about how wonderful it is to work with the great athletic commission of whatever state the fight is in. Then they introduce the fight sponsors and a representative of whatever casino the fight is at. After that, you have a bunch of people who hang around the fighters. These are people who've never accomplished anything on their own in their entire life and now, all of a sudden, they have a platform so they talk forever. It's insulting to the fighters to make them sit there and listen to that garbage.'

Don King has been known to hold press conferences replete with midgets, clowns and jugglers. Last year at a Chinese restaurant in New York, King entered the room carrying a traditional incense offering to the gods while a troupe of lion dancers followed behind him, banging drums and clanging cymbals; all this to promote King's soon-to-be-cancelled heavyweight extravaganza in Beijing. The promoter, Evander Holyfield, John Ruiz and Hasim Rahman then posed for a photo op, holding what looked like makeshift fishing poles with heads of wilted lettuce attached. The high point came when Ruiz's lawyer, Tony Cardinale, told the media, 'When the dust settles, everyone will agree that John Ruiz is one of the greatest fighters who ever lived.' A lot of dust will have to settle before people agree on that one.

King's press conferences also seem endless. The over-under line on most of them is in excess of two hours. Indeed, at the kick-off press conference for Felix Trinidad versus Mamadiou Thiam, King invoked the names of 47 clergymen and politicians. Thus, the tale of a six-year-old boy who attended a Don King press conference. When the boy returned home, his mother asked, 'What did Don King talk about?' And the boy answered, 'He talked about four hours.'

'Don talks too long,' concedes Eric Gelfand (Madison Square Garden's Vice President of Public Relations for Sports Properties). 'But he always gets you your TV sound-bite.'

By contrast, Murad Muhammad's press conferences are as long as King's, but with less entertainment value. Lou DiBella once opined, 'Murad Muhammad is Don King without brains.' He might have added, without a sense of humour either.

Bob Arum is a control freak. His press conferences are orderly and to the point, but aren't particularly well thought of by members of the media since they're also notoriously short on food. 'Every now and then,' observes Michael Katz, 'Arum will splurge on a pitcher of ice water.'

New York is the favoured location for kick-off press conferences because of the media concentration in the Big Apple. Traditional sites include Madison Square Garden and the now-defunct All-Star Cafe, but venues have run the gamut from the Plaza Hotel and Waldorf-Astoria to the battleship USS *Intrepid*. Michael Blutrich used to hold kick-off press conferences at a mob-controlled adult club called Scores, and Tony Paige (then President of the Boxing Writers Association of America) regularly boycotted Blutrich's sessions. It's unknown whether Blutrich was offended by Paige's absence, and it's now impossible to ask him since Michael has vanished into the federal witness protection programme.

Memorable moments are few and far between at kick-off press conferences. Most of the gimmicks are pretty corny, such as George Foreman having a platter of hamburgers delivered to him at the kick-off for Holyfield–Foreman. Sometimes the unexpected enlivens the scene. Mike Tyson showed up at a press conference to announce a fight on HBO wearing an ABC Wide World of Sports T-shirt. On the advice of Steve Lott, he turned the shirt inside out before the festivities began. However, that was nothing compared to Iron Mike's performance at the 14 September 2000, kick-off for Tyson–Golota.

'I don't care about living or dying,' Tyson told the assembled media. 'I'm a dysfunctional motherfucker... Bring on Golota; bring on Lewis. They can keep their titles. I don't want to strip them of their titles, I want to strip them of their fucking health... I'm in pain, so I want them to be in pain. I want their kids to see pain. Fuck 'em... You don't know me; you can't define me. I'm a convicted rapist, a hell-raiser, a father, a semi-good husband. I raise hell. I know it's going to get me in trouble or killed one day, but that's just who I am. I can't help it...Listen, I'm a nigger. No, really, really, listen to me. I'm a street person. I don't even want to be a street person; I don't like typical street people. But your grandchildren will know about me. They'll be like, "Wow, wasn't that a bizarre individual?"'

Then the subject of Zoloft was raised, and Tyson responded, 'I'm on it to keep from killing you all. I don't want to be on it. I'm jacked up. My sex life is jacked up. My dick don't work.'

In January of this year, Iron Mike outdid himself when he bit Lennox Lewis on the thigh at the kick-off press conference for what was to have been, and may still become, the largest-grossing fight in boxing history. Once order was restored, Tyson moved to the front of the stage, grabbed his crotch, simulated masturbation (one hopes it was simulated), and screamed obscenities at the media.

In other words, the script isn't always followed. At the kick-off for Sugar Ray Leonard versus Marvelous Marvin Hagler, promoter Bob Arum told the media that Leonard would not answer questions regarding the detached retina he'd suffered several years earlier. Leonard himself put an exclamation point on Arum's words with the declaration, 'The eyes are no longer an issue.' Whereupon Pat Putnam of *Sports Illustrated* shouted out, 'How many fingers am I holding up?'

Lou DiBella, then of HBO, also departed from script at his employer's press conference to publicise Lennox Lewis versus Oliver McCall II. 'This fight shouldn't happen,' DiBella told the media. 'McCall is unstable. He's on drugs. He's been throwing Christmas trees around hotel lobbies.' And of course, McCall suffered a breakdown in the ring against Lewis in one of boxing's more embarrassing moments.

Lennox Lewis and Roy Jones Jr are virtually always late for press conferences. Hector Camacho once went to the wrong hotel by mistake, decided he was hungry, and stayed for lunch, thereby blowing off the entire event.

As of late, kick-off press conferences have become more elaborate than in the past. Madison Square Garden spent $30,000 to announce the first Holyfield–Lewis fight and the same amount for Lewis versus

Michael Grant. In each instance, there were flashing lights, smoke, mirrors, and sound effects. The kick-off for Holyfield–Lewis I was particularly interesting because Garden officials neglected to seat representatives of the WBC, WBA, and IBF at the dais, which prompted Don King to throw a tantrum of Shakespearean proportions.

In early 2001, King returned to Madison Square Garden to kick off his middleweight championship series, which was being televised by HBO. The spotlight was supposed to shine that morning on Felix Trinidad, Bernard Hopkins, Keith Holmes and William Joppy. But instead, King spent the first twenty minutes talking about John Ruiz, who had just won the WBA heavyweight championship on Showtime. Then the promoter posed Ruiz and Trinidad together for a five-minute photo op, while the HBO executives in attendance burned.

Still, when all is said and done, it's clear that boxing's kick-off press conferences are here to stay. So let's give Eric Gelfand the final word as he defends them with the explanation, 'Kick-off press conferences are an opportunity to create a feel for the fight. And it makes my day to go home and see a clip from one of our press conferences on ESPN or CNN, or pick up a newspaper the next morning and see a story with a photo of the fighters beside it. A good press conference sets the tone for the entire promotion of a fight.'

I'd planned to put this story online in conjunction with a dinner that was to be held in Eddie Futch's honour. Instead, it became his eulogy.

Mr Futch

Every once in a while, it's nice to have a 'feel good' story about boxing. Eddie Futch, who died today at age ninety, was always a feel good story. Whenever one talked with him – or better yet, listened – one heard words of wisdom. If the world lived by better standards, he would have been a king. As it is, it's a sign of the respect he was accorded within the boxing community, and particularly among fighters, that he was often addressed as 'Mr Futch'.

Great trainers have a unique talent; the ability to recognise and develop talent in others. Futch began training fighters in 1938, and worked with 22 world champions including Joe Frazier, Larry Holmes, Michael Spinks, Riddick Bowe, Ken Norton, Bob Foster and Alexis Arguello. There would have been more, but for an admirable quirk in Eddie's personality. 'I never take on a fighter I don't like,' he once said. 'If I find myself with a fighter I dislike, I get rid of him no matter how much profit there is in it. I've seen managers who subconsciously hate one of their fighters and enjoy seeing him beat. You've got to love your fighter. Otherwise, it's dangerous. You'll send him out and get him mangled or killed.'

Futch was also a disciplinarian. In the late 1930s, he was working with amateurs in Detroit. 'There was a twelve-year-old who'd come to the gym,' he remembered. 'He wasn't there to train; just hang out with his friends and make noise. One day, he made so much noise that I chased him out of the gym and told him not to come back until he was ready to behave himself. About six months later, his family moved to New York and he began fighting as an amateur.'

The story bears repeating, because the young man's name was Walker Smith Jr, later known to the world as Sugar Ray Robinson.

'Ray had it all,' Futch said with a trace of awe in his voice. 'Boxing skills, punching power, mental strength. He did things in the ring I've never seen anyone else do, before or since.'

Like many of his brethren in boxing, Futch moved into the lime-light as a result of Muhammad Ali. He was in Joe Frazier's corner for all three of Smokin' Joe's bouts against Ali, and saw something in Ali's style that could be exploited. 'It was the way Ali pulled his head back from punches,' Futch explained. 'Not in the centre of the ring, but when he was on the ropes. He would pull his head back from punches in a way that left his body exposed, so the body attack was the key. Most fighters, when they boxed Ali, when he went to the ropes they'd go immediately to the head. Ali would pull back so the punches passed in front of him. And once he made you miss, he'd come off the ropes and hurt you. So Joe was instructed, when Ali was on the ropes, to work the body with both hands. Let Ali pull his head back, because if he leaned back against the ropes, he'd expose his body to hard shots.'

In Ali–Frazier I, it worked. 'I might have cut the diamond,' Yank Durham (Frazier's first trainer and manager) said afterward, 'but Eddie polished it.'

After Durham's death, Futch became Frazier's trainer and manager. In that capacity, he's best remembered for stopping Ali–Frazier III after fourteen brutal rounds of carnage in Manila.

'Joe kept getting hit with the right hand,' Futch said later. 'His left eye was completely closed; his right eye was closing. It had been a gruelling fight, and that's when fighters get hurt; when they get hit with good clean punches they don't see. I didn't want Joe's brains scram-bled. He had a nice life and a wonderful family to live for; so I decided at the end of the fourteenth round to stop it. I just didn't think Joe should go on any more.'

Futch was also with Ken Norton for the first two Ali–Norton bouts, and devised the strategy for Ali–Norton I which led to Norton breaking Ali's jaw.

'It was the way Ali held his hands,' Futch recalled. 'Not that they were too low, but the placement of his right hand when he threw the jab. When a man throws a jab, his right hand should be by his chin to parry the jab that's coming back, but Ali didn't keep it there. He'd move it to the right. Norton had four inches more height than Frazier, so I told him to step toward Ali with his jab. Norton's right hand being in proper position, Ali's jab would be blocked by Norton's right. And Norton's jab would hit Ali in the middle of the face, because Ali's right hand would be out of position.'

It's no wonder that, when Ali reflected back on his own career, he acknowledged, 'Whenever I fought someone who was trained by Eddie Futch, I knew I was in for a hard fight.'

Futch ranked Joe Louis as the greatest heavyweight of all time, with Ali and Jack Johnson in a virtual tie for second place.

'I have great memories of Joe Louis,' Futch reminisced. 'We came out of the same amateur club in Detroit. Joe was a light-heavyweight at the time, and I was a lightweight. But we sparred together about a dozen times, because Joe liked to work with fast fighters. He never hurt me with a punch to the head, but blocking his shots let me know how devastating his power was even then. I was too small to force him back, so I had to lead him into things. And I hit him a few times. Yes, I did; I hit Joe Louis. But he was a smart fighter, getting smarter, and his hands were so fast.

'I remember, one time we were sparring,' Futch continued. 'I hit Joe. He stepped back and looked at me and asked, "How'd you do that?" I told him, "Joe, it doesn't matter how I did it. I'm too small to hurt you." And he said, "I know. But if you can hit me with it, someone bigger than you can hit me with it too."

'Maybe I'm prejudiced,' Futch said in closing, 'but I think Joe Louis would have beaten Ali. People remember how hard Joe punched. What they don't remember is what a good boxer he was. I always thought that Joe would have seen the flaws in Ali's style and been able to take advantage of them.'

With Mr Futch in Joe Louis's corner, it would have been quite a fight.

Meanwhile, looking back over the course of his career in boxing, Eddie Futch could say that he sparred with Joe Louis, was in the corner with two guys who beat Muhammad Ali, and kicked Sugar Ray Robinson out of the gym. That's quite a life.

Most boxing writers have a story to tell about seeing a fighter killed in the ring. I've seen it happen twice. This was the first time.

A Dangerous Game

When I started writing about boxing, Mike Jones told me something that always stayed with me: 'If you go to the fights often enough, eventually you'll witness a tragedy.'

Mike had been in Wilford Scypion's corner on 23 November 1979, when Scypion fought Willie Classen at Madison Square Garden. Classen was knocked out in the tenth round and died several days later. I mentioned to Mike that I'd seen Emile Griffith pummel Benny 'Kid' Paret on television in 1962 and Ray Mancini against Duk Koo Kim, again on the small screen, twenty years later.

'It's different when you're there in person,' Mike told me.

On 20 November 1999, Mike Jones's prophecy came true for me. I witnessed a tragedy. Stephan Johnson suffered injuries in a fight against Paul Vaden that led to his death two weeks later. I've said many times that television cosmetises a lot of what goes on inside a boxing ring. On 20 November, there was no filter. When Johnson collapsed to the canvas, I was sitting with Spider Bynum (a NABF official on site that night) at the edge of the ring apron. We were as close to Johnson as it was possible to be.

Stephan Johnson was a decent man, who had been fighting professionally for twelve years. Given the fact that he was under medical suspension in Canada at the time of his death, there are serious questions as to whether he should have been in the ring against Vaden. But that's an issue for another time. The point to be made here is that, even under the best of circumstances, boxing is a dangerous sport.

Ironically, boxing is also a marvellous showcase for the brain. Skilled fighting requires balance, coordination, speed, reflexes, power, instinct, discipline, memory and creative thought. These assets enable a professional fighter to deliver blows that smash an opponent's head backward and twist it violently from side to side. The human brain is a jelly-like mass suspended inside the skull in cerebrospinal fluid. A hard blow shakes the brain, sending it careening off the inside of the skull. In extreme cases, blood vessels snap and the brain begins to bleed. Since there is no room inside the skull for anything except the brain and cerebrospinal fluid, the pressure of the added blood compresses the brain, causing unconsciousness, coma, and sometimes death. Fighters understand this. They know that getting punched in the head is an integral part of their business and that sometimes bad things happen. 'People say a lot of things,' Roy Jones Jr once noted. 'But most people have no idea what it's like to be on the receiving end of what goes on in a boxing ring.'

Personally, I believe that, when boxing is properly regulated, its risks are acceptable in relation to what is gained. Yes, it's inherent in the sport that some people will take a beating and others worse. To discount this danger is to deny young men like Stephan Johnson the full measure of credit they deserve for the courage they display every time they step into a boxing ring. But it would be a disservice to the memory of Stephan Johnson to use his death as an argument against the continuation of boxing.

There was a time in our nation's history when young men enlisted in the military for glory. Now they do it as a job. Fighters, like soldiers, fight for glory and money. One can argue that war is necessary, whereas boxing is not. But the truth is, many of our nation's wars have been avoidable, with both sides fighting for economic gain or some other non-essential cause. The 'good wars' such as the Allied effort in World War II have been few and far between.

However, Stephan Johnson's death does put further into perspective the ugliness of corruption in boxing. Every time a sanctioning body takes a bribe to raise a fighter in its ratings; every time a ring judge renders a biased decision; every time a state athletic commission gives a job to an inept political appointee who doesn't know the first thing about protecting fighters; those powers that be will be desecrating the memory of Stephan Johnson, who made the ultimate sacrifice in pursuit of his dream.

By the year 2001, the New York State Athletic Commission had become a microcosm of incompetence and corruption culminating in the death of Beethavean Scottland. I'd like to think that the following article and others like it were part of a rising tide that called attention to the situation and led to the resignation of the NYSAC's chairman and several of his top operatives.

A Scandalous Tragedy

It began as a festive occasion. On the night of 26 June 2001, Duva Boxing was promoting the first professional fights ever held on the deck of the USS *Intrepid*. The 900-foot aircraft carrier went to sea in August 1943. It saw extensive action during World War II, and was involved in numerous other military missions such as the blockade of Cuba during the 1962 missile crisis and naval operations off the coast of Vietnam. The *Intrepid* also served as a prime NASA recovery vehicle for the Mercury and Gemini space capsules. It was decommissioned in 1974 and opened to the public as a museum in 1982.

The ring was set up on the flight deck surrounded by folding chairs with aluminium bleachers (tiers of aluminium seats) on two sides. Arriving fans were greeted by roundcard girls styled as World War II pin-ups. Wherever one turned, there were panoramic views. To the east, the towering skyscrapers of midtown Manhattan; to the north, the George Washington Bridge; south, New York Harbor and the World Trade Center; west, the Hudson River and New Jersey Palisades. But a boxing ring is a boxing ring wherever it is.

There was a patriotic picnic-like atmosphere. Red, white and blue ring ropes cordoned off the red, white and blue ring canvas. Everything sparkled. The sky was a perfect, almost surreal, backdrop for the fighters; aquamarine at first; after that, dark with just enough haze to resemble a black velvet curtain.

Then tragedy struck.

Beethavean Scottland entered the ring against George 'Khalid' Jones for the first of the evening's two co-featured bouts. Scottland, regardless of what he tipped the scales at, was a super-middleweight. Jones had weighed in for all but two of his last twelve fights at more than 180 pounds. It was Scottland's first fight in 329 days.

Scottland took a beating. On three occasions in three different rounds, he came back from the brink. And rather than just try to survive, he kept trying to win, but the danger signs were there.

During round five, Max Kellerman, who was commentating for a national television audience on ESPN2, cried out, 'That's enough! That's it; that's it; that's it! This is how guys get seriously hurt, as we saw with Jimmy Garcia, who wound up dying.'

NYSAC Chairman Mel Southard, NYSAC chief neurologist Dr Barry Jordan and Dr Rufus Saddler (the ring doctor assigned to Scottland's corner) sat there and watched.

In round seven, Kellerman voiced his concern again: 'You know what I don't like about the way he's getting hit. About four or five times a round, Jones lands two or three good sharp punches right in his face, snapping his head around, and those are the cumulative punches that lead to things you don't want to hear about after the fight. That's bothering me. I don't like it.'

Mel Southard (the $101,000-a-year NYSAC Chairman) looked on. What did he think was happening in front of him?

At the end of round seven, Kellerman's voice grew more urgent: 'I don't like it. I don't like it. If you're in Scottland's corner, you have to ask yourself, is it worth it, the damage he's sustaining right now? Is it worth it for the kid's life in the future, sustaining this kind of damage?'

Still, no doctor took it upon himself to visit the corner.

In round ten, Kellerman was pleading, 'I don't like what I'm seeing; how much he's getting punched in this fight; how many clear shots to the head he's taking in this fight.'

Then Scottland's condition went beyond taking a beating. His eyes wandered. Clearly, he was no longer functioning properly. And referee Arthur Mercante Jr let the fight continue to its brutal knockout end.

Scottland lapsed into a coma seconds after the bout and was taken in critical condition to Bellevue Hospital, where he underwent emergency brain surgery. Six days later, he died.

Duva Boxing reports that the New York State Athletic Commission demanded 45 credentials to 'regulate' the fight card. In addition, NYSAC officials requested and were given 'fifteen to twenty' free tickets. In other words, on the night of 26 June, there were 45 credentialled officials from the NYSAC on board the USS *Intrepid*. A man was beaten to death in front of them. And they did nothing to save him.

The tragic death of Beethavean Scottland underlines the problems that permeate the New York State Athletic Commission. Many ring deaths are unavoidable. This one was not.

Any examination of the Scottland tragedy has to begin with the man who refereed the fight, Arthur Mercante Jr. Arthur is a gentleman. I like him. I think he's a good person. He might be the best referee in the country but for one serious flaw. There are times when he allows fights to go on too long. It happened with Razor Ruddock against Michael Dokes in 1990. It happened with Pernell Whitaker against Diobelys Hurtado in 1997. It happened with Michael Bennett against Andrew Hutchinson early in 2001. And it happened again on the night of 26 June.

Mercante's situation is analogous to that of a dedicated police officer. Picture a cop who cares about the community, is fearless in fighting crime, makes important arrests and does his best to serve society. But once every few years, he fires his police revolver under questionable circumstances. One time, he fires at a fleeing mugger on a crowded street. Another time, he fires when he thinks a suspect has a gun that is actually a cellular telephone. The incidents go on, but no one is hurt. Then, one day, he fires at a fleeing bank robber who's running past a school playground, and a ten-year-old is accidentally killed.

Long before a cop reaches that point, the police department should sit him down and talk with him. Yet no one at the NYSAC sat down with Arthur Mercante Jr to talk about his philosophy of refereeing and improve his otherwise sterling ring performance. Several times since the tragedy, Mercante has said, 'I never thought of stopping the fight.' But if Arthur didn't at least think about stopping the fight, something in his thinking was wrong. His desire to let Scottland finish the fight is understandable. Again and again, Beethavean had come back from the brink; and rather than just try to survive, he kept trying to win. Indeed, after taking a beating in round seven, Scottland won rounds eight and nine.

But the first and foremost concern of a referee during a fight must be the safety of the fighters. And here, the thoughts of Arthur Mercante Sr are instructive. In arguing against the use of a standing-eight count for fighters in trouble, the elder Mercante once opined, 'I'm opposed to the standing-eight count, because the point at which a referee is supposed to use it is precisely the point at which a fight should be stopped. The fighter's knees are weak; his eyes are rolling. So why prolong his agony?' And Jerry Izenberg of the *Newark Star Ledger* echoed Mercante's reservations when he observed, 'A fighter can be an inch away from getting knocked out; then he's brought back; and then he can go an inch away from getting knocked out again. That's not good for the fighter.' Yet that's precisely what happened to Beethavean Scottland in the fourth, fifth and seventh rounds. Then, in round ten, Scottland stopped functioning properly. This was the point at which stopping the fight became an urgent imperative rather than a judgment call. Yet Mercante let the destruction go on.

To Mercante's credit, he hasn't gone into hiding. He has answered inquiries about the tragedy as forthrightly as possible. It has been suggested that he retire from the ring. Should he? I can't answer that. If he referees again, will he go in the opposite direction and stop fights too soon? I don't know. I'll say simply that I feel sorry for the situation that Arthur finds himself in. Whatever course he pursues, he'll carry this tragedy with him for the rest of his life.

The men in Beethavean Scottland's corner are also to blame. Did they care about their fighter? I'm sure they did. But they saw what was happening to him and let the fight continue. However, the ultimate responsibility for Scottland's death lies with the New York State Athletic Commission, which is currently chaired by Mel Southard.

The NYSAC is a microcosm of incompetence and corruption. Yes, some dedicated public servants work there. But by and large, the most qualified employees – men like Joe Dwyer, Bob Duffy, Tony Mazzarella and Tom Hoover – have been forced out or chose to leave the commission because of the lack of professionalism that surrounded them. Those four men cared about the fighters; they understood boxing; and they're gone.

After Beethavean Scottland underwent the second of three unsuccessful surgeries to repair the damage to his brain, Michael Katz asked Southard if any of the commissioners or other ranking NYSAC personnel had gone to the hospital with Scottland. 'No,' Southard told him. 'Why not?' Katz queried. 'Because the main event was coming up,' Southard responded, 'and we had to be there in case something happened.' 'What for?' Katz countered. 'Something happened in the fight before, and you didn't do anything.'

Not enough people at the NYSAC do their job. Or phrased differently, too many commission employees today view their job as one of Republican Party service rather than public service. They know next to nothing about professional boxing and care less. The result is that there's a shortage of qualified personnel at the NYSAC. Many of its referees, judges, and inspectors are poorly chosen and poorly trained. No one takes charge, because no one in a position of responsibility knows what has to be done.

On the night of 26 June, Mel Southard should have gotten up from his seat, walked around the ring to the physician assigned to Scottland's corner, and told him to examine the fighter. If he had, Scottland might be alive today. Instead, Southard's office now says it's conducting an investigation by reviewing a videotape of the tragedy. And Dr Barry Jordan, chief neurologist for the NYSAC, explains, 'We're asking, were there any opportunities to stop the fight?'

That's an idiotic question. Of course there were opportunities to stop the fight.

Jordan observed the Jones–Scottland bout from a neutral corner outside the ring. He says that, after round seven in which Scottland took a bad beating, he told Mercante, 'Don't let him take too many more blows.' Mercante says that Jordan's words were, 'Let's keep a good eye on him.' The difference is immaterial. Jordan's observation of the carnage from a distance was hardly a substitute for a closer look at Scottland by a qualified doctor.

Dr Rufus Saddler was the ringside physician assigned to Scottland's corner. Reporters in the press section observed, and

Mercante later confirmed, that Saddler examined Scotland only once during the fight. He went to the fighter's corner to check on a cut after the fourth round. No one has ever bled to death in a boxing ring. Saddler later told Dr Jordan that he was concerned about Scotland's condition, but was close enough to the corner to see and hear what was going on. I wonder if Dr Saddler examines the patients who come to his office from across the room.

Dr Michael Schwartz is Chairman of the American Association of Professional Ringside Physicians. Schwartz says that, 'During a fight, the most important thing the ring doctor can do is visit the fighter in the corner.' Dr Ferdie Pacheco, who knows a thing or two about medicine and boxing, is more direct. 'The main job of the ringside doctor,' says Pacheco, 'is to figure out when enough is enough. If he doesn't go into the ring to examine Scotland, what's he there for?'

Dr Margaret Goodman is a physician who works for the Nevada State Athletic Commission. She and Dr Flip Homansky (a former ring-side physician, who is now an NSAC commissioner) recently edited a book entitled *Ringside And Training Principles*. The book should be mandatory reading for all fight personnel. One of the essays in it is enti-tled 'What the Ringside Physician is Looking for in Determining Whether or not a Fight Should Continue'. In that essay, Dr Goodman notes that, when the physician visits a corner between rounds, 'He has already seen something during the round that led him to believe there was a potential injury... Using a penlight, the doctor looks to see how the fighter's pupils react. If they are unequal or slow to constrict, this can indicate a potentially serious brain injury.' Nowhere in the book does Dr Goodman recommend that a between-rounds examination be conducted from a seat outside the ring while the fighter is staring in another direction. Goodman also states in a section of her book dealing with acute head injuries that there does not have to be a loss of consciousness for a concussion to have occurred. 'LET ME RESTATE THIS FOR EMPHASIS,' she says in capital letters. 'Someone can function with a concussion, but continuing to take punishment with one can lead to permanent brain damage.'

Much has been made of the fact that Scotland told both his corner and Mercante that he wanted to continue. Here again, the Goodman–

Homansky book is instructive. 'The roles of the referee and doctor are vital,' it states, 'because a fighter usually doesn't know when he is hurt. He cannot think cognitively and doesn't realize his body is not functioning properly. The decision to continue should not be left up to the fighter.' And to that, one can add the thoughts of Arthur Mercante Sr, who once opined, 'The last thing you do is ask a fighter who's been beaten up or is dazed, a fighter who might be hurt, if he wants to continue; because if he's any kind of fighter at all, he'll say "yes".'

In sum, a fighter should be allowed to decide that he wants to quit. A fighter should not have the final say on whether he is allowed to continue in a fight. Dr Jordan now says, 'This is just one of those unfortunate things that happens every once in a while. Occasionally, a boxer gets hurt despite regulatory policies.'

No! In this case, a fighter was killed because too many people at the NYSAC didn't do their job properly. And it all traces back to the top, although there's a school of thought that Mel Southard doesn't even run the commission. After the Scotland tragedy, several NYSAC officials spoke on condition of anonymity. 'The assignments are coming from Albany,' said one. 'The politicians have to be satisfied that the right people are in the corner and in the ring, particularly when a fight is on television.' Another commission official was more specific in his complaint, stating his belief that assignments for major fights are often dictated to Southard by Republican Party officials through State Senator Michael Balboni.

Balboni represents the seventh state senatorial district, which includes most of the north shore of Nassau County. Arthur Mercante Sr is Balboni's personal trainer. Mercante describes the legislator as 'a handsome, bright, intelligent guy, who's going to go a long way.' Both Balboni and Southard were unavailable when interviews were sought for this article. But regardless of Balboni's role, it's clear that the New York State Athletic Commission is now an arm of the New York State Republican Party.

'We're not even a commission anymore,' one NYSAC official acknowledges. 'All we are is a slush fund for the party. Our primary guideline is, what will this fight or this appointment do for the party? Any guy in a local Republican club can say, "I want to be an inspector for a night," and it's done. Most of the inspectors have no idea what they're doing. There are a few good ones left, but the great majority just stand in the corner and have no idea what's going on. Anyone who gives enough money to the Republican Party can get a job for his son or his son's friend. It's disheartening for the few decent people who are left at the commission, and it's dangerous beyond belief for the fighters.'

Tragedies happen in boxing. They're more likely to happen when a state athletic commission is run for the primary purpose of supporting a state political party. There's a need for a full house-cleaning. A man getting beaten up on the street would have received better protection from strangers that Beethavean Scottland got from the New York State Athletic Commission on the night of 26 June.

Marilyn Cole Lownes and I collaborated again on a look at Don King's jewellery.

The King of Diamonds

Long before Michael Jordan wore a diamond stud in his ear, long before it was fashionable for professional athletes to resemble a walking version of the Crown Jewels, there was Don King.

King is a large bulky man: six-feet-two-inches tall, weighing 270 pounds. Charismatic, flamboyant, spellbinding, ostentatious; he has dominated professional boxing since the mid-1970s.

'Like me or dislike me, my longevity is unquestioned,' King says in a voice as rich as his bank account. 'I've been on top for 25 years; number one against insurmountable odds. Others try to emulate and imitate me, but I'm the trailblazer and the pioneer. I've set the tone for the whole business of boxing, and there ain't no stopping me now.'

'The jewellery started when I became a promoter,' King explains, speaking in rushes. 'I determined that it would be to my advantage to dress the part of success. People like shiny things, so I put on shiny things to attract attention. I couldn't afford what I can afford now. But sparkling gems, real or not, were my entree. Now,' King continues, 'I wear them for show business. If you've got it, flaunt it. The baubles get attention. You see, the system puts diamonds at the top. If I wear diamonds, I get the ear of those within the system who are less fortunate than I am and who want to get to the top like I did. It's like the bait going on the hook for the fish. Young pugilists see the glitter and sparkle, and it draws them to me like a moth to a flame. Then, once I do my job properly, the job supersedes the baubles.'

King's collection includes his famous diamond-studded crown-logo necklace, a larger crown-logo necklace, and assorted diamond-studded crucifixes, bracelets, watches and rings.

'I have an array of jewels,' the promoter says. 'But without question, my favourites are the crown necklaces, which were designed by

236

my wonderful wife Henrietta. I love them because they're beautiful and because they're the symbol of kings and the symbol of my achievement and success.'

Is the jewellery real?

'Some of the baubles are more valuable than others,' King acknowledges. 'It's in the perception. Some say they're real; some say they're not. Sometimes people give me imitation and, if the gift comes from the heart, I accept it as though it's real because what comes from the heart is priceless. But I will tell you, I do like quality.'

The jewellery is insured. Not long ago, King was robbed at gunpoint in Mexico City. Reimbursement for a $125,000 watch followed.

Most of the jewellery that King buys today comes from a jeweller in Las Vegas. Before that, he bought in New York.

'Jewellers come to me in droves,' King reports. 'They're always bringing me sacks filled with baubles and doo-dads, showing me their wares. But I'm reluctant to treat dollars with reckless abandon; particularly when they're mine. You see, the Queen of England inherited her jewels, but I worked for mine. I wasn't born with a silver spoon in my mouth. So when faced with temptation, my number-one rule is, "Keep common sense." You know, the value of jewels doesn't go down if you buy wisely. You've heard the saying, "Diamonds are a girl's best friend." It's the same for a man.'

And then King adds one final thought: 'The jewels are grand. But the jewels don't make me. I make the jewels.'

While researching Muhammad Ali: His Life and Times, *I travelled with Muhammad to Indonesia where, among other things, we attended a Larry Holmes singing engagement. Later, I wrote a concert review that appeared in* The National. *Thereafter Larry telephoned and screamed at me for 45 minutes. Part of me was honoured. I told myself, 'Larry Holmes, one of the greatest fighters of all time, thinks my writing is important enough to spend 45 minutes on the phone with me.' And part of me was worried: 'Larry Holmes, one of the greatest fighters of all time, is really pissed.'*

Larry Holmes in Concert

'Super Show '90', as it was known in Indonesia, featured music, boxing and Larry Holmes singing in the Grand Ballroom of the Sahid Jaya Hotel. 'I take my music very seriously,' Holmes told reporters in Jakarta. 'Any time someone comes to hear me sing, I don't want them to go away disappointed.'

The evening began with Holmes lumbering on stage wearing three diamond-and-gold rings, a diamond-and-gold chain, a diamond-and-gold watch, and an outfit that resembled the uniform worn by bus driver Ralph Kramden on the *Honeymooners*. Given the fact that Holmes was considerably over his fighting weight, he also looked somewhat like Kramden. Then the singing started.

Round One: The first song was about boxing, but Larry's five-man band drowned out all the lyrics except for the phrase 'boxing ring'.

Round Two: The second song sounded very much like the first, except the audible lyric was 'she's built'. Holmes suffered from apparent jock itch during this number, and tugged periodically at his crotch.

Round Three: Midway through 'I Feel Good', someone in the audience threw a white dinner napkin towards the stage in a gesture of surrender.

Round Four: 'Stand By Me' – 'When the night have [sic] come, and the moon is clear.' If it were a fight, at this point the referee would have stopped it.

Round Five: Medley – 'You Really Got A Hold On Me' and 'Bring It On Home'. It was here that James Tillis, who was in Jakarta to box an exhibition with Holmes, opined, 'I'm having fun, but Larry can't sing.'

Round Six: Once again, the lyrics were unintelligible. By now, Larry was sufficiently behind on points that he needed a knockout to win.

Round Seven: 'Lean On Me' – Holmes was sweating profusely, and instead of lumbering, he'd begun to lurch.

Round Eight: I don't know what song this was either, but true to his fighting spirit, Larry finished on his feet. Whereupon one onlooker declared, 'Float like a butterfly, sting like a bee; Holmes can't sing as well as Ali.' Or as Ali himself might say:

> 'If there's ever a concert in Malaysia,
> Instead of Holmes, I want Joe Frazier.'

As a general rule, when I put an article online, I get a dozen E-mails in response. This one, written after Lennox Lewis and Hasim Rahman engaged in their now infamous studio brawl, engendered more than 300 letters.

The Bigot

Five years ago, Muhammad Ali and I co-authored a book entitled *Healing: A Journal of Tolerance and Understanding.* In explaining our purpose, we wrote, 'We want to make a statement about bigotry and prejudice. We believe that most people are tired of the hating. We believe that most people are saying, "If there's a way to solve this problem, let's solve it." '

Last week, Hasim Rahman became part of the problem. Referring to the fact that Lennox Lewis sued to force him to live up to a rematch clause in their contracts, Rahman declared, 'It was gay to take it to the court.'

There are a lot of things wrong with Rahman's comment. First, it was a nonsensical non-sequitur. In the ugly world of bigoted stereotyping, Jews are typecast as 'money-grubbing' and African-Americans are typecast as 'shiftless and lazy'. But prior to Rahman doing his imitation of an intellectually challenged Ku Klux Klan member, I'd never heard anyone suggest that gay people are particularly litigious.

Moreover, Rahman didn't even have the moral courage to acknowledge the nature of his remark. In the next breath, he feigned innocence with the words, 'I don't know why [Lennox] was so offended.'

Hasim might be stupid, but he's not that stupid. He has to know that his statement was an ugly, overtly bigoted taunt.

Stan Hoffman (Rahman's manager) took advantage of a contract loophole and betrayed his friend Cedric Kushner for monetary gain. Was that a 'Jewish thing' to do? Mike Tyson was convicted of rape. Was that a 'black thing' to do? Roberto Duran said 'no mas'. Was that a 'Panamanian thing' to do? Hasim Rahman says he's a devout

Muslim. Was seeking to break his contract with Lewis a 'Muslim thing' to do?

Maybe Rahman is fixated on the movie *Philadelphia*. Or maybe he's embarrassed by the fact that he's the one who sought to avoid a rematch with Lewis, and Lennox had to sue to force him into the ring again. Either way, Hasim's words and subsequent protestations of innocence last week remind me of a scene I saw many years ago when a white man in a mob threw a rock at a ten-year-old black girl being escorted by federal marshals into a previously all-white public school in the Deep South. After throwing the rock, the man hid his hand behind his back.

What makes this all particularly sad, of course, is that Rahman is currently heavyweight champion of the world. By virtue of his position, he's a role model. Prejudice is learned. It's not a self-winding watch. Some of the things that lead to prejudice might be human nature, but prejudice itself is not. Babies don't know prejudice; they have to be taught. And the lesson Hasim Rahman taught last week was that gay-bashing is all right.

It's incumbent upon every decent person to speak out against overt expressions of bigotry. Let's see if the people who have condemned Bernard Hopkins for throwing a Puerto Rican flag to the ground are as vehement in their criticism of Rahman. Initially, it's easy to hate. For some people, being prejudiced might even be fun at first. But after a while, hating becomes a full-time job and the hours suck.

The jury is still out as to how good a fighter Hasim Rahman is, but he's starting to look like a shabby human being. People can speculate all they want regarding whether or not Lennox Lewis is gay. What we know for a fact is that, last week, Rahman acted like a bigot.

There's one honourable road for Rahman to travel. He can sincerely and genuinely apologise. If he does, he'll redeem himself and raise his stature. Meanwhile, the slur he uttered last week tells us far more about himself than it does about Lennox Lewis.

The volume of, and thoughts expressed in, my reader mail led to the following column.

More on Hasim Rahman's 'Gay' Comment

Two days ago, I posted a column on this website entitled *The Bigot*. In it, I criticised Hasim Rahman for his comment that it was 'gay' for Lennox Lewis to sue him. Since then, I've received hundreds of e-mails in response. Many were supportive of my thoughts. Others voiced disagreement. As expected, some of the e-mails were ugly and blatantly homophobic. Others expressed disagreement in a way that was intelligent and carefully thought out. I'd like to continue the dialogue with this latter group of readers.

Most readers who disagreed with me voiced one or more of the following objections to my thoughts:

1. Rahman's use of the term 'gay' wasn't intended as homophobic. Rather, it was street slang commonly used by people who are younger than I am.

    It might be street slang. But given the rumours about Lennox's sexuality, the remark wasn't innocent. I thought it was intended as a taunt; and obviously, Lennox thought so too. Also, just because something is street slang, doesn't mean it's acceptable. Various readers have advised me that, in street slang, 'gay' means 'weak... wimpy... poor effort... etc.' That, to me, is no better than saying, 'He tried to jew me out of ten dollars,' or 'There's a nigger in the woodpile.' Oftentimes, prejudice is spread through the careless use of language.

2. Lennox's reaction was inappropriate.

    I agree. Saying that he was 'one hundred per cent man' and suggesting that Rahman bring his sister for a demonstration was not a good way to handle the situation.

3. Muhammad Ali once called white people 'devils' and was merciless in deriding Joe Frazier as ignorant, an Uncle Tom, and a gorilla. That's worse than anything Rahman said.

Ali stepped far over the line when he was young, and I've commented on that at length. So has Muhammad. Twelve years ago, Ali told me, 'I'm sorry Joe Frazier is mad at me. I'm sorry I hurt him. Joe Frazier is a good man. I couldn't have done what I did without him, and he couldn't have done what he did without me.' Also, in the book on bigotry and prejudice that Ali and I co-authored, Muhammad wrote, 'When I was young, I followed a teaching that disrespected other people and said that white people were devils. I was wrong. Color doesn't make a man a devil. It's the heart and soul and mind that count.'

4. Homosexuality is a choice.

I'm not an expert on the subject, but I don't think being gay is a choice. One might choose to act or not act on sexual desires, but people are what they are. I'm heterosexual. That's not a 'choice' I made. It's what I am. Given the 'choice' of a sexual liaison with a roundcard girl or a male fighter, I'll take the roundcard girl every time. People don't choose their sexual preference the way they choose a political party or their religious beliefs.

5. I shouldn't have said that Rahman is 'stupid'.

Actually, I didn't say that Rahman is stupid. I said he 'might be stupid'. Regardless, it was a poor choice of words, and I retract them. I should have written, 'Hasim isn't stupid. He has to know that his statement was an ugly, overtly bigoted taunt.'

I could go on at length; but at this point, I've pretty much had my say. What I'd like to do, however, is quote from one of the many letters I received in response to my first column on this subject. It's from a reader in South Africa, who wrote as follows:

Dear Mr Hauser,

Thank you for addressing the core issue surrounding the
fracas that ensued on television between Rahman and Lewis.
It seemed that nobody in boxing had cottoned on to the simple
fact that Rahman had essentially committed an act of
prejudice. Just because you're black does not mean that you
are naturally exempt from committing prejudice against other
people. I'm a black South African, and we suffer very much
from the same mentality in our society. Everybody is
prejudiced. While the roots of the prejudice may lie in slavery,
subjugation, and colonial rule, it does not mean that the
victims of prejudice are innocent of the very same crime.
Rahman, as a black Muslim in America, should at least carry
himself with enough grace not to engage in bigoted stone
throwing in an attempt to ruffle his opponent. If he himself is
not enough to inspire fear or doubt in Lennox, then he has no
business dragging in and abusing some already marginalised
sector of society. Gay people are easy to pick on. They're
characterised as weak effeminate men and have traditionally
made easy targets for abuse. Rahman has chosen them as his
target. Maybe some part of him thought that nobody would
really mind if he picked on gay people, and sadly, he's
probably right.

Those words speak volumes. And there's one last thought I'd like
to add to them. After Hasim Rahman defeated Lennox Lewis in South
Africa, both men were invited to meet with Nelson Mandela. Lewis
was bitterly disappointed by the loss of his title, but he stayed in South
Africa to meet with Mandela. Rahman, by contrast, said he was 'tired'
and returned to the United States.

Nelson Mandela is one of history's great men. His peers are true
heroes like Martin Luther King Jr and Mahatma Gandhi. Rahman
should have met with Mr Mandela. He might have learned something.

The structure of professional boxing deserves criticism. But there are also some very nice things that can be said about it.

Boxing – The Open Sport

'Boxing,' Seth Abraham once declared, 'always has a cold. It's never completely healthy.'

Actually, forget about the cold. Herpes is more like it. The sweet science has long been known as the red-light district of professional sports. Yet, for all its failings, boxing is also the most democratic and most open of all sports. Let a few comparisons suffice.

Throughout the first half of the twentieth century, baseball and boxing were intertwined in America's consciousness as the nation's only truly national sports. Indeed, one of boxing's most treasured moments – the Dempsey–Tunney 'long count' of 22 September 1927 – occurred a mere eight days before Babe Ruth's mythic 60th home run. Yet if one compares racial progress in the two sports, the contrast is clear. Joe Gans, Jack Johnson, Henry Armstrong, Joe Louis, and Sugar Ray Robinson all held world championships before Jackie Robinson set foot on a major league baseball field. Were the odds stacked against black fighters? Absolutely. But at least they had a chance to prevail.

The second half of the twentieth century has witnessed black dominance on the playing field in many athletic endeavours. It has been 22 years since a white player led the National Basketball Association in scoring. Last season (1998–1999), sixteen of the top seventeen scorers in the NBA were black. It has been 37 years since a white player led the National Football League in rushing. Last year, there were twenty 1,000-yard rushers in the NFL. All of them were black.

Yet for all these statistics, the residual effects of old prejudices remain. Doug Williams is the only black quarterback to have led his team to victory in the Super Bowl. At the start of the 1997 season – a full fifty years after Jackie Robinson's debut – only eight black pitchers had been credited with a victory in World Series play. And perhaps more important, the ownership councils in baseball, football, basketball and hockey are almost exclusively white, as are the television executives and other behind-the-scenes power brokers.

Contrast that with boxing. Don King, the sport's dominant power broker over the past twenty years, is black. Larry Hazzard and Wilbert McClure are among the state athletic commission chairmen who are black. Bob Lee, Murad Muhammad, and numerous other fistic powers that be are black.

Boxing, more than any other sport, offers open access. One doesn't need 800 million dollars to buy a franchise. A college education is unnecessary to manage or promote. All you need is a dollar and a dream. On 8 March 1971, Don King listened to reports of the first Ali–Frazier fight from a prison cell in Marion, Ohio, where he was incarcerated for manslaughter. Four years later, King co-promoted Ali–Frazier III.

My own experience with professional boxing confirms its open nature. In 1983, I finished writing a book about Beethoven. Being a lifelong sports fan, I wanted to write next about sports. But which sport? Baseball was my first love. But I couldn't just walk into Yankee Stadium and start talking with Don Mattingly. I was a basketball fan, but there was no way I could go to Madison Square Garden for an in-depth conversation with Larry Bird when the Celtics were in town. Bill Parcells? No way. Wayne Gretzky? Not a chance. But I could walk into any gym in the city and start talking with fighters.

My first day out, I visited the Times Square Gym. Davey Moore and Saoul Mamby (both former world champions) were training there. Each man spoke with me for an hour. The next day, Emile Griffith came by. Soon, I was on a first-name basis with Ray Arcel, Gil Clancy, Arthur Mercante and dozens of others who populated the sweet science. John Condon gave me a press credential so I could sit at ringside at Madison Square Garden. Writers like Michael Katz and Jerry Izenberg shared their knowledge with me. One year later, I had written *The Black Lights*.

Over the years, I've authored two dozen books and hundreds of articles on a wide range of subjects. But the sweet science is never far from my heart. It has taken me around the world with Muhammad Ali and seated me at ringside for some truly great fights. It has introduced me to some of the best people I've ever met; and also, to some of the worst. But whatever happens, I'll always appreciate the fact that the door to the sport was open to me. It's one of the reasons I agree with fight manager Mike Jones, who once said, 'You can knock promoters; you can knock trainers, managers, even fighters. But don't knock boxing. It's the purest sport there is; and anyone who's ever been involved will tell you, it's an honour to be associated with boxing."

After the 11 September terrorist attack, Michael Katz, Tom Gerbasi and I co-authored the following editorial regarding the upcoming middleweight championship fight between Felix Trinidad and Bernard Hopkins.

Reschedule the Fight

Thirty-eight years ago, an assassin tore at the fabric of the United States when John F Kennedy was assassinated in Dallas. Two days later, the National Football League played its regularly scheduled contests. Pete Rozelle, the NFL commissioner at the time, later acknowledged that it was the biggest mistake he ever made.

That bit of history is relevant now in the wake of today's horrifying terrorist attack. The most important, most exciting fight of the year, Felix Trinidad versus Bernard Hopkins, is scheduled for this Saturday night at Madison Square Garden.

It should be postponed.

Reasonable arguments can be made in support of holding the fight as planned. Disrupting the rhythm of everyday life is a form of collateral damage that, in a way, plays into the hands of terrorists. Economic losses will result from a postponement. And a postponement will weigh particularly heavily on the fighters' shoulders.

But even if all the logistical problems caused by today's events are overcome, there are compelling reasons why the fight should not take place on Saturday night. Prior to today, there were safety concerns regarding the fight. These concerns pale following today's events. Madison Square Garden sits on top of Penn Station, which has been evacuated as a prime terrorist target. And more important, there can be no joy in a fight that is contested this Saturday night. The loss of life that occurred today is simply too great. Two men punching each other in the head is an inappropriate memorial to the thousands of men and women who died this morning.

American enterprises from Major League Baseball to Disneyland have shut down today. This is not a time to play. Fights are often rescheduled because of injury to one of the participants. Felix Trinidad versus Bernard Hopkins should be rescheduled because the nation has suffered a grievous wound.

After Trinidad–Hopkins was postponed, I visited an empty Madison Square Garden on the night that would have been.

Madison Square Garden: 15 September 2001

This was to have been 'ground zero' tonight. Bernard Hopkins versus Felix Trinidad for the undisputed middleweight championship of the world. Screaming partisans had been expected to turn Madison Square Garden into a sea of red, white and blue flags. Puerto Rican flags. The cops would have been here in full force because of security concerns stemming from incidents in which Hopkins was perceived as having disrespected that flag. It was feared the night would turn ugly. But another four-letter word – EVIL – intervened.

Tonight was a perfect mid-September evening. Clear skies, temperature in the low sixties, a hint of autumn in the air. No events were listed on the Garden marquee; just the digital image of an American flag at half-mast. A giant multicoloured banner advertising the fight stretched from the first floor to the top of the building. Inside the Garden, three box-office windows for advance ticket sales were open. The main arena itself was dimly lit, its floor still covered with ice put in place for New York Rangers practices earlier this week.

A half-dozen uniformed New York City cops stood outside the employees' entrance at the corner of Eighth Avenue and 33rd Street. 'Normal security,' they said. Other cops were sprinkled in and around Penn Station, which lies beneath the Garden.

Eventually, things will return to normal in America, although the definition of 'normal' will change. There will be added security. But no matter what measures are taken, seeing the World Trade Center towers sliced in two by a handful of madmen leaves all of us feeling vulnerable.

We are.

Maybe we'll find a way to make our own airlines secure. But what about foreign airlines? What about personnel who work for Pakistan International Airlines, Saudi Arabia Airlines, Royal Jordanian Airlines, and Egypt Air? What about car bombs, biological warfare, poisoned reservoirs, and other acts of terrorism? Are there pilots on domestic carriers who admire Timothy McVeigh?

The acts of terror that occurred on 11 September make us realise how insignificant our games are. All of us who live in New York know someone who perished in the World Trade Center. We just don't know yet who they were.

When Bernard Hopkins and Felix Trinidad ultimately meet, American flags will be waved along side their Puerto Rican counter-parts. Fans will be shouting 'USA! USA!' Let's hope the flags are waved in unity. This fight was never about Bernard Hopkins versus Puerto Rico or Puerto Rico versus the United States. It was always a fist fight between two men; nothing more.

Meanwhile, there's a horrible feeling in waking up each day and knowing right away that something is wrong. The mourning over this week's events has barely begun. The implications are far from fully understood. It feels like a death in the family.

When Bernard Hopkins and Felix Trinidad finally fought each other, reminders of 11 September were everywhere.

Madison Square Garden: 29 September 2001

Autumn is the nicest time of year in New York. Summer is too hot, winter too cold, and spring too short. Autumn is glorious. From the middle of September until the days just before Thanksgiving, the skies are often cloudless. Autumn leaves fire the imagination, and the temperature is just right.

The weather was glorious on 11 September; the day the World Trade Center was attacked. On 29 September, the skies alternated between sunlit and overcast. The mood at Madison Square Garden was festive one moment and sombre the next. Normally, big fights are the boxing community's version of a family holiday. Hopkins–Trinidad was both holiday and wake.

Meanwhile, two blocks away from the Garden, the Empire State Building was bathed in red, white and blue.

For those of us who grew up in an earlier era, the Empire State Building was the most visible symbol of New York. King Kong met his destiny there with Fay Wray at his side. The Kong who perished at the World Trade Center decades later after a liaison with Jessica Lange was a pale imitation.

In 1945, a B-25 bomber lost in blinding fog crashed into the 79th floor of what was then the world's tallest building. Thirteen people were killed. The Empire State Building survived. Now it gives every appearance of standing guard over New York.

On 23 November 2001, Lou DiBella held a boxing fundraiser for victims of the World Trade Center attack. The following article was written for that night's programme.

11 September 2001

I'm very down on the overall state of boxing. From top to bottom, the sport is a mess. The business is endemically rotten. People lie and misrepresent and cheat as much on 20,000-dollar club-fight cards as they do on the multimillion-dollar pay-per-view shows. There's endless scheming and plotting to hurt other people. The negative energy is overwhelming. One of the few good things about it for me so far has been dealing with the fighters. A lot of people told me that being on the side of the business that I am now would teach me that the fighters are as bad as everyone else. But that hasn't been the case. So far, I've found most of the fighters to be very special decent individuals. There have been disappointments, but I love working with most of them. I enjoy the mentoring aspect of my relationship with the Olympians. There are times when I'm proud to be a member of the boxing community, and November 23rd will be one of them.

– Lou DiBella

Roseland, where tonight's fights are being held, stands a block from Broadway. For a long time, in New York's theatre industry when someone died young, the question asked was, 'Did he die of AIDS?' Now, for a horrible ten weeks, when we hear of someone dying young, the question asked is, 'Did he die at the World Trade Center?'

The human mind is capable of conjuring up evil that, for some of us, is literally unimaginable. Any individual can end another person's life and wreak havoc on the lives of the victim's loved ones. A small group of plotters, indeed a lone assassin, can cause incalculable harm.

Once something has happened, we can't change it. We can't undo what has been done.

Yet one day can change the world. It happened in 1914, when Archduke Ferdinand was assassinated in Sarajevo, lighting the

conflagration that became World War I. It happened at Pearl Harbor.
And it happened again ten weeks ago.

On 11 September, we all died a little. America was the target, but
the entry point for the wound was New York.

We are aware of the twin towers more now in their absence than
ever before. We're also uncomfortably aware of the fact that evil lurks
just beneath the surface of our lives. There are places in the world
where the type of violence we've just experienced is part of everyday
life. But Americans have been largely immune to such cares. Most of
us have had the luxury of going through life confident that the sudden
ending, the tragic accident, the unspeakable horror, won't happen to us.
To a friend; perhaps. To someone we know; probably, as a matter of
statistical likelihood. But not to me.

Now the certainty we seek in our lives has been undermined, and
in its place we have fear. The fear that someone wants to kill us; the
fear that, just as terrorists were trained as pilots here in the United
States, their brethren might be learning the nuances of lethal biology at
universities and laboratories in America; the fear that this is the start of
a long, hard, difficult time.

Many of us have been traumatised by the visual image of United
Airlines Flight Number 175 hitting the south tower of the World Trade
Center more than we understand. 'People keep saying "'like a movie,
like a book," Stephen King wrote recently. 'And I keep thinking, "No,
not at all like a movie or a book. This is what it really looks like when
an actual plane filled with actual human beings and loaded with jet fuel
hits a skyscraper. This is the truth."'

That scene will stay with us for ever. It is the signature image of
horror in our times.

Now comes the response. Makeshift shrines to honour lives lost
have sprung up outside fire stations across New York. People seem
friendlier, warmer and more polite. They smile and nod in acknowl-
edgement to one another more now than before. They look at cops and
firefighters with new appreciation and respect.

One of the ironies of our democratic society is that, in recent
decades, only one segment of society has been called upon to do the
hard, dangerous, dirty work. In World War II, people of all classes

fought in the military. But since then, America's armed forces have been comprised largely of men and women who come from poverty and see the military as a form of upward mobility.

The World Trade Center attack struck at Americans of all classes. With terrorism, we are all soldiers. And on 11 September, we were reminded of who our real heroes are. Now, we say to the perpetrators of this horror as Winston Churchill once spoke to Adolph Hitler, 'We will have no truce or parlay with you or the grisly gang who do your wicked will. You do your worst, and we will do our best.'

That brings us to tonight's fights. Everyone talks about how super-star athletes are heroes and role models. But most professional athletes, like the rest of us, do first and foremost for themselves.

The fighters on tonight's card are making a true sacrifice. Like cops and firefighters, boxers know what reality is. In our video-game culture, every time they enter the ring they put themselves on the line. They know that a single moment of violence can change everything. Yet many of the fighters here tonight are entering the ring for free, and their opponents are appearing for greatly reduced purses. That's part of the good in boxing.

I've often said that, if I went to war, I'd want professional fighters beside me. Professional fighters and trainers like Teddy Atlas and a young Eddie Futch. I still believe that to be true. Meanwhile, conventional wisdom dictates that a fighter isn't considered truly great until he has gotten up off the canvas to win. New York will rise from the canvas and win.

Some Thoughts on Boxing

The difference between a champion and an also-ran is that an also-ran does things almost right and a champion does them exactly right.

True champions are fighters who do what has to be done when it needs to be done.

There's no 'when' in boxing; only 'if'.

Some words of wisdom from Sugar Ray Robinson: 'You always say, "I'll quit when I start to slide." Then, one morning, you wake up and you done slid. You can't choose your ending in boxing.'

Some words of wisdom from George Foreman: 'Look at what happens to the head in boxing. The head is what's getting hit. And there aren't any push-ups or sit-ups or roadwork you can do to get the head in shape.'

In a street fight, the combatants always look for an edge; a gun, a knife, the first punch, whatever. In the ring, the playing field is supposed to be level. But too often, it isn't. Too many people in boxing learn the rules simply so they can break them without getting caught.

In the ring, a fighter can submit to pain or he can resist it.

'Pound for pound' belongs to Roy Jones Jr. Nobody else can fight like Jones does, and nobody else is as good. At times, his bouts look like a Sugar Ray Robinson highlight film. Ask fifty fighters today, 'Pound for pound, who's the best fighter in the world right now?' Forty-nine of them will answer 'Roy Jones Jr.'

Some words of wisdom from Don King: 'There's something I learned a long time ago. You don't get what you deserve in life. You get what you negotiate.'

Some words of wisdom from Angelo Dundee: 'My greatest moment in boxing was with a club fighter named John Holman. Every time we were together, John would tell me about his dream. He wanted a house with shutters on the windows and a white picket fence around the lawn. One night, John wasn't doing well. He was getting the crap knocked out of him. After the eighth round, I told him, "You're blowin' it, son. That man on the opposite side of the ring, the one you're fighting, he's taking away your house with the shutters and white picket fence." John went out and knocked the son-of-a-bitch out in the ninth round.'

Christy Martin is a shot fighter, but she's a fighter.

Oscar De La Hoya knows how to win rounds, but sometimes he's unwilling to pay the price.

A heavy underdog has to go into the ring asking himself, 'How do I beat this guy?' – not, 'How do I keep from getting hurt?'

Some words of wisdom from Larry Holmes (explaining his participation in a 'legends' boxing event): 'I've got a lot of common sense. I just don't use it.'

Some words of wisdom from Billy Costello (explaining his participation in the same 'legends' event): 'I'm not fighting because I need to fight. I'm fighting because I need the money.'

A fighter should only continue his career if he can make enough money by fighting to fundamentally change his life.

In the toughest of fights, a champion hangs on when a lesser fighter would let go.

Some words of wisdom from Bernard Hopkins: 'I won't fight Shane Mosley. It's personal. Fights sometimes get nasty, and I like Shane. I have too much respect for him to let it get that way. Of course, if the money is right and Shane gets nasty first –'

There's no way that Arturo Gatti will lose a fight on cuts again. He's all out of blood.

There are times when Roy Jones Jr makes putting together a fight deal seem like root canal work. But it's even more unpleasant to fight him. Jones is beatable, but he's the hardest person in boxing to beat since Muhammad Ali in his prime. When Roy Jones Jr is at his best, bad things happen to the other guy.

Some words of wisdom from Mickey Duff: 'I've managed ordinary fighters through thirty or forty wins without a loss, because I found worse opponents and that was the way it seemed right to do things at the time. But sooner or later, you're faced with a moment of truth when your guy has to fight a real fight. That's when you realise it's a lot easier to be successful with a quality fighter. It's the difference between managing Frank Sinatra and managing some guy who sings at weddings and bar mitzvahs.'

Some words of wisdom from Don Elbaum, explaining why a fighter he'd advertised as being seven feet, one inch tall was really only six-seven: 'He's short for his height.'

A boxing promoter is a man who lends you his umbrella when the sun is shining and wants it back when it starts to rain.

Boxing is a great sport and a lousy business.

It takes great pride to be a great fighter.

John Ruiz looks like an affable department store security guard.

The young Mike Tyson was a great fighter. He could hurt you with any punch in a combination. He could hurt you with every punch in a combination. And when he hurt you, it was like a shark smelling blood. The young Tyson was relentless in his assault. His opponents were in danger of being knocked out every second of every round. Sure, if you took him into the seventh or eighth round, he might get a bit tired. But by then, you didn't feel so good either. And by the way – even today, the consequences of making a mistake against Mike Tyson can be devastating.

Some words of wisdom from Roy Jones Jr: 'If I fought Mike Tyson I'd key on his power because, if Tyson catches me with a big punch, I'm losing out. I'd have to avoid his big punches and make sure I landed all my punches so he couldn't counter. That wouldn't be easy, because Tyson bobs and weaves and he's quick. One area where I'd have an advantage is, I'd work on his footwork. I'd make him chase me because his footwork is ordinary. If I get past three rounds, Tyson's in trouble. I doubt if I'd knock him out, but if it goes past three rounds, I'd win a decision.'

A competitive fight isn't necessarily an entertaining fight. That's why matchmakers are important.

People talk about the pressure that a 'big fight' atmosphere puts on a fighter. But the pressure doesn't come from everything that surrounds a big fight. It comes from the fact that top-quality fighters aren't used to fighting an opponent who's as good as they are.

Some words of wisdom from Evander Holyfield: 'If you hit someone, they're gonna hit you back. My momma taught me that when I was a little boy.'

Some words of wisdom from Chuck Wepner (after being knocked down by Sonny Liston and then asked by the referee how many fingers he was holding up): 'How many guesses do I get?'

Boxing is such a chaotic mess that it belongs on the internet.

Think about what it takes for a fighter to get up off the canvas. He's being beaten up. He's hurt. He's groggy. His ribs ache. He's getting punched in the face. And he's asking for more.

Some words of wisdom from Alex Stewart: 'Some fighters, when they knock an opponent down and see him struggling to get up, they want him to make it so they can hit him again. I'm not like that. I want the guy to stay down so I can win. Hey, if I wanted him standing up, I wouldn't have knocked him down to begin with.'

Some words of wisdom from trainer Donald Turner (on whether he objects to his fighters having sex while in training for a bout): 'Sex is fine. It's the chase that kills them.'

No matter how good a fighter is, most likely in the end, he'll break your heart.

Fighters get careless. But the truly great fighters do it less often than the rest and take they advantage of their opponents' mistakes.

Some words of wisdom from George Foreman: 'Mike Tyson talks a lot about doing bad things. But all you have to do is go into prisons and you'll hear that stuff all the time.'

Some words of wisdom from Larry Holmes: 'None of us is promised tomorrow. If I go 25 more years, that's a blessing. But if I don't, I've done my thing.'

If a ring judge lacks the courage of his convictions, he'll score close rounds for whichever fighter is favoured going into a bout. A ring judge who's mentally weak is as unsuited for his job as a fighter who's mentally weak.

The world sanctioning organisations are like arthritis. After a while, you get used to the pain. But every now and then, one of them flares up in a particularly troublesome manner.

Some words of wisdom from Roy Jones Jr: 'I don't have to satisfy the media. The media is cool. I like the media. But my job is to win, and I have to do what's comfortable for me and gets me ready. If I win, the media has something to write about. And you and I both know that, if I lose, the media won't be interested in me.'

Some words of wisdom from Bernard Hopkins: 'I respect Roy Jones, even if Roy hasn't given proper respect to me. But I don't know about Roy. Roy plays basketball; Roy feeds his chickens. That's a sign of being punchy, when you follow animals around like a big flood is coming.'

Fighters get old in a particularly cruel way.

When a fighter loses three fights in a row, either he's being badly managed or he should retire from boxing – or both.

Some words of wisdom from Billy Costello: 'A champion doesn't have to measure himself against the world. All he has to do is measure himself fight by fight against one opponent at a time.'

Some words of wisdom from Cedric Kushner: 'Ike Ibeabuche telephoned me at three o'clock one morning to tell me that he was seeing demons. I understand why Ike was seeing demons. What I don't understand is why he called me.'

Boxing is going to be boxing. No one will ever change it.

Ageing fighters are like ageing lovers. As their bodies get older and their physical prowess wanes, they try to get by on technique.

The business of boxing is like a chess game that goes on and on and on.

The following incidents, reported in various postings, confirm that there's a humorous side to professional boxing.

Insights and Nuggets

Andrew 'Six Heads' Lewis will make the first defence of his WBA welterweight title against Larry Marks at the Hammerstein Ballroom in Manhattan on the night of Saturday 28 April 2001. The fight will be promoted by Top Rank in association with Cedric Kushner Promotions and telecast by HBO as part of its *KO Nation* series.

According to Bob Arum of Top Rank, HBO was insistent that the show emanate from the Hammerstein. Unfortunately, the ballroom had already been booked for a bar mitzvah on the same night. 'No problem,' said HBO, which agreed to pay $30,000 to the young man and his family on the condition that they relocate their ceremony to another venue. This is believed to be the first instance of 'step aside money' being paid to a thirteen-year-old in conjunction with a world championship fight.

* * *

Bob Arum waxed eloquent recently about Oscar De La Hoya, who is engaged in ongoing litigation with the promoter. 'I have to make a conscious effort to put him out of my mind and stay busy with other promotions,' said Arum. 'Otherwise, it will eat me up.'

Arum was then asked about rumours that De La Hoya has said he wants Arum to return the Olympic gold medal he gave to the promoter. According to at least one report, the Golden Boy claims Arum promised to return the medal if there ever came a time when he was no longer Oscar's promoter.

'Not true,' said Arum. 'The little motherfucker gave it to me at my sixty-fifth birthday party. It's all on tape. Now he wants it back, and I'll tell you what. If Oscar wants to return gifts, he can give me back the Ferrari I gave him and I'll give him back his medal.'

* * *

Prior to the first fight between Lennox Lewis and Hasim Rahman, many people felt that Lewis was looking past his opponent. At least, that was the opinion of some observers, who said that Lewis didn't prepare seriously and arrived in South Africa too late to adjust to the high altitude.

Two weeks before the fight, Lewis was still training in Las Vegas and spent several days on the set of *Ocean's Eleven*. The Rat-Pack Era Hollywood film was being remade with Julia Roberts, George Clooney, Matt Damon and Andy Garcia in starring roles. The plot revolves around a plan to rob several Las Vegas casinos coincidental with a city-wide power blackout at the start of a heavyweight championship fight. Initially, the producers wanted to cast Lewis against Mike Tyson. But there were fears that Iron Mike might not show; or worse, that he would show and the make-believe fight would become real. Thus, Lewis was put in the ring with WBO heavyweight champion Wladimir Klitschko.

All of this led to an unscripted scene when Lennox was in the make-up trailer, chatting animatedly with Matt Damon and Julia Roberts. Klitschko walked into the trailer. Dead silence followed. No one said a word. Wladimir stood by awkwardly, with Lewis following his every move in the mirror.

Finally, Roberts spoke. 'Have you two guys fought each other?' she queried.

'Not yet,' Klitschko answered.

'Actually,' Lewis told her, 'the fight just began.'

* * *

One of boxing's finest legends concerns an unsavoury manager who brought a Latin American fighter named Marcos to New York in the early 1960s, changed his name to Marcus, and began touting him in ring circles as 'The Star of Zion'. The Star, it was widely advertised, was of Orthodox Jewish vintage, fought to bring honour to the Jewish people, and would some day be a superb champion. He blew his cover at a B'nai B'rith luncheon when, hungrily eyeing the matzo, he said politely, 'Please pass the tortillas.'

* * *

On 6 February 1993, Ray Mercer fought Jesse Ferguson at Madison

Square Garden on the undercard of Riddick Bowe versus Michael Dokes. The high point of the evening occurred when Jesse Jackson walked into the arena and took his seat. Soon after, the crowd was chanting, 'Jesse! Jesse!' Jackson's chest swelled with pride, and he stood up to wave – at which point the guy behind him tapped the good reverend on the shoulder and pointed towards Jesse Ferguson in the ring. Score a unanimous upset decision for journeyman Jesse Ferguson.

* * *

Mike Tyson's co-manager Jim Jacobs was fond of recounting an incident that occurred when Cus D'Amato was seventy years old. Jim and Cus were walking down a street in Manhattan one night when two muggers, knives in hand, approached and demanded money. Jim was in the process of reaching for his wallet when Cus raised his fists, glared at the thugs, and snarled, 'Get out of here, you punks, or I'll tear you apart.'

The muggers fled. Shaken, Jim turned to D'Amato and said, 'Cus, you're absolutely crazy. That's how people get badly hurt.'

'There was nothing to worry about,' D'Amato answered calmly. 'I knew exactly what I was doing, and I had no intention of hurting either one of them.'

* * *

Some managers are predatory in nature, but others look after their fighters with hearts of gold. Take, for example, manager Mike Jones. After Billy Costello won the World Boxing Council super-lightweight championship from Bruce Curry and successfully defended it against Ronnie Shields, Billy borrowed $10,000 from Jones.

'I'm worried,' Mike told a friend. 'I know Billy has family obligations, but I've tried very hard to get him to save his money so he doesn't have to ask favours from anybody when his career is done. I want him to be financially independent.'

'I got money,' Billy said, when apprised of Mike's concern. 'I got an IRA [Individual Retirement Account]; I got a Keogh [retirement] plan; I got a bank account. But I figure, if Mike Jones is willing to loan me $10,000 interest free, I'll buy a treasury bill, keep the interest, and give him back his $10,000 later on.'

Each Christmas for the past few years, I've devoted a column to some thoughts from George Foreman.

Two Conversations with George Foreman

What's George Foreman really like? I don't pretend to have a definitive answer. But I'd like to share some thoughts regarding two days that I spent with him a dozen years apart.

The first day occurred in December 1988. I'd begun working with Muhammad Ali on a book entitled *Muhammad Ali: His Life and Times*, and was in Las Vegas for the taping of a documentary entitled *Champions Forever*. The producers had brought Ali, Foreman, Joe Frazier, Larry Holmes and Ken Norton together to reminisce, and it was an opportunity for me to talk with them.

Foreman's 'second ring career' had begun by then, and he'd amassed thirteen comeback wins against opposition like Tom Trimm, Guido Trane and Ladislao Mijangos. The common denominator among his opponents was that they were short, fat and out of shape. George said he was fighting them because they were 'the Mike Tyson type'. Tyson, of course, was the undisputed heavyweight champion of the world back then. Many considered him more powerful than Godzilla, and he was expected to reign well into the next millennium. Meanwhile, George had shed the surly image of his youth, and seemed to have a more promising future as a preacher than as a fighter.

George and I talked about Ali for several hours that day, and the generosity of his spirit shone through. He talked about falling in love with Ali as an adolescent, the evolution of his own career, and the night Ali knocked him out to regain the heavyweight championship in Zaire. 'After the fight, I was bitter,' George confessed. 'I had all sorts of excuses. The ring ropes were loose. The referee counted too fast. I was drugged. I should have just said the best man won, but I'd never lost before so I didn't know how to lose. I fought that fight over in my head a thousand times. Then, finally, I realised I'd lost to a great champion;

265

probably the greatest of all time. Muhammad won fair and square, and now I'm proud just to be part of the Ali legend.'

But what impressed me even more about George that day was something that happened after the documentary taping was done. I have a friend named Neil Ragin, who was about to celebrate his 48th birthday. Neil was, and still is, a huge boxing fan and a great admirer of George Foreman. He's five foot ten and, to his great dismay, had pushed past 200 pounds. As a birthday present for Neil, George taped a second interview with me. I asked who he wanted to fight next, and George responded as follows.

'Being that I want to fight Mike Tyson for the heavyweight championship of the world, I'd like a tune-up with Neil Ragin. They've got similar styles. All I need is to get Neil in the ring, and I'll show the world that George Foreman can beat the Mike Tyson type.'

Did George think he'd have trouble with Neil Ragin's speed?

'No trouble at all, because I'll cut the ring off and work on his body a lot earlier than I did with Muhammad. I went head-hunting with Muhammad. But with Neil Ragin, I'll start off on his body and stick with the body attack.'

What about Ragin's power?

'No problem. He'll try to hit me with those Joe Frazier/Mike Tyson type of punches, but I'll stay low, work the body to drain him of his power, use the left jab as much as I can, and eventually get him with an uppercut. You tell Neil Ragin that I'm going to knock him out.'

Neil loved it. So did I. Very few sports legends would have taken the time, or had the presence of mind, to perform a kindness like that.

Meanwhile, George's comeback continued. In 1990, he raised some eyebrows with a second-round knockout of Gerry Cooney. But Cooney had won only once in the previous five years, so the victory was discounted. There was a win over Alex Stewart and losses to Evander Holyfield and Tommy Morrison. Then came the night of 5 November 1994. George Foreman versus Michael Moorer – KO ten. And suddenly, at age 46, George was a beloved champion. The whole country fell in love with him.

George played his role well. 'The question isn't at what age I want to retire,' he told one interviewer. 'It's at what income.' Lucrative bouts against Axel Schulz, Crawford Grimsley, Lou Savarese and Shannon Briggs followed. But more significantly, George was parlaying his celebrity status and cheeseburger-eating image into a financial bonanza via 'George Foreman's lean mean grilling machine'. When the company that held rights to the grill was sold, George's take, according to the *Wall Street Journal*, was the staggering sum of $105,000,000.

During those interim years, I saw George on a number of occasions. But we never spoke at length, and he remained something of an enigma to me. In that regard, my experience was similar to those of other people who have spent considerably more time with him than I have.

Larry Merchant, who has teamed with Foreman at HBO for over a decade, admits, 'Personally, I can't say I know George well. I sense a toughness to him that's left over from the days when he was young, but there's no need for him to use it any more and he disguises it well. As a general rule, he's fun to be around. But I can't say that I socialise with George. Nobody I know does.

'George's persona when I've been with him is pretty much the way he is in public,' Merchant continues. 'As far as his work for HBO is concerned, he's a professional. He does his homework. He shows up for every production meeting and briefing session. He does little kindnesses for people and some pretty big ones too. I've heard people say – and it's true – that George has put a wall around himself through which nobody is allowed. One reason for that might be, he's become such a huge public figure that he has to do it in order to maintain his sanity. And I'm sure there are other reasons as well. But all in all, I think he's a good guy. If he's fooling me, it's an awfully good act.'

Jim Lampley (Foreman's other broadcasting partner) fills out the profile a bit more. 'George is unique,' says Lampley. 'I don't know anyone like him. It's not difficult to offend him if you're insensitive to who he is, because his principles are so rigid and powerfully felt. I remember, once after a fight, I brought a couple of beers into the limousine that was taking us back to the hotel. George didn't say a word to me about it but, next fight, he had his own limousine. Drinking and his view of Christianity simply don't mix. But if you respect George and his principles, you'll receive complete loyalty in return.

'Little things are important to George,' Lampley continues. 'I've never seen him really angry, but he can be easily hurt. He's very self-protective. He knows that, in life and particularly in boxing, people will use you if they can, and he guards himself carefully against that. In some respects, he's tight with money, but there are times when I've seen him be unbelievably generous. And more than anything else, except for his religion, George is adamant about maintaining his privacy. He has a powerful sense of privacy. He'll never give it up.'

All of which brings me to November 2000. I was in Las Vegas to cover Lennox Lewis versus David Tua. On 10 November (the day before the fight), I attended an HBO briefing session with Lewis and Emanuel Steward. When the session was done, I asked George if I could talk with him.

The subject was God. More specifically, why people believe in God and the differing beliefs that people have. I'm in the process of writing a book on the subject. Over the past year, I've done a lot of research; some of it scholarly, some less formal. One of the things I've done is talk at length with people who have a firm belief in God. George agreed to share his thoughts with me.

We live in an age when many believers of all faiths assert that their way is the only road to heaven. George has a contrary view. I won't write at length here about what he said. That's for another forum. But as we approach the first Christmas of the new millennium, I'd like to pass along a few of words of wisdom from George Foreman:

- 'Someone who has no faith in God should be embraced, not with doctrine, but with love.'
- 'A preacher can preach without a tongue and without a Bible by simply doing good works.'
- 'Good is good, whether or not one believes in Jesus. To be good is to be saved.'
- 'If I treat everybody nice, that's religion.'

So that's George Foreman. He's a legendary fighter, a shrewd businessman, and an intensely private person. He's deeply spiritual and, in the words of Jim Lampley, 'a Christian in the best sense of the word'. He's a good messenger for this holiday season and every other day of the year.

The tradition continues.

George Foreman on Christmas

George Foreman is one of boxing's best 'feel good' stories. His thoughts, recorded below, make a pretty good holiday message for the coming year:

- 'I'm low key about the holidays. In fact, I put all the holidays into one basket. Everyone has been so prosperous in recent years that the buying and gift-giving never stops. People are overly generous. The machinery of giving expensive things has gotten so well established that nothing stops it. It starts with birthdays and goes on through Christmas and every other day of the year. It's "Let's see how much we can buy," and a lot of people have forgotten about giving of themselves instead of giving things.'

- 'I got a giant music box from Motown last Christmas. Very expensive. You could see it was something they sent to the elite. But not a letter asking, "How are you? What's happening?"'

- 'I get Christmas cards in the mail from people I hardly know, and I know it's "Let's send him a card and him a card." My parents are dead and gone, and they still get Christmas cards from people who haven't checked for years to see how they're doing. I send out hellos and how-you-doings all the time. There's never one day a year that people have to wait for to hear from me.'

- 'You know, when I was growing up, Christmas was the most dangerous time of the year for me. We didn't have a tree or anything like that. We were poor. In the summer, we had a choice between electricity and gas, and we chose electricity. In the winter, we chose heat. Christmas trees cost money and, once you had a tree, you had to put something on it; so no tree at Christmas. But when I was young, I'd hear people saying, "I'm giving my mother this; I'm giving my girlfriend that." So I'd go out and prowl the streets; fourteen, fifteen years old, a mugger, to outdo people and get money for presents.'

- 'Even now, I don't have a tree at Christmas. Why not? Just because. And I don't get into gift-giving at Christmas. The only gift that really matters is the gift of love.'
- 'If a young child asked me what Christmas is about, I wouldn't say anything; I'd just hug him. Words can mess up anything, but a hug is always good. I'd hug him and spend the day with him. And the wonderful thing about a hug is, you don't have to wait for Christmas to give it. You can give hugs every day of the year.'

A Christmas Eve Visit from George Foreman

T'was the night before Christmas, and all through the home
Big George was eating at the start of this poem.
A holiday banquet; burgers with cheese
Pizza and chocolate, tacos and peas.
Then it was time to take out the trash
And up on the roof, George heard a loud crash
Followed by moaning and groaning: 'Oh, my!
I've broken my leg,' he heard Santa Claus cry.
George carried Santa Claus down from the roof.
'Oh, what a blunder! Oh, what a goof!
Oh, what a mess,' Santa Claus wailed.
Then Santa's shiny red rosy cheeks paled.
'Can't travel,' said Santa. 'My leg hurts real bad.
Children all over are gonna be sad.
No presents this Christmas, that's how it will be.
It's the worst thing that ever has happened to me.'
'Oh, this is awful; it's tragic,' George cried.
'This will bring teardrops to children worldwide
Isn't there anything that I can do
To help in this moment of crisis for you?'
Then George sat with Santa Claus right by the fire
And stared at the flames as they rose ever higher.
He furrowed his brow ever deeper in thought
And clenched his fists like he once did when he fought.
'I've got it,' George said. 'I know what I'll do.
I'm big and I'm strong and I'm built just like you.
I can handle a sleigh; I'm still kind of cute
And I can fit into that Santa Claus suit.'
So Santa Claus took off his holiday wear
And gave it to George, who took it with care.

Then George put it on; it fit him just right.
Said George, 'I'll deliver those presents tonight.'
'Fantastic!' cried Santa. 'But before you deliver
There are rules to be followed if you're the gift giver.
Now and then, someone will make a request.
I've got a long list of which presents are best.
As a substitute Santa, please take my advice.'
George took the list and read it through twice:
Mike Tyson wants to learn how to behave.
Bob Arum wants to give Mike Katz a shave.
Mike Katz, in turn, wants to give Arum tsouris.
Butterbean wants a defence that's less porous.
Andrew Golota wants true peace and quiet.
The Duvas want to put Lou on a diet.
Lucia wants Christy; MacGregor wants guys.
Julio writes, 'Please, not Willy Wise.'
Lou DiBella wants to escape from the greed
Of Pretty Boy Floyd and dream David Reid.
Mark Johnson would like to become better known.
Roger Levitt wants someone to float him a loan.
Rich Giachetti wants love and respect.
The Goossens want to see Main Events wrecked.
And here's a request that came in by fax;
Teddy Atlas would like a gun to shoot Max.
Don Elbaum would like to pick up a quick buck.
Frans Botha would like a change in his luck.
Jay Larkin wants a much bigger budget.
If Holyfield fights, he wants Jean to judge it.
Here's one that seems an improbable dream:
Erik Morales wants Prince Naseem.
Roy Jones would like a monster to fight.
The US Attorney wants to indict.
Bill Cayton wants joy for his lovely wife, Doris.
Showtime wants to forget Orlin Norris.
John Ruiz wants to continue to rate.
Cedric would like a real heavyweight.

Oscar wants Felix early next year.
Budweiser wants to sell fight fans more beer.
Arturo Gatti wants skin that is thicker.
Michael Grant wants to have hands that are quicker.
Art Dore has asked for a cute Playboy bunny.
Sulaiman, Lee and Mendoza want money.
And here's an attempt to bribe Santa's chief elf:
Don King wants all of the toys for himself.
'This list is confusing,' George said with a sigh.
'I'll never remember what goes to which guy;
So I'm gonna give out the best gift ever seen
Everyone's getting a grilling machine.'
And that night, Big George did just what he said.
With grilling machines piled high on his sled
He went round the world in the spirit of joy
Giving grilling machines to each girl and boy.
It made him feel good, and the part he liked best
Was wherever he went, to the East or the West
To the North or the South, lower or higher
People left cookies and milk by the fire.
George thought the snacks were a wonderful treat
He ate every one; a remarkable feat;
And I heard Big George say when he came home that night,
'My stomach is stuffed, and my pants are too tight.'